John Gilmary Shea, Richard Brennan

Christ in His Church

A Catholic Church History

John Gilmary Shea, Richard Brennan

Christ in His Church
A Catholic Church History

ISBN/EAN: 9783743399297

Manufactured in Europe, USA, Canada, Australia, Japa

Cover: Foto ©Lupo / pixelio.de

Manufactured and distributed by brebook publishing software (www.brebook.com)

John Gilmary Shea, Richard Brennan

Christ in His Church

Approbations.

This book, in my judgment, is well adapted for the use of Schools, and is calculated to impress upon youthful minds a knowledge of the salient points of Ecclesiastical History, and a profound reverence for the champions of the faith who in every age have illustrated the Church by their heroism, their learning, and their Apostolic lives. Mr. SHEA'S Supplementary History will not fail to inspire the young student with an increased admiration for the pioneers of the faith in our own country, and a greater love for our holy religion, which has fostered such noble characters.
✠ JAMES GIBBONS, *Archbishop of Baltimore.*

This book is **a compendium of most useful information** for Catholics in general, comprising as it does in brief compass and admirable plan the variform life of the Church in history, in dogma, and moral teachings, in sacraments, in liturgy, in hierarchy and religious orders, in saints and holy doctors, in arts and science, in persecutions and trials and in triumphs; showing in all these the presence and workings of Christ and the Holy Spirit in and with the Church. **The work is a valuable addition to our English Catholic literature.**
✠ THOMAS L. GRACE, *Bishop of St. Paul.*

I hope this **useful and excellent work** will have a wide circulation.
✠ J. SWEENEY, *Bishop of St. John, N. B.*

"CHRIST IN HIS CHURCH" is indeed an appropriate title of your Church History translated by the gifted Dr. Brennan from the original of the Rev. L. C. Businger, author of the exquisite "Life of Christ." * * * the perusal of your History is sufficient to convince any impartial reader that the Catholic Church is a divine institution, and the only one which fulfils and verifies the words of Christ, "The gates of hell shall not prevail against it."
✠ E. O'CONNELL, *Bishop of Grass Valley.*

I beg to thank you for the copy of the work "CHRIST IN HIS CHURCH," with which you have favored me. I find it an excellent work of its kind, presenting the facts of Church history in a clear, concise, and yet comprehensive manner. It is an interesting, edifying, and instructive book, **admirably adapted for the use of Catholic families** and as a prize-book for our Colleges and Convents. I wish it an extensive circulation. ✠ JOHN WALSH, *Bishop of London.*

An admirable compendium of Ecclesiastical History. The second part containing a clear and concise History of the Church in this country, must render the work of great interest and value to American Catholic readers. ✠ T. MULLEN, *Bishop of Erie.*

I am pleased to see the work of Fr. Businger in an English dress. **It is a valuable addition to our English Catholic literature.** I need hardly add that the "History of the Church in America," by John Gilmary Shea, which you published with Rev. Fr. Brennan's translation of the above work, must make the volume doubly acceptable to American Catholics and doubly valuable, especially to the rising generations. ✠ S. V. RYAN, *Bishop of Buffalo.*

Father Richard Brennan, already **so favorably known** by his many literary labors, has done another **most meritorious work** by giving us in an English dress the celebrated book of the Rev. L. C. Businger, "CHRIST IN HIS CHURCH." This Catholic Church History was received with such enthusiasm by the Catholic reading public when it first appeared in German, that we have no doubt it will prove **a genuine boon to the English reader.** The book comes to us with the very highest recommendations of those in authority, and it has received such flattering notices from the Catholic press, that we can but **add our humble approval,** and express our fervent hope that "CHRIST IN HIS CHURCH" may find a hearty welcome in every Catholic household. **It is the book for the people.**
✠ A. M. TOEBBE, *Bishop of Covington.*

This highly instructive and interesting work I consider **very useful for family use,** and therefore I heartily recommend it to the faithful of my Diocese.
✠ FRANCIS MORA, *Bishop of Monterey and Los Angeles, Cal.*

Fr. Businger's name as the author, and Fr. Brennan's as the translator, are in itself a great recommendation, and still more so is Bishop Lachat's letter. I must say that I wish it may have a large circulation in this country. **It is short, but contains all the essentials,** and is as instructive as it is edifying.
✠ RUPERT SEIDENBUSH, O. S. B., *Bishop.*

Whatever comes from the pen of Father Businger is well written. The reading of this book makes a Catholic feel proud to belong to a Church which in time of persecution and peace is evidently the work of God. ✠ F. JANSSEN, *Bishop of Natchez.*

This Church History is very comprehensive, and contains an immense amount of knowledge in a condensed form. Though the book is principally designed for American use, it is not unlikely to be much in request here when its merits are known. In type, arrangement, and illustrations it may compete with anything that can be produced by the best European presses.—*London Tablet.*

PREFACE.

ANY history of the Catholic Church, if impartially and truthfully presented, forms one of the best and most striking human evidences of its divine excellence. When Pilate would offer to the unbelieving Jews a demonstration of the innocence of Jesus, he simply pointed to the suffering Saviour and said, "Ecce Homo"—"Behold the Man."

In venturing to present to the Catholic readers of this country an English translation of Father Businger's admirable Church History, I would simply say; Behold the Catholic Church and you behold the Church which Christ established, for in every page of its history you 'Behold the Man,' the Son of God, living and acting in that Church, and giving constant and unfailing evidence of its divine origin and supernatural life upon earth.

We would have but a very crude and unworthy perception of the Incarnate Son of God were we to imagine Him to have been a merely historical personage, who seemed to lay the foundation of His Church, then ascended to the right hand of His Father, leaving that Church without a guide or protector.

In His divine wisdom, he made His work of Redemption perpetual. And it is perpetual in this sense, that it is to extend to generations that did not exist at or before His coming.

If it is said that this satisfaction for the sins of the world was consummated and completed on Mount Calvary, how would that benefit the generations that have passed over the earth ever since that hour of divine atonement? What would it avail us, who were not born? How would its merits reach our sinful souls? For, before we could be redeemed by the Son of God, we must have an existence.

There are two modes given. One is to suppose—and, though a dismal, an awful supposition, it has gained credit—that God had, by an unchangeable decree, determined all through eternity that certain persons only should have the benefit of Redemption. But this never entered into the message which the Apostles were to carry to mankind. On the contrary, they taught, as Christ had taught them, that he would be with them all days, even to the consummation of the world : not indeed physically, as during his mortal life ; nor yet typically, as under the Old Dispensation ; but that He would be present in His Church truly, mystically, and actively. He was to be, as it were, the vital principle of that Church; which, like the human body in its dependance on the human soul, was to be the medium or channel of applying to the souls of men during all ages the benefits of the atoning sacrifice on Calvary.

He is mystically and efficaciously present in each and all of her Seven Sacraments.

Indeed we can nowhere discover that Christ has forsaken His Church. He is the guardian of her truth, the guide of her counsel, the perpetuator of the application to the souls of men, of the merits of His atoning death.

Some one may preach. But that is external. The grace, the inward grace, that accompanies the legitimate preaching of those whom Christ sends, is His special gift. In that sense Christ is the preacher.

He appoints His ministers to govern the Church, and the successor of St. Peter is the head of that ministry and government. But Christ is there as the higher Head. He is there to suggest and direct the course best fitted for the purpose which He had in view, when He became man and died on the cross in order to redeem that human nature, and to raise it from grovelling with its crimes in the very dust of the earth, and thus reconcile it and reunite it to an outraged God.

This sublime purpose of Christ has always been the main object pursued by the Church. It is the highest aspect and aim of Christianity. But Christianity has two aspects: one, partially described above, is all divine, and looking to God; contemplating man, not in his temporal existence, but in the eternal state of being. This is the direct object of the existence of the Church. But it may be easily shown that the Church, which appears to have been intended exclusively for our happiness in a future life, is also to serve for the furtherance and maintenance of our well-being here below.

This latter constitutes the indirect effect, the temporal effect, the civil and social aspect and influence of the Church.

Now in this aspect also Christ is really visibly present.

Every event in the world's history is connected with that Church. Every action of man has been wrought either for or against it. The Church is the good. Evil exists only for the purpose of attacking her, and is evil only inasmuch as it opposes her.

So it was with regard to Christ her founder, who in the land of Judea entered the lists against evil and iniquity, and from that time till the present day has kept up the conflict through the medium of His Church. We do not say too much when we assert that every triumph over evil has been won by the Catholic Church. All the improvement that has taken place in the social and religious condition of mankind, ever since the birth of the Saviour at Bethlehem, is to be attributed to the Catholic Church, which alone has received from her Teacher the divine lessons which He inculcated in reference to a brighter and better world than this. Until the appearance of Christ and His

Church, the selfishness of man was his ruling law of action. He knew no restraint, till the Church by word and example succeeded in instilling into his heart the lessons of poverty, of self-denial, of love of God, of love for neighbor for the sake of God. "Whatsoever," says Jesus Christ, "ye do unto one of these little ones, ye do even unto me." Who can estimate the importance of this element of love for God and neighbor infused into the human heart? The Church acting outwardly through the inward inspirations of Christ, her life and her soul, makes man love that spirit of sacrifice by which the world's selfishness has been abashed and abated. What calamity to which man may be exposed has not found a remedy under the impulse of the teachings of the Church? Have not old age, once so neglected; infancy, once abandoned by its criminal authors; the family, domestic law, the orphan, the outcast of society, the soldier and the statesman—have they not all felt the hallowed influence of Christ's teachings as reduced to practice by the Church? Yes, the law of Christ, as executed faithfully and to the letter in the Church, has infused that power by which (when reading the history of the Church) we see man, and above all woman, who comprehends this power in all its divine delicacy, devoting year after year to the service of their fellow-beings a life which in pagan times was wholly wasted in the empty vanities of the world, or worse.

Christ is everywhere visible in the Church: whether we study the lives of her apostles, or of her martyrs, of her rulers, her virgins, her members of mendicant Orders, her members of societies for befriending little children, weak old age, the crippled, the lame, the blind, the afflicted, Christ is still living, teaching and aiding His Church.

Now, more than ever before, perhaps, should the children of the Faith be made conversant with the history of the one true Church. Though bodily persecution is not directed against its members as in the olden time, yet they and their Church are charged in private circles, in public assemblies, in the public press, and even in the school book, with imputations of dishonor, with calumnies, with revilings, with slanders. Even those who should be and who are by their office the appointed guardians to regulate justice, have attempted to invade the rights and liberties of the Church of Christ. What do these assaults prove? They prove that ordinary means are now recognized as insufficient to arrest the progress of truth on the rostrum of free discussion. They prove that there is no way of putting down this hated teacher of the doctrine of the Son of God, this Representative of His own presence but by poisoning the minds of those who know nothing of her attributes and of her majestic beauty; by poisoning their minds beforehand, and making them believe that she is the enemy of the human kind, that she is the adversary of all that is enlightened or grand in conception or performance.

In studying the history of this Church, especially in the peculiar form in which it is briefly but graphically presented by Father Businger, we find our faith and love for her strengthened and intensified. We are pleased and edified at discovering how closely the history of her long life of nigh two thousand years resembles the history of the life of her divine Founder. Hers is a succession of trials and of triumphs. Hers is like His, an everlasting persecution from the hands of worldlings, of the enemies of truth; but from the side of God a perpetual triumph.

The present History of the Church is far more than a mere narrative of events. It is a bright living picture of Christ living, acting, suffering, through the medium of His Mystical Body, which in its turn acts, lives, and suffers through the lives of its members.

A history of the Church, thus presented, ought to produce in the heart of the impartial reader sentiments similar to those awakened in the hearts of the few followers of Christ who were present at that awful scene in Jerusalem, when the world, as represented by the promiscuous crowd in Pilate's hall, was told to "Behold the Man."

Yes, behold Christ's Church, as seen in the light of her own history, and you "Behold the Man," Jesus Christ, God himself, the author of all good, whether temporal or spiritual, and yet the recipient of all the opposition that can spring from hearts as impervious to the true, the beautiful, and the good, as were the hearts of those who, when told to "Behold the Man," cried out, "Away with Him; crucify Him, and give us Barabbas."

The second portion of this work consists of a clear, concise, and accurate history of the life of the Church in America. It is from the able pen of Dr. John Gilmary Shea, who, amid the many other labors of his long and industrious life has made Church History, and especially American Church History, the object of much careful research; the fruits of which have already appeared in his learned and authentic works on this and other subjects.

R. B.

St. Rose's Rectory, New York.
Feast of the Seven Dolors, 1881.

CHAPTER I.

THE CHURCH AND HER HISTORY.

1. What the Church is.

"Behold, I am with you all days, even to the consummation of the world."—MATTHEW xxviii. 20.

WHEN we read in the New Testament how our beloved Lord Jesus Christ "went about doing good" in the land of Judea, preaching heavenly truths, imparting saving grace to men of good will, and infusing peace into the hearts of all, we are apt to indulge in feelings of regret that we too did not live in those happy days, that we were not permitted to enjoy his sacred presence and to hearken to his voice.

Although, under the guidance of the holy Evangelists, we may in spirit accompany the Redeemer all through his earthly life from Bethlehem to Calvary; although we may see him attesting and sealing his words of truth and his works of power and mercy by his atoning death on the cross, we are apt to ask ourselves: What is Christ to us, or to all the generations who have lived and died during the long lapse of time since he dwelt upon earth? No one of our generation has looked upon him with corporeal eyes. No one of us has heard the words of wisdom uttered by his sacred tongue, or felt the touch of his blessed, grace-imparting hand. We have not been permitted to stand with Mary and John and Magdalen under the cross, nor to be sprinkled like them with his saving blood. He has ascended into heaven, and now sits in unapproachable majesty at the right hand of his Father, whilst we are living in exile upon earth. How then can we have any share in the truth, blessings, and graces of this Christ?

Our question is a vain and foolish one. If we but look with the eye of faith, we shall soon and easily discover that this same Christ, with all the fulness of his wisdom, power, and mercy, is still living in our midst, as he promised to do. "Behold, I am with you all days, even

Our Saviour appoints St. Peter the head of the Church.

to the consummation of the world," is the consoling assurance that falls from his own divine lips.

Let us therefore examine and study carefully the plan adopted by our Saviour whereby he continues still to dwell on earth, forwarding the work of salvation in all lands and during all time.

What method has Christ followed in order to effect this object?

He delegated his threefold office and character—namely,

his teaching office, his priesthood, and his kingly authority —to a number of chosen men, in union with whom he continues to act as Teacher, Priest, and King to the end of time.

It was in this threefold character, that Christ effected our salvation. He redeemed us as Teacher, as Priest, and as King: as Teacher, by preaching heavenly wisdom; as Priest, by the atoning sacrifice offered upon the cross; and as King, by enacting and inculcating laws or commandments. As Teacher, he rescued us from spiritual blindness by giving us the truth of heaven; as divine-human Priest, he redeemed us from the guilt of sin by offering himself in sacrifice on Mount Calvary; as God-man-king, he saved us, by his maxims and commandments, from the folly and wickedness of life.

This triple office he committed solemnly to a body of chosen men, a short time before his departure from earth. This truth can be plainly proven from holy Scripture. The divine Teacher sent forth his Apostles to preach to all nations, to teach all truth as he had imparted it to them, and to teach it with the same authority and infallible certainty as he himself taught it: "He who hears you hears me."

Our divine High-priest, on the eve of his Passion, instituted and offered up, in a mysterious manner and by anticipation, the saving sacrifice of the cross, saying: "This is my body which shall be delivered for you, this is my blood which shall be shed for you." He committed to the hands of the Apostles for all time to come this holy sacrifice of his body and blood, saying: "Do this," as I have just done, "in commemoration of me." He gave to the Apostles power to baptize, to forgive sins, to bless; in a word, to so dispense graces in his name, that these same Apostles were able to say later of themselves with truth, and with a consciousness of their power and dignity: "Let a man so account of us as of the ministers of Christ;

and the dispensers of the mysteries of God" (1 Cor. iv. 1).

Finally, our divine King transmitted his spiritual prerogatives of royalty to the Apostles, with the words: "All power is given to me in heaven and on earth. As the Father sent me, so I send you." It was by virtue of this charge that the Apostles prescribed for all the nations to whom they preached all those laws and regulations, and established all those institutions, which they deemed

The Apostles are appointed Shepherds of the Flock.

necessary for the spiritual welfare,* or conducive to the eternal salvation, of men.

Hence we see clearly that although Christ has returned to heaven, he has not left us orphans, but has been

---

* These laws and ordinances of the Apostles and their successors appertain to spiritual things, and not to civil affairs nor civic regulations. If, therefore, the management of political affairs has been in the hands of ecclesiastics from time to time, it was in consequence of divine providence, or on account of the confidence which Catholic princes and peoples reposed in their clergy.

pleased to remain mystically with us, carrying on, through his Apostles as his chosen instruments, his threefold office of Redeemer till the end of time. In union with St. Peter, their visible Head, the Apostles were to traverse the earth, preaching, dispensing graces, ordaining, and becoming fishers of men, in order to bring all men to a share in the benefits of truth, grace, and salvation through Christ. They were to unite them to Jesus himself in oneness of life, and to join them together in one large and glorious mystical body, of which Christ was to be the invisible Head.

Such was the duty imposed by Christ on his Apostles. But the Apostles were mortal, and died, one after the other, during the first century of Christianity, whilst the threefold office of teacher, priest, and ruler committed to them by Christ should endure till the end of time. Hence it is clear that when the divine Founder of our Church imparted this threefold power to his Apostles in order to perpetuate his Church, he meant not only the twelve men standing there and then in his presence. His divine gaze extended to all their lawful successors, the Popes, bishops, and priests to the end of the world, as if they all stood in his presence when he spoke. In this sense it was that he said to them all: "Lo, I am with you all days, even to the consummation of the world."

The Apostles, therefore, and their legitimate successors are the persons to whom Christ entrusted the duty of forming in his name, among all nations and in all ages, a holy community or spiritual society; or, rather, of extending and strengthening the original society established by himself.

This spiritual society, consisting originally of the Apostles, disciples, and a few devout believers, became like the mustard-seed of the parable, a great tree whose branches were spread over all the earth. And this is the universal or Catholic Church, in which Christ, by the instrumentality of his Apostles and their successors, perpetuates forever his work of salvation and applies it to each individual soul. His truth, his saving grace, his redeeming sacrifice, all his merits as God-man from his birth to his death—these are the glorious treasures of this society, the riches of that grand corporation in which each member, who has been duly admitted by baptism, has a right to participate. Therefore, when we speak of the Church we understand that holy society in which Jesus Christ exercises throughout all ages, by the instrumentality of the Apostles and their successors, the bishops and priests, his threefold office of Teacher, Priest, and King.

If the Church were a mere association of persons holding the same tenets, differing in no way from any other human society, it would not be the "mysterium fidei," or the mystical body of Christians united to Christ. But the Church embraces, besides the *visible*—that is to say, the laity of all nations and their ecclesiastical authorities—also the *Invisible;* namely, the inheritance of Christ's merits and the merits of his Saints, the treasures of truth and goodness, as well as supernatural guidance. It thus becomes a sublime mystery of faith, and hence the Christian can truthfully say, and with meaning, "I believe in one Holy Catholic Church."

2. Why the Church is the Pillar and Ground of Truth. Why she shall always continue such.

"The house of God, which is the Church of the living God, the pillar and ground of the truth."—1 TIMOTHY iii. 15.

It is beyond all doubt that our divine Founder entrusted to the Apostles and their successors the duty and the power of directing his holy Church in sanctity and truth, and of leading all men into her fold. They had a very difficult and onerous duty to perform. The work was far above human strength and sagacity, while the Apostles themselves, as well as their successors, the bishops and priests of the Church, were mere men, liable to death and sin, and exposed to error and changes. How could such incapable men accomplish this superhuman task? And granting that the Apostles had been confirmed in their faith, in sanctity of life, in zeal for God's kingdom upon earth, by Jesus Christ himself, and hence succeeded in preserving pure and unchanged his sacred legacy of truth and holiness among the nations of their times, how could their successors in the course of centuries be expected to enjoy similar strength and holiness? Whence were they to draw it? Alas! poor human nature is sadly prone to whims, to passion, to instability and change. And will not this corruption of human nature so affect the leaders in God's Church that in a few years after the death of the Apostles the work of Christ will languish, die, and be forgotten?

How many societies have been established within the lapse of eighteen hundred years, many with the very best and most laudable ends in view; founded, too, in the wisdom and experience of wise men, and carried on with prudence and sagacity! Yet in the course of time evil crept in, they changed, became corrupt, fell to pieces, and have long since been forgotten even in history. Will not the society of the Church encounter a similar fate?

Certainly not; for, glory, honor, and praise be to God! this society has not only been *founded* by Christ, but he has moreover infused into it for all time *a divine vital power*. He has sent truly his own Holy Spirit, as is related in the Acts of the Apostles in the following words of the Evangelist St. Luke:

"And when the days of the Pentecost were accomplished, they were all together in one place. And suddenly there came a sound from heaven, as of a mighty wind coming, and it filled the whole house where they were sitting. And there appeared to them parted tongues as it were of fire, and it sat upon every one of them. And they were all filled with the Holy Ghost, and they began to speak with divers tongues according as the Holy Ghost gave them to speak. Now there were dwelling at Jerusalem Jews, devout men, out of every nation under heaven. And when this was noised abroad, the multitude came together, and were confounded in mind,

The Descent of the Holy Ghost.

because that every man heard them speak in his own tongue. And they were all amazed, and wondered, saying: Behold, are not all these that speak Galileans, and how have we heard every man our own tongue wherein we were born? Parthians, and Medes, and Elamites, and inhabitants of Mesopotamia, Judea, and Cappadocia, Pontus and Asia, Phrygia and Pamphilia, Egypt and the parts of Libya about Cyrene, and strangers of Rome, Jews also, and proselytes, Cretes and Arabians;

we have heard them speak in our own tongues the wonderful works of God. And they were all astonished, and wondered, saying one to another, What meaneth this? But others mocking, said: These men are full of new wine. But Peter, standing up with the eleven, lifted up his voice and spoke to them: Ye men of Judea, and all you that dwell in Jerusalem, be this known to you, and with your ears receive my words; for these are not drunk, as you suppose, seeing it is but the third hour of the day. But this is that which was spoken of by the prophet Joel: And it shall come to pass, in the last days (saith the Lord), I will pour out of my Spirit upon all flesh; and your sons and your daughters shall prophesy, and your young men shall see visions, and your old men shall dream dreams. And upon my servants indeed, and upon my handmaids, will I pour out in those days of my Spirit, and they shall prophesy. Ye men of Israel, hear these words: Jesus of Nazareth, a man approved of God among you by miracles and wonders and signs, which God did by him in the midst of you, as you also know; this same, being delivered up, by the determinate counsel and foreknowledge of God, you, by the hands of wicked men, have crucified and slain. This Jesus hath God raised again, whereof all we are witnesses. Being exalted therefore by the right hand of God, and having received of the Father the promise of the Holy Ghost, he hath poured forth this which you see and hear."

From all this, we can understand why the Catholic Church is the only one among all the institutions upon the earth that remains unchanged and unchangeable; why, with her, truth has never been adulterated or obscured, even in the ages of darkest ignorance in the world; why her saving graces, amid all the corruptions of men, have never been weakened nor diminished. She was made immortal for all time by the infusion of God's breath, the Holy Ghost, on the day of Pentecost. Yes, the Holy Ghost dwells really and truly within her; that Spirit which renews the face of the earth as the Psalmist sings; that good and comforting Spirit mentioned in the book of Wisdom; that Spirit of wisdom and understanding, of counsel and fortitude, of knowledge and piety, foretold by Isaias; that Spirit which comes to aid us in our weakness, as St. Paul writes to the Romans; that Spirit promised by Christ to his Apostles, who was to teach them all things and to lead them to all truth.

Since the Catholic Church has really received this Holy Spirit as her own peculiar life and soul and strength, the personal faults and failures of her visible rulers and leaders can do her no real harm.

Although some few weak, unhappy priests may have gone astray, although even in remote ages of the Church bishops themselves may have fallen into error and false opinions, although a few Popes have made lamentable mistakes individually, nevertheless no general Council of the Church has ever erred, never has any Pope when speaking officially contradicted any Council or any previous decision of his predecessors in the chair of Peter. Never has any Pope uttered heresy. The divine power, which dwells and acts in the Church with mysterious and miraculous force and wisdom, is able and knows how to overcome, at all times, decay, error, and vice.*

No! Christ did not wish by any means to extinguish and annihilate the human in the bosom of his Church.

---

* That such corruption may taint not only laymen, but even ecclesiastics, has never been denied. Thus, in the year 1521, at the assembly, in Worms, of the German princes, Aleandri, the papal nuncio, exclaimed plainly: "In Rome itself there have been abuses, even among prelates. Some of the earlier Popes made mistakes, some were culpable, some were even wicked. All this is admitted, not with pride, but with sentiments of humiliation." Then he adds: "And yet this Rome it was which a few centuries ago declared the great St. Bernard to be a saint, although in his writings he had rebuked and reproved these same vices."

As by the sending of the Holy Ghost he did not intend to dispense and free the Heads of the Church from the duty of employing the human means of prudence and reflection, of study and of worldly cleverness, in order to settle and fix and decide truth, and guide the Church; so, too, he did not see fit to make it impossible for any one individual person to fall into sin and error. But the Church herself is always intact, pure, blameless, and immortal, even if some few individual members perish of error and wickedness. She remains the pillar and ground of truth, as St. Paul styles her; and the gates of hell shall not prevail against her.

3. What is Church History?

"In the world you shall have distress: but have confidence, I have overcome the world."—JOHN xvi. 33.

As the holy Evangelists relate the life and actions of Jesus Christ, so does Church history describe the life and works of his spouse, who is the Catholic Church. Now as Jesus Christ continues to live in his Church, it follows that the history or description of that Church is certainly the mirrored reflection of the holy Evangelists. The history of our divine Redeemer's life is one of continued struggle and suffering. The same is true of the history of his Church, and herein lies a powerful and undeniable evidence of the truth of our beloved Church.

But as Christ, in the midst of this opposition, suffering, and contest, constantly manifested his glorious divinity, completed his work, and triumphed over death and hell, so does Church history exhibit to us, in the midst of persecution, conflict, and martyrdom, the triumph of truth and grace over the dark powers of this world.

1. It shows us how Christ manifested himself to all nations by the preaching of his representatives and messengers, and how his Church spread throughout all

nations. This forms the history of the Christian missions, or the growth of the Church.

2. It shows how Christ continues to live in his Church as the Redeemer and High-priest in the holy sacrifice of the mass, in the sacraments and other means of grace, which by a believing people are surrounded with ever-increasing solemnity, heightened beauty, and significant ceremonies. This forms the history of divine worship in the broad sense of the word.

3. It shows how Christ has ever lived in his Church as Teacher of truth and heavenly wisdom, by leading the fathers and teachers of that Church into a miraculous knowledge of the mysteries of his kingdom, by guiding the Councils through the Holy Ghost, and by saving the Popes from error in their definitions of faith. This forms the history of the Fathers of the Church, or of the Councils.

4. It shows how Christ has ever reigned in his Church as King, by clothing his representatives, the priests, according to their various ranks with divine authority, and by maintaining through their instrumentality God's kingdom on earth in discipline, peace, and tranquillity. This forms the history of the Hierarchy, of Church rights and of Church penalties.

5. It shows how Christ has always dwelt in his Church as the Holy One, by leading individuals to extraordinary holiness, and creating, especially in the monastic life and other religious associations, schools of the highest virtue and evangelical perfection for those whom he calls to holiness of life. This forms the history of the saints, and of religious life.

6. It shows how Christ has lived in his Church as the Despised One, inasmuch as his doctrines have been misrepresented, denied, and rejected by misguided and wicked men in all ages as in his own lifetime. This forms the history of heresy.

7. It shows how Christ has suffered in his Church as the Crucified, inasmuch as his faithful followers individually,

and his holy Church in general, have been, in private and in public, violently attacked and persecuted, wronged and misrepresented by declared enemies and treacherous friends. This forms the history of the persecutions.

8. It shows how, finally, Christ has triumphed in his Church as the glorious Conqueror. For the Church, even in the midst of her greatest trials and under severest oppression, has won victory after victory, triumph after triumph; and the miraculous promise of heaven shall be fulfilled for all time as it has been in the past: "In this sign of the cross thou shalt conquer." This constitutes the history of the triumph and glory of the Church.

Such are the contents of Church history.

As the Bible history of the Old Testament describes to us how the human race was prepared for the Redemption, and as the Bible history of the New Testament shows us how the work of that Redemption was actually accomplished, so does Church history describe that Redemption still going forward and being accomplished in the Church. It shows how Christ, even after the lapse of centuries of time, is still mysteriously going about among men, as their invisible King and Saviour, and, in spite of the efforts of the powers of hell and of wicked men, is drawing the elect to himself, and sanctifying and saving them by the interposition of the Holy Ghost.

4. Whence are derived the Truthful and Genuine Recitals of Church History?

"Many have taken in hand to set forth in order a narration of the things that have been accomplished among us: according as they have delivered them unto us, who from the beginning were eye-witnesses and ministers of the word."—LUKE i. 1, 2.

The most ancient of Church historians is St. Luke. In the Acts of the Apostles he describes, though briefly, the lives of the first Christians, the most important events in the primitive Church, as well as the doings of some of the Apostles and of their disciples. But the real father of Church history is Eusebius, bishop of Cæsarea, who died about the year 340. His "Ten Books of Church History" are of most incalculable value; for in them he gives us a quantity of ancient decrees, of lengthy narrations, and of decisions of Councils from the first three centuries of the Church; all of which but for his care and industry would have been irretrievably lost.

The works of the great Church fathers, who for the most part have put into writing the oral traditions coming down from the first ages of the Church, contain numerous well-attested narrations of Church history.

Next to these come the chronicles of pious and learned bishops and priests who, at the time of the great invasion of the northern tribes, from the year 350 to 500, and also in the middle ages, from the time of Charlemagne, about the year 800, to the sham reformation in 1518, have set forth the ecclesiastical events of their respective ages in a creditable and credible manner.

Besides these we must count the well-preserved decisions of the ancient Councils of the Church, the Briefs of Popes, and the antique inscriptions which have been discovered and deciphered on ecclesiastical and architectural monuments, especially those discovered in the Roman catacombs. From all these one may understand how, even at this late day, we possess positive knowledge of the early condition of the Church and of events occurring in the earliest ages.

In modern times many able and learned Catholic writers, from Baronius down to Stolberg, Möhler, Hefele, Alzog, Rohrbacher, and others, have undertaken, for the most part in very comprehensive works, to compile Church histories chiefly based on and drawn from these ancient decrees. They have thereby merited the gratitude of the

Catholic world. For by their researches they have proved that many things written, by enemies, against the Popes and other prominent persons in the Church were misrepresentations and calumnies.

They have thus successfully vindicated the honor and good name of the Church against these malicious falsifiers.

5. False Church History.

"There shall be a time when they will heap to themselves teachers, having itching ears. These will turn away their hearing from the truth, but will be turned to fables. But avoid foolish and old wives' fables."—1 and 2 TIMOTHY 4.

In the ninth book of his Church history, Eusebius relates: "Under Maximinus the fury of the persecution against us"—that is to say, the Christians—"was renewed. And although he had full power to do as he pleased, having lately assumed the dignity and authority of emperor, yet he wished to keep up an appearance of acting upon just grounds. For this purpose he caused to be prepared certain 'Acts' such as might have been used by Pilate in his treatment of the Saviour. Into these 'Acts' were embodied all that could be conceived blasphemous against Christ. Into all the provinces of his kingdom he sent these 'Acts,' with the command that they should be distributed through all the cities, villages, and hamlets. The school-teachers were ordered to dictate them to the children in school, who had to learn them by heart as exercises for the memory."

What was here done by Maximinus, the persecutor of the Christians, has been practised against the Church in all ages by his imitators. Even in very early times heretics have endeavored, with cunning and insolence, to falsify not only the teachings but also the history of the Church. They have fabricated false "Acts," and attributed to the authorities of the Church follies and crimes well calculated, if true, to render the clergy both ridiculous and hateful in the eyes of the world.

This contemptible mode of acting was practised to a great extent, more especially in the latter part of the middle ages, by certain chroniclers in the pay of governments or kings who were at variance with the Popes. In this manner there accumulated in course of time an immense amount of spurious, unreliable, and disgraceful chronicles which, then and during the so-called reformation, and in the wars which followed, were still further increased and more widely diffused.

Superficial or evil-minded writers seized upon these fables and, without questioning their historical value, reproduced them in their books. Although in our day these falsifiers of Church history have been unmasked by learned Catholics and by honorable and truth-loving Protestant writers, yet thousands of unscrupulous novelists continue to reproduce these fabulous stories about the Church, merely changing the mode of expression, and serving up the same unwholesome diet in a later style of preparation. But the same treatment must be bestowed by the enemy on the Church as was bestowed of old on her divine Founder: "For many bore false witness against him, and their evidence were not agreeing" (Mark xiv. 56).

CHAPTER II.

THE HISTORY OF THE CHRISTIAN MISSIONS.

CHRIST IS MADE MANIFEST TO ALL NATIONS BY THE PREACHING OF HIS MESSENGERS. HIS CHURCH IS EXTENDED THROUGHOUT THE WORLD.

6. The First Congregation at Jerusalem.

"Now, therefore, O my sons, be ye zealous for the law. Call to remembrance the works of the fathers."—1 MACHABEES ii. 50.

CHRIST chose St. Peter to be his Representative and the Visible Head of his Church on earth, and formally appointed him with the words, "Thou art Peter" (which means rock), "and on this rock I will build my Church, and the gates of hell" (that is to say, the evil powers of error and vice) "shall not prevail against it. To thee I give the keys of the kingdom of heaven. Feed my lambs. Feed my sheep."

In his sermon on the day of Pentecost, addressed to the multitude assembled in Jerusalem, St. Peter spoke with such supernaturally effective powers of persuasion that many accepted baptism, and the first Christian congregation in a short time numbered five thousand members.

In the beginning, the early Christians continued to observe the Jewish rites, and used to go at stated intervals to the temple to pray. Soon, however, they began to hold separate assemblages for worship, at which the Apostles used to conduct divine service according to the ordinance of Christ, and to dispense the sacred mysteries of salvation.

The Acts of the Apostles thus describe the mode of life followed by the members of this first Christian congregation:

"They were persevering in the doctrine of the Apostles, and in the communication of the breaking of bread" (that is, the holy mass and Communion), "and in prayers.

"Many wonders also and signs were done by the Apostles in Jerusalem.

"And all they that believed were together, and had all things common.

"Their possessions and goods they sold and divided them to all, according as every one had need.

"And continuing daily with one accord in the temple, and breaking bread from house to house, they took their meat with gladness and simplicity of heart, praising God, and having favor with all the people. And the Lord increased daily together such as should be saved."

Thus, during the first years after Christ's ascension into heaven, the Apostles remained together in Jerusalem, partly to fortify the new Christians in their faith and in a Christian life, and to organize them as a model for future congregations; partly, also, in order to comfort and protect the faithful in the persecutions which soon broke forth, and partly, too, in order to encourage and fortify each other by the most confidential mutual intercourse, and also to prepare each other for the great work of the mission.

For the Church of Christ was not to be confined to the country of the Jews. The day was approaching when the Apostles, in obedience to the charge given them by their divine Master, were to preach the Gospel to all nations, and to carry the kingdom of Christ to all parts of the world.

7. The Life and Mission of St. Peter.

"The first: Simon who is called Peter. The twelve Jesus sent, saying: 'Behold, I send you as sheep in the midst of wolves.'"— MATTHEW x.

What a glorious army of brave and self-sacrificing spirits rise before our vision as we enter upon the contemplation and study of the stupendous growth of the Church of Christ! At their head march Peter and Paul, with their immediate followers, the Apostles and Evangelists, to be succeeded century after century by hosts of holy bishops, zealous priests, and devoted monks, all chosen by God to carry the light of his Gospel into every quarter of the globe. On the very day of Pentecost this rapid diffusion of the truth began. For those God-fearing Jews who had come from many countries, and were then sojourning in Jerusalem carried the news about Christ and his Church back to their own homes, and prepared thousands of eager souls for the reception of the Christian doctrine, which the Apostles, in pursuance of their high vocation, would soon carry into every city, town, and hamlet.

The most glorious of all was the missionary life of St. Peter, the Prince of the Apostles, at whose first sermon, on the day of Pentecost, about three thousand persons were converted and enrolled under the banner of the cross. And this number was increased soon after to five thousand, on the occasion of the healing of the lame man at the gate of the temple of Jerusalem.

But the Prince of the Apostles, besides being the first to establish the Christian Church amid the Jews, had also the privilege of founding the first Christian congregation among the Gentiles. Being directed by Heaven to seek Cornelius, a certain heathen centurion, at Cæsarea, Peter went and preached before him and his household concerning the death and resurrection of Christ. The Holy Ghost came down upon all those who were listening to the Apostle's inspired words, and they were converted and baptized by Peter. Thus he to whom the keys of the kingdom of heaven had been given was the first to open the doors of God's kingdom upon earth to the pagan world. We find him soon after presiding as first bishop over the first large congregation of converted heathens in the city of Antioch, where the disciples and followers of

Sts. Peter and Paul in Prison.

Christ were first called Christians. Later we discover this fisherman of Galilee, whom the Lord had marked out to be the head of his Church, travelling incessantly through Judea, Galilee, Samaria, Asia Minor, Italy, and other places; everywhere diligently casting his net to bring the souls of Jews and Gentiles into the knowledge of Christ crucified. His most important mission, however, was to the imperial city of Rome, where, by divine dispensation, he was to establish the centre of the Christian Church.

LIFE AND MISSION OF ST. PETER. 31

This proud pagan capital, hitherto the seat of corrupt though refined superstition, was henceforth to be a beacon-light of pure Christian faith and piety. The peaceful throne of the Prince of the Apostles was soon to rise on the ruins of the blood-stained throne of the emperors of the world. Tradition assures us that St. Peter governed

The Crucifixion of St. Peter.

the Church at Rome for twenty-five years, from the year 42 till the year 67 after the birth of Christ; although during this time he went frequently to preach the Gospel in other lands, and to visit the newly established Christian communities. At last, on the 29th of June, in the year 67 of Christ, he sealed his faith and mission with his blood on the hill of Janiculus in the city of Rome; and the prophetic words of Christ concerning the Chief of the Apostles were fulfilled: "When thou shalt be old, thou shalt stretch forth thy hands, and another shall gird thee: Follow me" (John xxi.).

The executioners of the cruel Nero "girded" the gray-haired man of God with bands, and fastened him to a cross, as had been done thirty-three years before to his divine Master. Willingly, and even cheerfully, the faithful Apostle stretched out his arms upon the cross, only too happy to be permitted to imitate his Master even in death. Yet, deeming himself unworthy the privilege of dying in the same posture as Jesus, he begged his executioners to permit him to be crucified with his head downward.

The martyred Apostle's body was laid in the Vatican catacombs, near Nero's circus.

8. The Conversion of St. Paul.

"He who persecuted us in times past doth now preach the faith which once he impugned."—GALATIANS i. 23.

Intimately associated and closely identified with the glorious name of Peter is the honored name of Paul. This great Apostle of the Gentiles, who is also sometimes called Saul, is the one of whom Christ himself bore testimony when he said: "He is a vessel of election to carry my name before kings, to the Gentiles, and to the children of Israel."

Trained in the schools of the Pharisees, he was at first a violent enemy of the Christian religion, and had obtained letters from the high-priest in Jerusalem authorizing him to search for the Christians living in Damascus, and to bring them before the Jewish courts. He was on his way to put these designs into execution, when a ray of God's grace struck him. "And as he went on his journey, it came to pass that he drew nigh to Damascus; and suddenly a light from heaven shined round about him. And falling on the ground, he heard a voice saying to him: Saul, Saul, why persecutest thou me? Who said: Who art thou, Lord? And he: I am Jesus, whom thou persecutest; it is hard for thee to kick against the goad. And he, trembling and astonished, said: Lord, what wilt

"Saul, Saul, why persecutest thou me?"

thou have me to do? And the Lord said to him: Arise and go into the city, and there it shall be told thee what thou must do. Now the men who went in company with him stood amazed, hearing indeed a voice, but seeing no man. And Saul arose from the ground, and when his eyes were opened he saw nothing" (Acts ix.).

Paul remained three days in Damascus, blind and without food, and crying to the Lord from the inmost depths of his soul for mercy and pardon. On the third day God sent Ananias, whom many suppose to be one of the seventy-two disciples, to Paul, to say to him: "Brother Saul, the Lord Jesus hath sent me, he that appeared to thee in the way, that thou mayest receive thy sight and be filled with the Holy Ghost" (Acts ix. 17). And immediately Saul recovered his sight, stood up, and received baptism.

With what astonishment and chagrin the Jews in Damascus looked upon this once bigoted Pharisee and bitter foe of Christianity, as he went into their synagogue, and with superhuman eloquence preached that the crucified Nazarite was the veritable Messias! He very soon left their city, however, and retired into the solitudes of the Arabian deserts, in order more freely to prepare himself for his high duties of an Apostle to the Gentiles.

9. The Missionary Labors of St. Paul.

"I am appointed a preacher and an apostle, a doctor of the Gentiles in faith and truth."—1 TIMOTHY ii. 7.

St. Paul set out on his first great mission in the year 45, starting from Antioch, and accompanied by St. Mark and St. Barnabas. This expedition consumed more than four years, and covered a vast extent of territory by sea and land. During this mission he established Christian churches in the island of Cyprus and in many cities and villages of Asia Minor; and with prayer and laying on of hands ordained priests and bishops to instruct and govern the new congregations.

St. Luke the Evangelist gives us, in the Acts of the Apostles, a remarkable example of the struggles and varied experiences of this indefatigable Apostle:

"And the multitude of the city was divided; and some of them indeed held with the Jews, but some with the Apostles. And when there was an assault made by the Gentiles and the Jews with their rulers, to use them contumeliously, and to stone them, they, understanding it, fled to Lystra and Derbe, cities of Lycaonia, and to the whole country round about, and were there preaching the Gospel. And there sat a certain man at Lystra impotent in his feet, a cripple from his mother's womb, who never had walked. This same heard Paul speaking; who looking upon him, and seeing that he had faith to be healed, said with a loud voice: Stand upright on thy feet. And he leaped up and walked. And when the multitudes had seen what Paul had done, they lifted up their voice in the Lycaonian tongue, saying: The gods are come down to us, in the likeness of men. And they called Barnabas, Jupiter; but Paul, Mercury; because he was chief speaker.

"The priest also of Jupiter, that was before the city, bringing oxen and garlands before the gate, would have offered sacrifice with the people; which when the Apostles Barnabas and Paul had heard, rending their clothes, they leaped out among the people, crying and saying: Ye men, why do ye these things? We also are mortals, men like unto you, preaching to you to be converted from these vain things to the living God, who made the heaven, and the earth, and the sea, and all things that are in them. And speaking these things, they scarce restrained the people from sacrificing to them. Now there came thither certain Jews from Antioch and Iconium, and persuading the multitude, and stoning Paul, drew him out of the city, thinking him to be dead. But as the disciples stood round about him, he rose up and entered into the city, and the next day he departed with Barnabas to Derbe."

About the year 51 we meet St. Paul at the council of the Apostles in Jerusalem, whence he set out soon after on his second great missionary voyage to Asia Minor, Macedonia, and Greece. His visit to Athens was specially important, where he thus addressed the highly educated and learned members of the highest court, called the Areopagus:

"But Paul, standing in the midst of Areopagus, said: Ye men of Athens, I perceive that in all things you are too superstitious. For passing by and seeing your idols, I found an altar on which was written: To THE UNKNOWN GOD. What therefore you worship, without knowing it, that I preach to you. God, who made the world and all things therein, he being Lord of heaven and earth, dwelleth not in temples made with hands; neither is he served with men's hands, as though he needed anything, seeing it is he who giveth to all life, and breath, and all things, and hath made of one all mankind, to dwell upon the whole face of the earth, determining appointed times and the limits of their habitation; that they should seek God, if happily they may feel after him or find him, although he be not far from every one of us. For in him we live, and move, and are. As some also of your own poets said: For we are also his offspring. Being, therefore, the offspring of God, we must not suppose the divinity to be like unto gold, or silver, or stone, the graving of art and device of man. And God indeed, having winked at the times of this ignorance, now declareth unto men that all should everywhere do penance. Because he hath appointed a day wherein he will judge the world in equity, by the man whom he hath appointed, giving faith to all, by raising him up from the dead."

On hearing mention made of the Resurrection, most of the Athenians began to sneer and to laugh. Some, however, agreed with Paul and believed; among others, Dionysius, a celebrated and respected member of the Areopagus.

This second voyage of Paul consumed about two years, and extended over a distance of more than a thousand leagues. On his third missionary voyage, lasting from the year 54 to the year 58, St. Paul tarried a long time

ST. PAUL PREACHING AT EPHESUS.

in Ephesus, a city of Asia Minor, where his new converts gave touching and instructive evidence of their strong Christian feeling. In that city fortune-telling and magic prevailed to a great extent, and the people had squandered large sums of money in the purchase of books which treated of these diabolical arts. But after Paul had preached with great eloquence and power on the one true God, the people, entering into themselves and discovering their errors, brought out all their books of magic, to the value of about 50,000 silver drachmas or about six thousand dollars, and burnt them to ashes in the public square. Would that Christians of our day might adopt a similar plan to rid society of many of the worthless, dangerous, and immoral books and newspapers with which we are deluged!

From Ephesus St. Paul journeyed into Macedonia, Illyria, and Greece, and returned finally to Jerusalem, after having traversed a distance of more than twelve hundred leagues, and gathered in abundant harvests for Christ.

10. Imprisonment and Execution of St. Paul.

"To me, to live is Christ, and to die is gain: having a desire to be dissolved and to be with Christ."—PHILIPPIANS i. 21, 23

The public feeling of the Jews in Jerusalem against St. Paul was again aroused to such a height that he was sent in chains to Cæsarea, where he passed two years in confinement. As he had but little hope of gaining his freedom, the more so as the Jews were continually clamoring to have him brought before their courts in Jerusalem, he appealed to the Roman emperor. Very soon after, King Agrippa came from Jerusalem on a visit to the Roman governor Festus at Cæsarea, and, as he remained some days, Festus had Paul brought before the king. In the court-room, besides King Agrippa, were his sister Bernice and Festus, the governor, together with a large concourse of the military and of the chief persons of the city; all of whom listened with profound attention to the eloquent words of the apostolic prisoner. Paul related so touchingly and so ably the wonderful circumstances of his conversion, his subsequent labors, his sufferings, trials, and tribulations in his newly adopted cause, that King Agrippa cried out, "Thou art almost able to persuade me to become a Christian;" and Festus, the governor, observed, "Paul, thou art beside thyself; too much learning hath made thee mad."

As Paul had appealed to the emperor, he was ordered to Rome in the autumn of the year 61; and, after many delays, he reached the imperial city about Easter-time the following year. Here he remained in prison for two years, but, being under very mild restraint, the Christians of Rome had access to him and were permitted to receive instructions in the new faith.

Having once more regained his liberty, he travelled westward as far as Spain; returned again to the East, founding the churches of Crete, visiting Ephesus, and traversing Macedonia for the third time, and finally, about the year 67, he went with St. Peter back to Rome. Here chains were again waiting for him; but this time they led to a crown of victory. This fate the Apostle had anticipated. "For I am even now ready," he writes to his dearly beloved friend Timothy, "to be sacrificed, and the time of my dissolution is at hand. I have fought the good fight, I have finished my course, I have kept the faith. As to the rest, there is laid up for me a crown of justice, which the Lord, the just Judge, will render to me in that day of mercy." (2 Tim. iv.) He was not wrong in his foreboding, for he and St. Peter were soon after thrown into the Mamertine prison. Even here they turned their dungeons into pulpits, and continued to preach to their fellow-prisoners the truths of religion, of salvation and redemption in Christ Jesus, till the final hour struck in which these heroes of Christ were to receive the crown of martyrdom. Whilst St. Peter was hurried off to crucifixion on the Vatican hill, St. Paul was being dragged along the Ostian road and beheaded. An inscription marks the spot where these two fellow-sufferers saw each other for the last time on earth, and bade each other farewell in the following touching words. St. Paul said to his companion: "Peace be with thee, thou foundation-

The Beheading of St. Paul.

rock of the Church, shepherd of all the flocks of Christ." The Prince of the Apostles replied: "Go in peace, thou teacher of all piety and virtue, counsellor of the good and virtuous, guide to salvation." The sumptuous Basilica of St. Paul stands over the grave of St. Paul, as St. Peter's on the Vatican hill shelters the tomb of St. Peter. Something more than a mile to the south-east of St. Paul's Basilica stands the church of "St. Paul with the Three Fountains," on the spot where St. Paul was put to death.

Old tradition has it that the head of the Apostle, on being violently severed from his body, bounded and struck the earth three times, and that at each point of contact a spring of pure water bubbled up which continues to flow till the present day.

11. The Missionary Labors of the Other Apostles.

"Their sound hath gone forth into all the earth, and their words unto the ends of the world."—PSALMS xviii. 5.

While Peter and Paul were thus laboring to advance the cause of Christ, the other Apostles were no less active and devoted in the great work of spreading the name and religion of Jesus Christ, and in founding and building up Christian congregations in all directions. St. James the elder proclaimed the tidings of salvation throughout Judea. So earnest was his zeal, and so great his success, that he drew upon himself the wrath of the wilfully blinded Pharisees, to please whom Herod Agrippa had the Apostle seized at Jerusalem and put to death by the sword, about nine or ten years after the ascent of Christ from the earth. According to tradition, the body of this holy martyr was brought into the Spanish province of Gallicia, where it is to this day visited by countless pilgrims at the shrine of Compostella.

St. John the Evangelist, brother of James, labored first in Judea. Soon after we meet him in Ephesus, the centre-point of Christianity in Asia Minor, where he gathered about him an assemblage of distinguished disciples, watched over the growing congregations of the neighborhood, and shielded the legacy of the faith, keeping it intact from the innovations of the Gnostics. Tradition teaches that St. John came also to Rome, where, being thrown into a caldron of boiling oil, near the Latin gate, he was, by the power of God, miraculously preserved unhurt, and afterwards banished by his enemies to the island of Patmos, where he wrote the books of the Apocalypse, or Revelation. Returning to Ephesus, he compiled his Gospel, and, although very old and infirm preached with untiring zeal the great law of charity, "My little children, love one another." He slept in the Lord about the year 100.

St. Andrew, the brother of St. Peter, preached in Scythia; that is, in Southern Russia, and along the shores of the Black Sea, and in Byzantium, the Constantinople of those times. At Patras, in Greece, he was brought before the judgment-seat of the proconsul Ægeas. "Sacrifice to the gods," was the order of the heathen proconsul. Andrew replied in these significant words: "Daily do I offer to the Almighty God, not indeed the flesh of oxen nor the blood of goats, but the immaculate Lamb of the altar; that Lamb with whose flesh thousands are fed, and who yet remains living and entire." At these words, he was condemned to be crucified. When the illustrious confessor came in sight of the instrument of his martyrdom, he greeted it lovingly and with cheerfulness, saying: "O dearest cross, honored as thou hast been by the body of my Master, long desired by me, my most cherished friend whom I have sought for constantly, take me hence from men and give me to my Lord!" After an agony of two days' duration, he calmly departed in the peace of the Lord.

St. Philip travelled through Scythia and Phrygia, preaching faithfully and successfully, and finally closing his saintly career by a martyr's death on the cross, at Hierapolis, in the eighty-seventh year of his age.

St. Bartholomew, that same Nathaniel of whom our Lord once said, "Behold a true Israelite, in whom there is no guile," went on his missionary duties as far as "India," which means, probably, Southern Arabia. He suffered martyrdom in the capital city of Armenia, having been first flayed by his executioners.

St. Matthew, who before his calling was named Levi, was the son of Alpheus, and preached the word of God in Ethiopia, Arabia, and Persia. He was the first among the four Evangelists to write the history of the public life of our Lord Jesus Christ, which he did in Palestine before beginning his missionary labors.

St. Thomas, after having carried the light of the Gospel to the Parthians, Medes, and Persians, penetrated into India, where, by the command of the king, he was pierced by a lance at Calamina.

St. James the younger, the cousin of our Lord and son of Alpheus, after the dispersion of the Apostles became bishop of Jerusalem, where, by his self-denial, strict integrity, and love of prayer, he not only edified and strengthened the infant Church in the spirit of the Gospel, but won over to the faith so many of the Jews that the chief-priests became exasperated and decreed the saint's death by stoning, in the year 63. He was finally slain with a fuller's club. He is the author of one of the apostolic epistles, in which he exhorts all the new Christians scattered through the country to the practice of the faith.

St. Jude Thaddeus, the brother of James, we meet as missionary in Arabia, Syria, Mesopotamia, and Persia, in which countries he labored faithfully, till, overtaken by the cruelty of the enemies of Christianity, he secured a martyr's crown. He too has left us one epistle.

St. Simon the Canaanite preached the kingdom of Christ to the inhabitants of Egypt and of other parts of Northern Africa, of Persia and of Babylon. He was crucified or, as some affirm, hacked to pieces at Suanir.

St. Matthias, one of the seventy-two disciples, was chosen Apostle soon after the Ascension of Christ, to take the place of Judas. Judea and afterward Ethiopia were the scenes of his apostolic activity and zeal; Sebastopolis, the place of his martyrdom.

St. Mark, or more properly St. John, accompanied

Paul and Barnabas to Antioch and Cyprus; and thence to Africa, where he afterwards founded the Church of Alexandria. We also find him in Italy, establishing the churches of Venice and Aquileia; and in Rome working side by side with St. Peter, who styled him his son, and under whose direction he wrote his Gospel.

St. Luke was a physician, and also a painter, from Antioch in Syria, and was chosen by St. Paul, in the year 53, to accompany him on the mission. Under the direction of St. Paul he compiled his Gospel, and afterwards the Acts of the Apostles. When far advanced in years, it was his privilege to seal with his blood that holy faith which he had taught so faithfully by word and writing.

Thus it was that our beloved Lord and Saviour Jesus Christ was pleased to manifest himself by his first messengers to the nations of the earth. How imperishable the glory and triumph of these chosen servants of God, these first pillars of the Christian Church! Little indeed has been written about their apostolic labors, but in the book of life their names are inscribed in letters of gold. On the great day of judgment we shall all discover how much these disinterested men preached, wrought, and suffered in their unceasing efforts to spread the Church of Christ throughout the earth. We may form some feeble notion of their arduous duties by reading and studying the address of St. Paul to the Corinthians, where he describes some of his own experiences, as well as some of the other Apostles':

"They are the ministers of Christ. (I speak as one less wise.) I am more: in many more labors, in prisons more frequently, in stripes above measure, in deaths often. Of the Jews five times did I receive forty stripes, save one. Thrice was I beaten with rods, once I was stoned, thrice I suffered shipwreck, a night and a day I was in the depth of the sea. In journeying often, in perils of waters, in perils of robbers, in perils from my own nation, in perils from the Gentiles, in perils in the city, in perils in the wilderness, in perils in the sea, in perils from false brethren. In labor and painfulness, in much watchings, in hunger and thirst, in fastings often, in cold and nakedness. Besides those things which are without: my daily instance, the solicitude for all the churches. Who is weak, and I am not weak? Who is scandalized, and I am not on fire? If I must needs glory, I will glory of the things that concern my infirmity. The God and Father of our Lord Jesus Christ, who is blessed for ever, knoweth that I lie not."

12. The Growth of the Church in Europe.

"But you are a chosen generation, a purchased people: that you may declare his virtues, who hath called you out of darkness into his marvellous light."—1 PETER ii. 9.

Rome is the centre of Christianity. Here the infant Church, baptized in the blood of the twin apostles, grew so rapidly that she counted in the third century one hundred and fifty priests besides her Chief Bishop. In the other cities, too, of Italy, Christian congregations sprang up and flourished in such numbers and piety that, among all the other countries of Europe, Italy possesses the enviable happiness and honor of being the first Christian nation in point of time.

In Spain the Church planted by St. Paul grew and flourished to such an extent that the cities of Toledo, Leon, Tarragona, Cordova, and Elvira were bishoprics as early as the year 250.

According to the traditions of the Churches of Vienne and Arles, in France, the faith was first preached in that country by some disciples of the Apostles themselves. It is beyond doubt, however, that some Christian emigrants from Asia Minor, under the lead of Sts. Pothonius and

Irenæus, brought the glad tidings of salvation permanently to France about the year 150. These founded the Church at Lyons, whence they afterwards sent out many zealous missionaries to convert other tribes among the Gauls. The infant Church of France, or Gaul, was threatened with destruction during the great and violent incursions of the Franks; but the Lord protected and saved his vineyard; for the French king, Clovis, immediately after the memorable victory on the plain of Zul-

The Baptism of Clovis.

pich, became converted to the true faith, and was baptized, together with the chief officers of his court, on Christmas-day, 496.*

* Previous to this date, all the efforts made by Queen Clotilda to convert the king to the true faith had proved fruitless. In the midst of the battle of Zulpich, fought against the Allemanni tribes in 496, Clovis, finding the fortunes of war going against him, and his troops beginning to yield, fell on his knees in the battle-field and petitioned "Clotilda's God" for assistance. Victory came to him unexpectedly. Full of gratitude, he put himself under a course of reli-

The light of our Lord's Gospel shed its rays as far as England, and tradition makes mention of a Christian king of that country, named St. Lucius, as early as the year 180. About the middle of the fifth century that country was overrun by the pagan Anglo-Saxons, and the feeble Church was in great danger of extinction. Pope Gregory the Great,

St. Patrick.

however, came to its rescue by sending, about the year 596, the Abbot Augustine, together with forty missionaries,

gious instruction, and counselled all his soldiers to turn towards that one true God who had led them on to victory. Accordingly, on Christmas-day of the same year, the king, together with three thousand of his subjects, received baptism at the hands of the saintly bishop Remigius, who immediately after the ceremony spoke to the king the following significant words: "Bow down thy head, proud Sicamber; burn what thou hast hitherto adored, and adore in future what thou hast hitherto burned." For, until that time, King Clovis, who was descended from the family of the Sicambri, had been an idol-worshipper and an enemy of the one true God.

to regenerate the people. In less than fifty years after St. Augustine's arrival we find many bishoprics, churches, and monasteries in England, who in her turn sent out countless holy missionaries to the other nations of Europe.

Ireland was added to the list of Christian nations by the great St. Patrick. His efforts were so blessed by Heaven that in a few years the whole people had become most faithful and fervent Catholics; and so numerous were

St. Columban.

the holy, learned, and indefatigable missionaries whom she sent abroad that she received the glorious title of the "Island of Saints." Amongst the countless missionaries from Ireland was St. Columkille, who went to Scotland in 565, and at his death, in 597, left the whole country Catholic.

In the same century St. Aidan carried the treasures of Ireland's faith and piety into Northumberland, in England.

St. Columban, like Abraham of old, left his native Ireland during the seventh century, and traversed Gaul, Switzerland, and Italy, preaching Christ crucified to the still unconverted inhabitants of those countries. St. Gall, who accompanied St. Columban in his missionary travels, was the chief founder of Christianity in Switzerland. All through the seventh, eighth, and ninth centuries the sons of Ireland continued to preach Christ crucified throughout most of the unconverted portions of Europe, and to supply abundant proof that the life of Christ had been prolonged in the "Island of Saints." That land of St. Patrick, St. Malachy, and St. Brendan was indeed a home of faith. In days when paganism and desolation still reigned where Christianity is now triumphant, Ireland had its saints ruling their flocks, its well-ordered hierarchy, its schools of Christian science. Armagh, Lismore, Clonfert, and other seats of learning and piety were known throughout Europe. Teachers from Ireland were held in high honor in the universities of Oxford, Paris, Pavia, and Bologna.

Even in the days of the northern invasions we find the monasteries of Europe, those ramparts behind which religion and civilization took shelter from the furious incursions of northern barbarians, defended in a great measure by those heroic sons of Ireland who had caught the impulse of their apostle's sanctity and zeal.

A learned and holy writer of the present day thus eloquently describes the spiritual and mystic life of Christ as manifested in Ireland before the days of persecution: "The image of that fair island rises before me, rock-bound and lashed by the mighty waters of the west, green with living verdure, with its blue mountains, its fruitful plains and exhaustless rivers. I seem to see some old picture, such as is hung over the altars in our sanctuaries, and in which the skill of the painter is even less than the sanctity of his idea. It is such as we often see when in the background there is a gentle landscape, bounded by dark, tranquil mountains, shaded by tall and spreading trees, in the midst a calm water and clear bright air; here is a company of saints musing on Holy Writ, and there a multitude of upturned faces drinking in the words of an evangelist; on one side a crowd by a river's brink receiving the sacrament of regeneration; on the other, the Holy Sacrifice of the altar is lifted up before the Eternal Father; beyond is a mystic ladder reaching up to heaven, on which angels are ascending and descending, and communing with saints in vision; and in the foreground, rising over all, is Jesus on his throne, and on his right hand Mary crowned with light and beauty."

In Germany, the country along the Rhine was the first to receive the light of the Gospel. As early as the year 150, Christian congregations were in flourishing and well-ordered condition; and when, in the year 336, St. Athanasius, bishop of Alexandria, came during his exile to Triers, he found Catholic bishops in Strasburg, Cologne, Speyer, Worms, and Trier. In South Germany, too, on the banks of the Leck and the Danube, the cross of Christ was firmly planted at a very early period; whilst renowned saints such as Bishop Maximilian of Lorch, Florian of Ems, Dionysius of Augsburg and his niece St. Afra, Victorinus of Petau, and many others, consecrated and fertilized the soil of Germany with martyr-blood about the year 300.

Switzerland honors as her first apostle St. Beatus, who died in the year of Christ 112. In very early days this land had episcopal sees in Augusta, afterwards called Basel; Avanche, afterwards called Lausanne; in Constance, Geneva, and Chur.

The invasion of the Huns, Allemanni, and other barbarous tribes had well-nigh destroyed the Church in Germany and Switzerland; but, in order to firmly and permanently restore and re-establish it, the Almighty raised up, during the sixth and seventh centuries, a body of holy, zealous, and able men, such as Fridolin, Columba, Gall,

Trutpert, Pirmin, Severin, Rupert, Emeran, Corbinian, and Killian.

Germany's chief apostle, however, was St. Boniface. He was a man of untiring zeal, high intellect, and childlike simplicity; a very hero in his faith, in his dependence on Providence, and in his charity; yes, a vessel of election like St. Paul. Born in England about the year 680, he received at his baptism the name of Winifred, and entered,

St. Boniface.

at an early age, the order of the Benedictines. Hearing in his soul a voice from heaven saying, "Carry the light of my Gospel to the people who sit in darkness and the shadow of death; I will there show thee how thou must labor and suffer for me," Winnifred promptly responded to this interior voice of God. Fortified with the blessing of his abbot and the prayers of his fellow-religious, he entered on his missionary labors, first in Friesland and afterwards in Thuringia and among the Hessians. Here he hewed down the sacred oak-tree to which the inhabitants used to pay divine honors, and with the timber built a chapel in honor of St. Peter. Paganism in this district fell with its sacred oak, to rise no more. Our saint afterwards labored in Bavaria, in the Rhine countries, and even in France itself, where, by the permission and authority of the pope, he anointed Pepin king of France in 752. When far advanced in years, the ardent wish of his early youth returned to him; namely, the desire to become a missionary in Friesland. He travelled towards the north, baptized many in the true faith, and for his zeal received the crown of martyrdom at Dorkum, on the 5th of June, 753.

This apostle of Germany made three wearisome journeys to Rome in order to obtain the sanction and blessing of the Vicar of Christ upon his labors, as well as to keep the Church of Germany in close union with the centre of Christian faith and unity. He received from the Pope the beautiful and significant name of Boniface, or *doer of good;* and also the dignity of archbishop of Mayence and papal legate for all Germany. Many dioceses and monasteries are indebted to him for their creation or restoration. His good work was continued by his faithful disciples, to the great blessing of Germany.

At the death of St. Boniface, the Saxons in Westphalia, Eastphalia, and Engern were the only large German tribe still in idolatry. But these also became subject to the yoke of Christ about the year 800; and the work begun by the sword of Charlemagne was completed by the untiring zeal, holy example, and profound knowledge of humble and self-sacrificing bishops and priests.

Our blessed Lord and Saviour wished also to take up his mystic abode among the people of the North; that is, among the Scandinavians in Denmark, Sweden, and Norway. To effect his loving designs, he chose as apostle for these people the holy monk Ansgar, afterwards archbishop of Hamburg-Bremen, who from this place travelled forth among the Swedes and Danes, preaching the Gospel and establishing the Church on a firm basis, by erecting dioceses and founding several seats of piety and learning.

The cross of our Saviour was carried in triumph into the countries of Sclavia; that is, among the peoples of Bohemia, Poland, and Russia. The chief apostles among the Sclavonic races were the Greek monks Methodius and Cyrillus, who lived about 870. The dioceses of Posen, founded in 968, of Prague, in 973, and of Gnesen, in 997, were the centres whence irradiated the glorious light of the Gospel into all the surrounding districts

Among the Magyars in Hungary we meet in the year 950, as first bishop, the monk Hierotheus. Two holy bishops, Piligrim of Passau and Adalbert of Prague, together with the king St. Stephen, completed, about the year 1000, the conversion of this warlike people; and the archbishopric of Gran became at this time the centre of Christianity in Hungary.

The last people in Europe to open their eyes to the light of the true faith were the Prussians. About the year 1000, the saintly Adalbert, bishop of Prague, and the holy Benedictine monk Bruno made an unsuccessful effort to convert Prussia, and both fell martyrs to their indomitable zeal. It was not until after the adjoining countries of Pomerania and Livonia had become Christian, about the year 1150, and when the monk Christian, of the monastery of Oliva, after having labored as bishop of the Prussians with extraordinary zeal and perseverance for their conversion, called to his aid, in the year 1226, the knights of the German order, under the lead of grandmaster Herman of Salza, that the religion of Christ struck a firm root in that country.

But after the short duration of less than three hundred years, the Catholic religion was overturned and discarded by these people; and from this land, which was the last to admit Christianity to its embrace, broke forth the disastrous storm of the so-called reformation, which in the sixteenth century carried away a large portion of Europe from the Catholic Church. In order to arrest the pernicious progress of this so-called reformation, but more especially in order to strengthen and vivify the faith and Christian virtue among the people who remained

St. Francis of Assisi.

steadfast to the faith, God called into existence the system of home-missions. For what did it avail to have preached the religion of Christ, or to have established his Church, if the spirit which quickeneth—namely, faith, hope, and charity—should gradually become dead, and if Christian life should degenerate into a mere external and profitless profession of religion? As a strong defence against such an evil, Christ raised up learned and holy bishops, and zealous, edifying priests to be their assistants in securing the salvation of souls. Nevertheless there have been occasions when this aridity of Christian life among men seemed to threaten the life of the Church itself in a most formidable manner. Then, indeed, were extraordinary men and means required, and Christ never failed to raise them up at the proper moment to protect his Church. Such, for instance, were the great penitential preachers, whose burning eloquence often aroused whole nations to a sense of their duty to God and to the practice of his saving truths and precepts, and infused a renewed Christian life into their hitherto deadened souls. Among these may be mentioned St. Bernard, St. Francis of Assisi, St. Dominic, St. Vincent Ferrer, St. Charles Borromeo, St. Francis of Sales, and many others. In more recent ages four great religious orders have flourished in a special manner, through whose exertions, in the conducting of popular home-missions in the parishes, many most salutary and profitable blessings and graces have been bestowed upon the faithful. These are the Society of the Jesuits, the Capuchin fathers, the Mission Priests of St. Vincent de Paul, and the Redemptorists.

13. The History of the Church in Asia.

"Thou knowest this, that all they who are in Asia are turned away from me."—2 TIMOTHY i. 5.

And now we direct our attention towards the second continent, called Asia, to learn how the Church of God has been spread over its boundless territory. Let us enter this region with reverence, for its soil is sacred. Here, of old, dwelt the patriarchs; here, for four thousand years, was the mystery of our Redemption in slow and solemn preparation; here Jesus Christ, the King of kings, lived in the form of a servant. Praise be to him for all eternity!

A rich and abundant harvest sprang up here from the seed sown by Christ and his Apostles. Antioch in Syria, Tyre in Phœnicia, Ephesus and Smyrna in Asia Minor, Nisibis in Mesopotamia, Sebaste in Armenia, Seleucia in Persia, Bostra in Arabia, Salamis in the island of Cyprus: all these places were flourishing gardens in the vineyard of Christianity during the first three centuries. Christian piety, morals, and knowledge not only flourished here, but were carried forth to every quarter of western and southern Asia. Even India[*] and China[†] were illuminated by the rays of the Gospel-Sun.

Who would have suspected in those days of Asiatic faith and piety that the dark night of infidelity would soon envelop that continent, and the Sun of Christianity, like the sun in the firmament, would take its way westward to European lands? Such are the inscrutable ways of divine wisdom, yea, rather of divine justice. Most of these eastern nations, gradually forgetting how deeply they were indebted to the Gospel of Christ, in place of a child-like faith cultivated pride of intellect and rebellion of heart—both leading to infidelity—and they soon began to look upon the maxims of Christianity as an intolerable burden. Then came the visitation of divine justice upon these ungrateful people. The first heavy blow of retribution was struck by the hands of the Persian kings, who during a period of three hundred years, till 620, persecuted the Church of Asia with fire and sword. These

---

[*] In the year 535 the monk Cosmas found Christian congregations in those countries, and even a bishop at Calliana.

[†] According to an old document written in ancient Syrian and Chinese, and discovered in 1625, a priest named Jaballah spread the faith here about the year 640.

people received their death-stroke from the hand of Mohammed.

This clever impostor, son of a pagan father and Jewish mother, was born in the year 570, at Mecca in Arabia. His fellow-countrymen, though they held a variety of religious views, were closely united in their common veneration for the Kaaba at Mecca, a kind of sanctuary in which, as they claimed, stood the so-called Altar of Abraham, a shapeless dark-colored stone. Mohammed, encouraged by Abdallah the Jew, and by Sergius, a heretical monk, inveighed forcibly against the idolatry of his countrymen, and preached the doctrine of "One God, and Mohammed is his prophet." Being persecuted by his neighbors, he fled on the 15th of July, 622, from Mecca to Medina, and soon afterwards he succeeded in bringing all Arabia under his power and made it conform to his religious teachings. His flight is still known by the term Hegira, or the Prophet's flight. His system of religion, which was based upon pretended revelations made by the Archangel Gabriel, and which consists even yet of a mixture of paganism and Judaism with a tinge of Christianity, was embodied in the Koran, after Mohammed's death in 632, and carried by dint of arms over all western Asia, throughout northern Africa, and even reached Spain through the emigration of the Arabs.

Since the rise of Mohammed, Asia has continued to be a dry and rotten branch, fallen from the Christian tree of life.

Throughout the middle ages the Popes never lost sight of the spiritual interests of Asia, nor even of Africa. During the thirteenth and fourteenth centuries several of the missionaries sent by the Heads of the Church to that part of the world penetrated even as far as China.

But the history of these Christian missionaries is shrouded in impenetrable obscurity. As the day set apart by an all-wise Providence for the conversion of these countries had not yet dawned, we may believe that the efforts of these messengers, though doubtless saving many souls, were not attended with much external lustre.

For many centuries Asia lay enveloped in utter darkness; till at last the Lord, who chastises and forgives, smites to the earth and raises up again, sent to them another apostle in the person of Saint Francis Xavier. This zealous and extraordinary man, leaving home and friends, was carried on the wings of love, about the year 1542, to

St. Francis Xavier.

the East Indies, where, like his divine Master, he called around him the children of ignorance and superstition, won their confidence and affection, and through these young people gained the heathen parents to Christ. He then founded churches and opened schools. The Indians styled him the Holy Man, the Great Father. From India he went to Japan, where in the short space of two years and a half he converted several thousand souls. He again set sail for China, with the hope of bringing its benighted inhabitants to a knowledge of the true faith, but died on the confines of that country on the 3d of December, 1552, after having baptized, according to reliable authority, more than three hundred thousand pagans.

His brethren in religion, the fathers of the Society of Jesus, continued the work of this illustrious missionary in India and Japan, building in the former country, from 1552 to 1590, about two hundred and fifty churches;

A Missionary among the Pagans.

while in China, by the holiness of their lives, the wisdom of their preaching, and the glow of their unbounded charity, they gained thousands upon thousands of souls to Christ. Notwithstanding cruel and bloody persecutions, especially in Japan, there have never been wanting, since that time, God-inspired men to devote themselves wholly to the Christian missions in Asia. Depending altogether upon the offerings of Christians in Europe, secular priests, Jesuits, Lazarists, Capuchins, and other devoted servants of God have worn themselves out in holy rivalry, in their efforts to spread the kingdom of Christ throughout heathen lands. At the same time, brave and self-sacrificing sisters of the various orders have given testimony before the eyes of the astounded and edified pagans of the power of Christian love, by their unceasing labors in hospitals, orphanages, and schools. Many of these missionaries met a martyr's death; some in bloody persecution, others in the excess of privation and of labor. But the gaps left by these are soon filled up, for Catholic Europe still sends its noblest and most disinterested sons as missionaries to the Orient, so that unbroken armies of new heroes of the faith take the places of the victors who have gone to rest.

14. The History of the Church in Africa.

"Before him the Ethiopians shall fall down. He shall deliver the poor from the mighty; and the needy that had no helper."—PSALM lxxi.

St. Mark the Evangelist had himself founded a Christian congregation with a bishop at its head in Alexandria, the chief city of Egypt. Very soon a large and flourishing school was established here, and the renown of its learned and pious professors gathered about them in great numbers from every part of Egypt and Asia Minor eager and docile disciples, whom they conducted through the paths of pagan knowledge into the realms of true wisdom and faith. The Church made such rapid progress in Egypt that about the year 300 there were more than one hundred bishops in that land.

The faith having been carried from Rome into the north-western portions of Africa, Carthage here became the centre of Catholicity. From this point the light and warmth of the true faith radiated with such good effect that an African priest, Tertullian, could say to the pagans as early as the year 200: "We Christians are of but yesterday, yet we occupy all the places once filled by you—the islands, cities, villages, council-halls, and military camps. We constitute the majority in every city." About the year 330 this north-west part of Africa, together with Abyssinia, counted more than three hundred bishops.

In the year 429, when the rude Vandals under their king Genserich came to Africa, a series of terrible persecutions overtook the Church, which lost vast numbers; till finally, in 533, the Greek commander Belisarius overthrew the Vandal power and re-established the authority of the Roman empire. But again in the seventh century Mohammedanism invaded Egypt and most parts of Northern Africa, and buried, as it did the Church in Asia, the once flourishing African Church out of sight.

But the memory of this once vigorous branch of the Church of God has never faded from the minds of European Christians. All through the middle ages, men zealous for the salvation of souls made repeated efforts to revive the knowledge of the Gospel in Africa. Thus, in the year 1212, five companions of St. Francis Assissi went with this intention to Morocco; but all the fruit of their efforts consisted in their own martyrdom. Similar efforts to the same purpose were made by the zealous Raymond Lullus, who, not satisfied with training young men in Europe to become apostles to the Mohammedan Saracens, went himself three times to Africa, where finally, on his third apostolic visitation, he purchased with his blood at Tunis, in 1315, the long-desired and ardently sought crown of martyrdom.

In later ages we again discover the sons of St. Francis, the Capuchins, as missionaries in Africa, both on the eastern coast, in Mozambique, Monomotapa, and Quiloa, and on the western coast, in Congo, Angola, Benguela, and in the islands of Bourbon and of France.

We see in the year 1838 a bishopric in Algiers, which

becomes an archbishopric in 1867. Later, also, three sees were established in the towns of Oran, Constantine, and Ceuta; and we also find missionary stations in Egypt, Abyssinia, in Central Africa, and along the coasts, at the various trading-posts.

But alas! what are these few struggling institutions, comprising as they do only four and a half millions of Catholics under the guidance of twenty-four bishops or apostolic vicars, in comparison with the glory of this same African Church in early times, when five hundred and fifty native bishops could assemble at one time in Carthage!

15. What America owes to the Catholic Church.

"Who in times past are not a people, but are now the people of God: who had not obtained mercy, but now have obtained mercy. I beseech you that having your conversation good among the infidels, whereas they speak against you as evil-doers, they may, by the good works which they shall behold in you, glorify God in the day of visitation."—1 PETER ii. 10.

The very name of America ought to fill the soul of every Catholic with joy and holy pride. To the Catholic Church America owes her discovery, her civilization, and, for the most part, her civil liberty and independence in the United States. Thus our beloved Church has justly earned for herself the most indisputable right to exist in the new as well as in the old world.

The discoverer of America, Christopher Columbus, was a son of the ancient Church, and indeed a loyal, devout, and practical member of that Communion. The motive which first inspired him, and led him on to his successful discovery, was a truly Catholic motive. In his last will and testament this devoted son of the Church expressly required his son Diego, or whomsoever should become his heir, to be prepared to offer his person, his influence, and his wealth in defence of the rights of the Holy See, in case an attempt should ever be made to alienate this portion of God's vineyard from the Vicar of Christ. He required his son, moreover, to spare no cost nor labor in bringing the Indians to a knowledge of the true faith. He also assures us that it was the wish of his heart at all times to see the revenues derived from his newly discovered country employed by his sovereigns in redeeming the holy city of Jerusalem from the dominion of the pagans.

Christopher Columbus.

Catholic priests were the truest friends and best aids to Columbus. He informs us: "When I was an object of ridicule to all, two monks remained steadfast in their devotion to me and my cause." These were the Franciscan friar Percy de Marchena and the Dominican Diego Deza. And for all the learning and science which led him to the discovery of the New World, was he not indebted to the Catholic Church, to her monastic schools, and to educational establishments founded and sustained by that Church?

Besides claiming the honor of having discovered America, the Church rightly lays claim to the honor of civilizing its people. She was the first to succeed in obtaining gentle treatment, and indeed freedom itself, for the native Americans. In 1537 Pope Paul the Third declared in an apostolic brief that the native Indians of

Bartholomew de las Casas.

America were really and truly free men who should not be reduced to slavery.

Throughout the four hundred years that have well-nigh elapsed since the cross of Christ was first planted in American soil, the Church has continued to send forth from European lands, heroes of faith and charity to bring the native Indians, as well as the bold European pioneers, into a state of civilization. Who does not know, and honor, and bless the name of that noble son of the Church, the illustrious Dominican monk, Father Bartholomew de las Casas? Five times this intrepid and devoted priest of God crossed the Atlantic Ocean in order to announce the glad tidings of eternal salvation to his beloved children, as he was wont to call the Indians. Five times he returned to Spain in order to plead the red man's cause, in words and writing, before the monarchs and great ones of the kingdom; to save his Indians from oppression, slavery, and even threatened extinction. With inexpressible pain and disappointment, he saw all his efforts towards obtaining freedom for the natives rendered abortive by the avarice and treachery of the Spanish authorities in America. He therefore resolved, as simple missionary, to conduct the sons of the forest at least to the freedom of the children of God. For this purpose he plunged into the vast and intricate forests of the unknown country, and continued his laborious and exhausting search after souls up to a feeble old age. His nights he passed in the open air, in lonely supplication for the blessings of heaven to descend upon his poor friendless Indians. His days were spent in their rude wigwams or at their public gatherings, where he spoke earnestly and eloquently to the wondering savages about a true fatherland and supernatural home, where, after the trials and tribulations of this life, they would enjoy freedom and happiness forever. He was called to his own true home of freedom and peace in 1566, in the ninety-second year of his age.

Finally, we fear not to assert that the irresistible advances of America towards religious and civil liberty are due to the influence and action of the Catholic Church. Its members were the first to set the example of religious toleration and of unrestricted liberty of conscience. Lord Baltimore, the founder of the first settlement within the State of Maryland, himself a Catholic, promulgated religious freedom to all settlers in the colony. This was in the year 1649, at a time when the Protestant authorities of the other American colonies were enacting penal decrees of banishment, of mutilation, and even of death itself against all Catholics venturing within the boundaries of their jurisdiction. From 1776 to 1783, in the war against Great Britain for American Independence, fervent and edifying Catholics were found in the front ranks and in the most honorable and gallant positions. It was a Catholic who led the Americans in their first naval battle, on the 11th of May, 1775. John Barry, a Catholic from Ireland, was the founder of the United States Navy. Washington's first adjutant, General Stephen Moylan, was a son of Catholic Ireland. Catholic priests lent their peaceful efforts to the success of Independence. Father John Carroll went on an embassy to the Catholics of Canada, and secured to no small extent their sympathy for the cause, and a valuable neutrality, if not an active co-operation. The patriotic Father Gibault was the first to pronounce a blessing on the American flag and mingle holy water with the "Stars and Stripes." Catholic France, "the eldest daughter of the Church," contributed not only her armies, commanded by brave and competent generals, but also many millions of money, as well as the incalculable moral support of her immense influence with the other nations on the Continent of Europe. Catholic gentlemen, such as Thomas Fitzsimmons and Charles Carroll of Carrollton, were eminently instrumental in bringing to a happy and peaceful union the thirteen colonies. Washington himself, after the proclamation of peace and triumph, did not hesitate to pay a generous, though well-deserved, compliment to these Catholics. In his reply to an address tendered by them, the great general said that "the country could never forget the patriotic stand assumed by the Catholics of America and France, nor the invaluable assistance which they had contributed towards the independence of the colonies."

16. The Church planted in America. Its Growth.

"These were men of mercy, whose godly deeds have not failed. Their posterity are a holy inheritance, and their children for their sakes remain forever, and their name liveth unto generation and generation."—ECCLESIASTICUS xliv.

After this hasty general glance at the sacred and close relations between the Church of Christ and America, the land of the future, let us direct our attention towards those noble and venerated missionaries, and contemplate the labors of those holy men who, by their supernatural zeal, faith, and charity, have proved that the life of Christ can be prolonged even in the New World.

To-day the two continents of North and South America contain upwards of fifty-four millions of European emigrants, Chinese, and Africans, with some twenty millions of Indians and mixed breeds, the great majority of whom belong to the Catholic Church. So devoted to Catholicity are the Indians, in some sections that a recent and well-informed writer has inscribed upon a mountain-rock the following sentiment concerning certain tribes: "When men say that these savages are simply religious, they convey but a very imperfect idea of the deep-seated piety and fidelity pervading their whole lives. They are more a nation of saints than a herd of wild savages." To save the emigrant from loss of faith, to guard him against the temptation of the proselyter, and to teach and baptize the Indian, has been the chief labor of the American missionary. So blessed by Providence have these labors been that the life of Christ has been continued in the wilds of America, reaching its highest perfection in the seraphic and virginal soul of St. Rose of Lima.

The very first year following the discovery by Columbus, twelve priests with the Benedictine abbot, Father Bernard Boyle, set out, like the twelve apostles under the leadership

A MISSIONARY IN AMERICA.

of St. Peter fourteen hundred years before, and crossed the Atlantic to extend the kingdom of Christ. On the 6th of January, 1494, they blessed, on the Island of Hayti, the first rude temple of the Most High in the New World. These were soon afterwards followed by the Sons of St. Francis and of St. Dominic. But the most numerous and most efficient of all were the black-gowned followers of St. Ignatius. The Jesuits were the first to penetrate into the remotest parts of the forests: the first to reach each and every tribe of Indians; the first to plant the cross in the wilderness, and to pour out their warm life's-blood at its foot. What a brilliant chapter in the history of the life of Christ has been written on the virgin-page of America's soil! The history of well-nigh every American city, of every American province, presents to us the picture of a soul-loving Catholic missionary, laboring first to erect his humble chapel, and then his own lowly home, and then gathering about him the sons of the forest, reinforced by the poor but devout and generous settlers from the old lands across the seas. Like magic, we see this humble beginning soon transformed into a centre of wealth and prosperity, but, better yet, into a stately seat of learning, civilization, and religion. But how describe the hardships, struggles, and privations of these men of God? With axe in hand, they hew their way through the primeval forests. They wander through the perplexing woodlands and over the lonely, pathless, boundless prairies. They ford the rushing stream on foot, and cross the impetuous river and stormy lake in the frail canoe or on the treacherous floating ice. They battle with supernatural energy against cold and heat, hunger and thirst, fatigue and illness, and often, too, against the treachery and murderous designs of the savage.

But a very few of these early missionaries, with the sole exception of the apostle of Brazil, Father Antony Vieyra, died a natural death, or found a last resting-place in soil consecrated by the blessings of the Church. Some, like Father Marquette, the discoverer of the Mississippi River, sinking beneath the crushing weight of their labors, lay down and died peacefully in the wilderness, surrounded only by their afflicted companions, who then dug the missionary's grave under some majestic tree or near the bank of a stream, and went away, leaving the place of sepulture silent and lonely. Others met death at the

Father Marquette.

bedside of the plague-stricken Indian, offering up their lives to God as an acceptable sacrifice of charity. Among these were the venerated Fathers Dablon and Turgis. Many died in the silent depths of the forests, unseen by any eye save God's; their bodies becoming a prey to the birds of the air. To many, too, was vouchsafed the more glorious death of the martyr. Among these were the venerable Fathers Corpo, Souel, Chabanel, Ribourde, Brebœuf, Lallemand, and others, who either fell before the piercing, poisoned arrow of the savage or were treacherously and unexpectedly assassinated, or else were burnt at the stake, surrounded only by the untamed redskins, who in their hideous war-cry drowned the feeble words of prayer uttered by the dying saints. The soil of the great State of New York was consecrated by the blood of Father Jogues.

The most striking evidence of what might have been attained by self-sacrificing and disinterested missionaries was seen in the "reductions" of the Jesuits on the river La Plata in Paraguay. Like the monks of old in Europe, after the devastating incursions of the Northmen, these intrepid Jesuits conceived the plan not only of converting the Indians to the Christian faith, but to organize them into free, independent, cultivated, civilized nations. Their grand enterprise received the approbation and aid of Philip the Third of Spain in the year 1610. During the next one hundred and thirty years about thirty "reductions," or colonizations of Indians, were set on foot, and established on a wise basis. Under the admirable management of the indefatigable Jesuits, the rude Indians were trained to agriculture and the trades, and even to the arts. Even the science of civilized warfare was not neglected, for the peaceful Jesuits drilled them in the art and mode of using all warlike weapons for the purpose of self-defence against aggressive neighbors. The missionaries were at once teachers, priests, fathers, and magistrates for the Indians, who were here gradually made to adapt themselves to the observance of correct morality, to moderation and the ways of civilized domestic life. The observance of the law was further assisted by the establishment of pious associations. In an incredibly short space of time the world saw these depraved and degraded superstitious savages transformed into gentle, chaste, patient, pious Christian communities.

Would you now desire, Christian reader, to know the results of all these apostolical labors? Let the works speak for themselves. See the many sumptuous cathedrals, the tens of thousands of churches large and small, the countless cloisters and many bishoprics, the hundreds of thousands of well-ordered parishes, with more than forty millions of souls, in North, Central, and South America; all, too, in communion with the Vicar of Christ, our Holy Father the Pope. Day by day the numbers grow more and more steadily.

The most remarkable increase in Catholicity has taken place in the United States of North America. In the year 1790 these States contained only three millions of inhabitants, of whom about fifty thousand, or the one-sixtieth part, were Catholics. In the year 1880, the Church in the United States counted 6,200,000 Catholics in eleven archdioceses, forty-eight dioceses, eight apostolic vicariates, and two apostolic prefectures, with about 5000 priests, 6000 churches and chapels, 600 colleges and academies, and 350 charitable institutions.

The first permanent organization of the Catholics of the State of New York into a congregation took place about 1785, with the Irish Franciscan, Father Charles Wheelan, as pastor. This congregation, which laid the foundation-stone of the first Catholic church in New York, St. Peter's, has since developed like the grain of mustard-seed into countless parishes, several bishoprics, and even a cardinalate of the Holy Roman Church.

The first bishop in the United States was Doctor John Carroll, a man distinguished for his piety, wisdom, and energy. In the year 1792 he held in Baltimore the first synod of the Catholic Church in the United States. Besides himself, there were present his three vicars, the director of his Seminary, and sixteen other priests. Seventy-four years later, in October, 1866, at the Plenary Council of Baltimore, Bishop Carroll's successor was attended by seven archbishops, thirty-six bishops, and many priests.

The whole of America counts about seventy-four millions of inhabitants, of whom about forty-three millions, or nearly two-thirds, are Catholics.

17. The History of the Church in Australia.

"For God who commanded the light to shine out of darkness, himself hath shined in our hearts, to give the light of the knowledge of the glory of God."—2 CORINTHIANS iv. 6.

The history of the Church of Christ in Australia, although showing forth the Life of Christ as still continued in the Mystical Body, throughout every portion of the world, does not present as brilliant a picture as we have discovered in that portion of the vineyard planted in America. Although the chief portion of that country has been known to Europeans since 1616, and although the bishopric of Manila had been established ninety years earlier on one of the Philippine Islands, it was not till within the present century that the Church made any perceptible progress in that remote land. The insalubrity of the climate, in many places so bad that the inhabitants could not survive for a great number of years, but more especially the persistent opposition of Methodist traders and speculators, who were growing rich on the ignorance of the natives, formed an almost insuperable barrier to the efforts of Catholic missionaries. Yet the blood of some martyrs, such as the venerable Fathers Chanel and Mozzuconi, Bishop Epal, and others, has watered Australia's soil and become the seed of Christianity.

In West Australia the flourishing and extensive missions of the Benedictines give promise of great success in the future. The Spanish Benedictine, Salvado, Bishop of Porto Victoria, and Serra, Bishop of Perth, accompanied by forty members of their Order, plunged into the depths of the primeval forests, with the view of founding a New

Nursia, as a nucleus of future civilization. What was considered in Europe an impossibility became a reality under the indomitable zeal and perseverance of the Sons of St. Benedict. The savage aborigines withdrew in great numbers from their wild nomadic mode of life, and under the mild and intelligent direction of the monks learned to till the soil, acquired a variety of trades, and to-day they constitute a model colony of religious, civilized people. A Protestant clergyman who had visited the settlement avers that what he saw there reminded him forcibly of the early ages of Christianity.

At the present time this continent of Oceanica, comprising New Zealand and other islands large and small, numbers about half a million of Catholics, governed and taught by some twenty-three bishops or apostolic vicars, and a large body of zealous, self-sacrificing priests.

18. The Catholic World.

"Thousands of thousands ministered to him, and ten thousand times a hundred thousand stood before him. He was given a kingdom, and all peoples, tribes, and tongues shall serve him."—DANIEL vii.

If we cast a glance at the condition of the Catholic Church at the present day, we discover that it numbers in Europe one hundred and forty-six million souls; in Asia, counting the adjacent islands, about three millions; in America, forty-three millions; and in Australia, about half a million of souls. In regard to the number of her chief pastors and rulers, we learn from the official register of May 1st, 1870, that at the Ecumenical Council of the Vatican in Rome there were present fifty-one Cardinals, eleven Patriarchs, ten Primates, one hundred and sixty-six Archbishops, and seven hundred and thirty-nine Bishops.

Thus has Christ manifested himself to all the peoples

of the earth: thus has he founded and built up his
Church. This glorious universal kingdom numbers two
hundred millions of faithful laity, under the guidance of
more than one hundred thousand chief pastors, and nearly
three hundred thousand priests, missionary and secular.
Besides, it counts more than seven thousand Religious
Houses, with one hundred thousand Religious men, and
above nine thousand convents with one hundred and ten
thousand Religious women, all serving God under the

The Kingdom of Christ.

evangelical counsels of voluntary poverty, unlimited obe
dience, and holy virginity, and steadily advancing in the
ways of Christian perfection.

What a glorious kingdom! How immense in its extent! Yet how well proportioned, and how closely connected and beautifully co-ordinate its many members!
All set in motion and spiritual life by Jesus Christ, governed and guided by one visible Chief Shepherd, the Infallible Pope. It is illuminated by the inextinguishable

rays of one only faith, inflamed and vivified by the fires of universal Christian charity. It is governed by the undisputed and undisputable authority of the same divine eternal law. It is animated into active healthful life by the seven-fold power of one and the same divine grace in the seven Sacraments. It imbibes a renewed vitality and courage from the living fountain of the one same Sacrifice of the Mass. Its members are tending towards one and the same goal, eternal happiness in heaven. Verily no such kingdom hath ever been built by the hand of mortal man. It is without a parallel in history.

Such is the kingdom of Jesus Christ, of the King of all kings, of our most adorable, most loving and lovable Lord and Saviour Jesus Christ; the glorious Church of Rome. Even to-day, upon this earth, he continues to live in his "Mystic Body," for worthy faithful members still live the Life of Christ. He is indeed the real and truly glorious Solomon of whom the Psalmist sings: "And he shall continue with the sun, and before the moon, throughout all generations. In his days shall justice spring up, and abundance of peace, till the moon be taken away. And he shall rule from sea to sea, and from the river unto the ends of the earth. Before him the Ethiopians shall fall down, and his enemies shall lick the ground. The kings of Tharsis and the islands shall offer presents; the kings of the Arabians and of Saba shall bring gifts; and all kings of the earth shall adore him, all nations shall serve him, and the whole earth shall be filled with his majesty."

This kingdom Jesus has built up for himself. He continues, amid all the opposition and persecution of the world, to build it up, and to maintain it day by day, now and forever.

"Why have the Gentiles raged, and the people devised vain things? The kings of the earth stood up, and the princes met together, against the Lord, and against his Christ. Let us break their bonds asunder, and let us cast away their yoke from us. He that dwelleth in heaven shall laugh at them, and the Lord shall deride them. But I am appointed king by him over Sion, his holy mountain. I will give thee the Gentiles for thy inheritance, and the utmost parts of the earth for thy possession."

In this kingdom Christ lives and reigns, and carries out his work of Redemption in a miraculous, mysterious, and real efficacy, and he will do so till the end of time. Blessed be the name of his majesty forever; the whole earth shall be filled with his glory.

CHAPTER III.

THE HISTORY OF CATHOLIC WORSHIP.

JESUS CHRIST LIVES IN HIS CHURCH AS REDEEMER AND HIGH-PRIEST.

19. What is Catholic Worship?

"Let us be glad and rejoice, and give glory to God: for the marriage of the Lamb," that is to say, Jesus Christ, "is come, and his wife," that is to say, the Church, "hath prepared herself. Blessed are they that are called to the marriage supper of the Lamb."—APOCALYPSE xix. 7 et seq.

JESUS CHRIST having established his kingdom for all ages and places in this world, all men are really his subjects; indeed they truly and actually belong to him; for, as high-priest and victim, he has purchased them by his bleeding sacrifice on the cross. And as he thus made them his own at the expense of his life's blood, he maintains his right to own them continually ; for he is constantly renewing his sacrifice, and thus continues to live in his Church as high-priest for all time. Hence the sacrifice of the Mass is the chief centre or focus of Christian worship ; and Christ is himself the sacrificing priest. He himself, by the hand and lips of the priest, renews his atoning sacrifice in a true and real manner, and makes it present in all places. Through the influence of the Holy Ghost, he moves the authorities of the Church to adorn and embellish this high-priestly service of God with symbolical ceremonies, tender devotional practices, glorious festivals, and sumptuous temples.

Christian worship is specially the continuation of the espousals of the heavenly bridegroom with his bride, of the High-priest with his Church. It is their mutual and mysterious interchange of love. The God-man bridegroom gives himself to his spouse through the sacrifice of his sacramental body and blood in the Mass, and the Church, his spouse, advancing towards the High-priestly bridegroom, gives herself to him by that adoration and homage of love so clearly expressed in her ceremonies, devout exercises, festivals, and temples.

---

20. Places of Worship.

"Indeed, the Lord is in this place. How terrible is this place! this is no other but the house of God, and the gate of heaven."— GENESIS xxviii. 16, 17.

The places in which the Apostles and their first successors assembled with the faithful for the celebration of divine service were simple rooms, or large halls in private houses. Many among the wealthy who had become converted to Christianity were glad to throw open their dwellings for the gathering of the small congregations of early Christians. But very soon the persecutions became so violent, that the faithful found themselves compelled to retire to obscure and secret hiding-places for the celebration of the sacred mysteries—even to caverns, cellars, and burial-places.

The most memorable of these places of refuge were the Roman catacombs: immense and intricate subterranean excavations, in which the Christians of the first three centuries used to bury their dead, and especially the holy martyrs. Into these gloomy homes of the dead the Christians fled in times of persecution, and here they excavated in the rocks large and sometimes very richly decorated chapels. The tomb of some holy martyr usually formed the consecrated altar-stone. A venerable and gray-haired man stands before one of these altars in the act of offering sacrifice. More than once has he suffered for the cause of Christ, and even now he bears on his venerable person the marks of persecution. This is the bishop of Rome, who has gathered about him in the silent gloom of the catacombs his pious and faithful flock, whom he prepares

Tombs in the Catacombs.

and strengthens against impending martyrdom, by imparting to them the heavenly Bread of Life. These catacombs beneath the soil of Rome were the subterranean, well-guarded retreats where the warriors of Christ used to arm themselves with the word of God, sacrifice, prayer, mutual intercession and exhortations, for the glorious victory soon to be won over Rome itself above ground. And lo, after a conflict of three hundred years, the early Christians gained the day. Prayer, sacrifice, and martyr's blood triumphed. Heathen Rome fell, and the Emperor Constantine the Great exalted the banner of the Cross above the Roman eagle.

From this time forward we everywhere see, both in the east and in the west, glorious temples of stately proportions and of various styles of architecture* rising aloft in honor of the world's Redeemer. The usual ground-plan of the early Christian church was in the form of a cross, to represent the cross of Calvary. The upper and shorter portion,

Mass in the Catacombs.

containing the choir and the altar of sacrifice, represented the head of Christ; the larger and longer shaft, occupied by the people, denoted the body of the saviour, while the two wings, one on the right and the other on the left, represented the extended arms of the dying Redeemer.

* These different styles are chiefly known as (1) the ancient Christian Basilica; (2) the Byzantine style, with its vaulted cupolas; (3) the Romanesque style, dating from the year 1000 to 1225; (4) the Gothic style down to 1525; (5) the Renaissance style.

Graceful columns, supporting the arches of the lofty and spacious vaults above, carried the hearts and souls of the faithful towards heaven. Mighty towers and airy domes announced to the distant traveller that here the King of kings had laid the foundations of his throne. Within these sacred edifices, on pillar and side-wall, on ceiling and window, painters and sculptors exhausted their skill in representing the glory of the Saviour and the excessive wealth of his mercy.

St. Peter's, Rome.

But who can enumerate all the temples erected to the honor of the one true God during the fifteen hundred years following the deliverance from the catacombs? and built, too, not merely by the munificence of kings and princes, but by the offerings of millions of poorer people, of pious workmen and artisans, who considered it a privilege and an honor to contribute their mite or give their labor to add to the glory of the great High-priest Jesus Christ, ever present in these temples. It is thus that the great cathedrals of our own day are erected. It was in this manner that, two hundred and fifty years ago, the most magnificent temple on earth, St. Peter's Church at Rome, was raised in all its costly and splendid proportions above the tomb of St. Peter, the Prince of the Apostles. The millions of dollars expended on this prodigy of architecture were the love-offerings of the whole Catholic world. And it has never occurred to the mind of any true Christian to term such generosity a useless extravagance, for he knows that where and when our great High-priest Jesus Christ is pleased to pour out his wealth of divine grace, it becomes the duty of rich and poor to consecrate to his service the best they have, and to give it joyfully and gratefully.

21. The Holy Sacrifice of the Mass.

"And the high-priest went up to the holy altar. He shone in his days as the morning star in the midst of a cloud, so did he shine in the temple of God, and he honored the vesture of holiness. And as branches of palm-tree, so they stood round about him, all the sons of Aaron in their glory. And the oblation of the Lord was in their hands, before all the congregation, and finishing his service on the altar, to honor the offering of the Most High King. And the singers lifted up their voices, and in the great house the sound of sweet melody was increased."—ECCLESIASTICUS l.

From the history of church-edifices let us now turn to ecclesiastical practices and ceremonies. Here, too, we shall discover a gradual and ever more glorious development and advancement; for the kingdom of God being like the mustard-seed must grow and spread.

The manner of performing divine service in the days of the Apostles is described by St. Luke in the Acts of the Apostles, and by St. Paul in his Epistles. The life and soul of the service was the commemoration of the Last Supper, the holy Sacrifice of the Mass. It was accompanied with common prayer, reading of passages from holy Scripture with explanations, chanting of psalms and Christian hymns, and a general love-feast. The manner in which all these exercises were united with the essential act of worship proper—namely, the offering of bread and wine, and the Transubstantiation—was not so unalterably appointed as it is in our time. But in the course of the first few centuries it became gradually fixed by the decrees of bishops, Councils, and Popes. Even as early as the time of Constantine the Great, about the year 325, the prayers and ceremonies of mass were much the same, and appointed in the same order, as we have them to-day.

Divine service, among the primitive Christians, was divided into two parts; namely, the Mass of the Catechumens, at which unbaptized candidates for Christianity, penitents, and even pagans, might be present, and the Mass proper, at which only the baptized faithful could assist. The Mass of the Catechumens began with a recital of psalms sung by the faithful in alternate choirs, and corresponding to the prayers now repeated at the foot of the altar by the celebrant with his ministers at the beginning of mass. Then was repeated a supplication for mercy, *Kyrie eleison*, followed by a hymn of praise, *Gloria in Excelsis*, to the thrice holy God; after which the celebrant greeted the people with the words, "The Lord be with you," *Dominus vobiscum*, or *Pax Vobis*, and then recited, in the name of all, the series of prayers called the "Collect." Then a lector ascended the pulpit to read a passage from the epistles of the Apostles or from the Old Testament. A psalm, *graduale*, was then chanted, and the gospel having been first sung by a deacon, was afterwards explained to the people by the bishop. Here ended the Mass of the Catechumens, and the deacon then directed them and the unbelievers and the penitents to retire.

The Mass proper began with the selection, from the offerings brought by the people, of the bread and wine for the sacrifice. The matter selected for the sacrifice was now offered up, the deacon poured water on the bishop's hands for the washing, and then came the repeated inquiry to the people whether any one amongst them had any ill-will in his heart against his brother. The bishop then sang the praises of God in the "Preface," closing it with the angelic hymn, "Holy, holy, holy Lord God of hosts," *Sanctus*, "The heavens and the earth are full of thy glory," and the whole congregation joined in the strain. Now began the most solemn part of the Mass, called the "Canon," a portion which, from the time of Gregory the Great—that is, about the year 600—to our own day, has remained unchanged. To the prayers for the living succeeded the Consecration, or act of transubstantiation, the elevation of the consecrated species, the prayers for the faithful departed, the *Pater Noster*, the *Agnus Dei*, the kiss of peace, and then holy Communion was administered, first to the celebrant by himself, and then to the faithful in attendance; a portion of the Communion being preserved in a vessel or tabernacle. Prayers of thanksgiving then ensued, and the people were formally dismissed by the deacon with the words, *Ite missa est*—"Depart, mass is over."

What intense feelings of reverence and of consolation fill our souls when we remember that the same holy sacrifice of the mass at which we assist to-day has been solemnized during fifteen, sixteen, or seventeen hundred years in precisely the same way by our ancestors in the faith! When, notwithstanding the very solicitous secrecy with which the Christians of the first four centuries concealed their holy mysteries from Jews and pagans, we learn from the writings of the most ancient church-fathers, as well as from venerable relics, from original inscriptions, and from images found in the catacombs, that even in those times the belief in the Real Presence of Christ in the Blessed Eucharist was held, and taught, and reduced to practice, our souls overflow with grateful feelings to

Jesus Christ for having permitted us to be members of that Mystical Body in which he has lived, in which he still lives, and in which he shall continue to live forever. What a comfort to know from all the above-mentioned evidences that our Holy Sacrifice of the Mass was, in all ages of Christianity just as in our own, offered up for both the living and the dead! It is a consolation and an assurance to know that not only has the essential portion of this

The Fountain of Grace.

Holy Sacrifice remained without change since the very hour of the Last Supper, but that even its very outward symbols and ceremonies as we have them to-day were strictly and permanently established during the earliest ages of the Church by such saintly and learned men as St. Basil, St. Chrysostom, St. Ambrose, St. Gelasius, St. Leo the Great, and St. Gregory the Great. Even in the smallest matters of ceremony we are in accord with primitive

Christianity. Thus it becomes evident that Jesus Christ still leads in his Church the real life of her great High-priest; whilst all her ritual is but a veritable though mysterious continuation of his great work of atonement. Thus the Life of Christ still goes on till the end of time, aye, even unto eternity.

In very early times it was permitted to offer up the Holy Sacrifice of the Mass in private houses. Thus, for example, St. Augustine, a holy doctor of the Church, tells us about a certain man named Hesperus, the members of whose household were annoyed by an evil spirit. "One day," writes the saint, "when I was absent, Hesperus besought our priests that one of them would come to his house and by prayer drive away the demons. A priest went, and offered up the sacrifice of the Body and Blood of Christ, fervently beseeching the Lord that the affliction might depart from the household. Through the mercy of God, the petition was granted." However, as in the course of time some abuses attended this custom, the Church forbade the celebration of mass in private houses. In America, in newly and sparsely settled districts, where the few Catholics are as yet unable to erect churches, the missionary priest, like his predecessor in the first centuries, is often glad to find an opportunity of offering the Holy Sacrifice, and of preaching the Word of God, in the humble home of some devout parishioner. As the Catholics increase in number and means, the little church with its permanent altar is taking the place of the poor man's cottage.

22. The History of Baptism.

"I will pour upon you clean water, and you shall be cleansed from all your filthiness, and I will cleanse you from all your idols." EZECHIEL xxxvi.

The graces resulting from Christ's unceasing Sacrifice of atonement, and which for well-nigh two thousand years have been poured out upon all Christendom, have come to us through the channels of the seven Sacraments. The Life of our Lord and Saviour Jesus Christ is still prolonged and continued in a mystical manner on earth, in and through these Sacraments. It cannot then be otherwise than agreeable, as well as profitable, to examine briefly whatever history furnishes us regarding the administration of these same cherished Sacraments.

According to the teaching of Christ, the Sacrament of Baptism was always considered not only as a deliverance from original sin, but especially as an admission into the kingdom of God, and to membership in the Church. In the early ages of Christianity the person to be baptized was immersed formally into the water; and from the fourth century, buildings adapted to this manner of administering the Sacraments were erected near the churches and were called baptisteries. The sick, however, and the feeble, and later all persons without distinction, were baptized by the pouring on of water. Although infant-baptism was practised at a very early period, yet this holy Sacrament was chiefly administered to grown persons who had been converted from paganism or Judaism to the Christian faith. These were required to spend a long time, sometimes two or three years, in preparation and in the study of the Christian doctrine, and were termed Catechumens. Originally bishops only were, according to rule, ministers of this Sacrament, though priests were permitted to baptize in very remote ages. Baptism was given on any day of the week, though mostly on Sundays. The appointment of Easter Saturday and Whitsun eve as special days for the solemn administration of this Sacrament was more recent. Even in the days of the Apostles it was customary to select sponsors as witnesses, and as sureties of fidelity to the faith on the part of the person baptized. The vows or promises, the use of blessed salt, of holy oil and the burning light, as well as the blessing of the baptismal water, have their origin in Christian antiquity. The candidate for baptism was required to turn towards the west when renouncing the devil and his works, and towards the east when promising allegiance to Christ. After baptism he was clothed with a long white garment. Similar garments were worn by those baptized on Holy Saturday during the ensuing week till the Sunday called Low Sunday, or Sunday in albis, when they laid them aside with certain ceremonies and prayers.

23. The History of Confirmation.

"And when Paul had imposed hands on them, the Holy Ghost came upon them."—ACTS OF THE APOSTLES, xix. 6.

Confirmation was at first regularly administered immediately after Baptism, and was therefore considered as a completion of that Sacrament. The Apostles usually imposed hands upon the newly baptized, in order to impart to them the gifts of the Holy Ghost and, besides making them children of God, to enroll them as soldiers of Jesus Christ. Joined to this imposition of hands, even in early times, we find the marking of the candidate with the sign of the cross, and the anointing with holy chrism; according to the statement of Tertullian: "The body is anointed in order that the soul may be healed; the body is signed in order that the soul may be strengthened; the body is overshadowed by the imposition of hands, that the soul may thereby be enlightened by the Holy Ghost." In regard to the use of chrism at confirmation, St. Cyril, a father of the Church, writes the following beautiful and significant words: "Be sure that you do not consider this oil of anointing to be common oil, or something of no account. For just as the bread of the Eucharist, by the invocation to the Holy Spirit, is no longer common bread, but the body of Christ, so this consecrated unction is, after the invocation, no longer simple oil, nor an ordinary anointing, but it makes the gifts of Christ and of the Holy Ghost effectual and operative through the presence of his divinity." In the fourth century the Church began to administer these two holy Sacraments of Baptism and Confirmation separately, and the administration of the latter was gradually reserved to the bishops. Of this, St. Jerome gives us clear proof, when he says: "It is a custom in the Church, when the priest or deacon in some small remote place administers the Sacrament of Baptism, for the bishop to visit those places, in order to impose hands on such baptized persons, and to call down the Holy Ghost upon them." The very name of the Sacrament, Confirmation, expresses a strengthening, and signifies that the faithful are fortified by this holy Sacrament, in a supernatural manner, to believe and profess their faith. Being a Sacrament of the living, it must be received only when the candidate is in a state of grace, and consequently those to be confirmed are to be prepared by a good confession.

24. The History of the Holy Eucharist.

"Neither is there any other nation so great that hath God so nigh to them as our God is present."—DEUT. iv. 7.

Of the profound reverence shown by the primitive Christians towards the all-holy Sacrament of the Altar, and of the love which they cherished toward it, we are informed by the holy Scripture; whilst pictures, signs, symbols, and inscriptions found in the catacombs, as well as innumerable passages from the works of the ancient Church-writers, give us indubitable proof. Strength for Christian life, comfort in tribulation, courage in persecution, joyous resignation to martyrdom, all these were sought and found by the firstlings of our faith in the heavenly food of the Eucharist. It was a universal custom to receive it daily,* as the daily supernatural bread. To those who were present at the " breaking of bread," it was placed upon their outstretched hands to be immediately consumed, while to the sick and imprisoned it was carried by the deacons. Travellers and hermits were permitted to carry the Blessed Sacrament away in a clean cloth. These last, as well as the sick, received Communion under one kind only, the form of bread ; because it was always firmly believed, from the very beginning, that the precious blood of our Lord was inseparably united to his body in the Blessed Sacrament, and hence that the entirety of Jesus Christ was received even under one form.

Gradually, for the most important reasons, Communion under only one form became more frequent for all the laity, and finally, since the fourteenth century, it has become general. In the beginning, the early Christians, like the Apostles at the last supper and afterwards, received in the evening; but as, in the course of time, many abuses crept in, it became the custom towards the end of the second century to receive Communion in the morning, before breaking fast. Since the fourth century this practice has been made a general law by the action of more than one Council.

In the days of the primitive Christians the Blessed Sacrament used to be most frequently carefully kept in a costly casket which hung over the altar, and had the form of a dove on the wing. Afterwards the so-called sacramentary shrines came into use. These usually stood on the Gospel side of the altar. Many of them were elaborately wrought and handsomely decorated towers, such as may be seen even at the present day in many Gothic

---

* It was only after the lapse of centuries that the Church was compelled to *command* her children to receive Communion at least three times a year; namely, at Christmas, Easter, and Pentecost. And even this precept was limited by the fourth Lateran Council to the one communion at Easter.

churches. Sometimes these shrines were imbedded in the wall of the church and had richly wrought doors. Finally, in later ages, the modern tabernacle, standing in the middle of the altar, has become the permanent repository of the most holy Sacrament of the Altar.

25. The History of the Sacrament of Penance.

"Peace be to you. As the Father hath sent me, I also send you. Receive ye the Holy Ghost. Whose sins you shall forgive they are forgiven them, and whose sins you shall retain they are retained."—JOHN xx. 21.

In all ages, as in our own day, holy Communion was administered to those who had been unhappily guilty of sin, only after a worthy reception of the Sacrament of Penance, by a sincere confession of their sins, a firm purpose of amendment, and a compliance with the penance enjoined. Thus we read in the nineteenth chapter of the Acts of the Apostles that in consequence of the miracles performed by St. Paul, not only Jews and pagans, but even Christians, were seized with fear, and came confessing their sins. To the very first Christians of antiquity, the holy Evangelist St. John, in his twentieth chapter, announced and declared that the Apostles had received from Christ the commission, and from the Holy Ghost the power, to remit sins. In the first chapter of his Epistle he imparts this consoling truth to sinners: "If we confess our sins, God is faithful and just to forgive us our sins, and to cleanse us from all iniquity" (1 John i.). In the year 200 we hear the learned Tertullian speaking and writing of Confession as something in general use, and of priestly absolution as a priceless treasure of grace. But he adds that even in his time there were many who tried to escape the duty of Confession entirely, or who put it off from one day to another, being more troubled about a false shame than about the salvation of their souls. Thus some individuals, known as Novatians, objected to the usage of the Church, saying that it was impossible for one man to forgive the sins of another. But the learned doctor of the early Church, St. Ambrose, answered them pointedly: "Why, then," said he, "do you baptize? Sins are forgiven in Baptism, and it is about the same thing whether the priest exercises the ample power given to him in Baptism or in Penance; in either of these two Sacraments the power exercised is the same."

Besides private confession we also meet in Christian antiquity the practice of a public confession of sins. This latter, on account of many abuses, fell into disuse in the fifth and sixth centuries. The penances imposed in early times for the commission of sins appear to us very severe. Murderers, adulterers, blasphemers, and other great criminals were not permitted, during several years subsequent to their crime, to be present at or take part in public worship. Standing or else lying prostrate before the public entrance to the church, they besought the prayers of those who passed in. They were denied the use of wine and of flesh-meat, and if they were rich they were required to devote large sums of money to the poor or to the Church, or to undertake difficult pilgrimages to Rome, Jerusalem, or some other distant place.

Gradually, in course of time, especially in the sixth, seventh, and eighth centuries, penalties formally proportioned and appointed for the different kinds and grades of sin were inscribed in the book of canonical penances, and they were strictly enforced for many subsequent centuries. How otherwise could the Catholic Church, in the early part of the middle ages, have subdued the savage and barbarous nations of heathendom and bring them to the freedom of the children of God? Moreover, great stress was constantly laid upon the truth that all these outward works of penance could have no value before God if they were not animated by a spirit of humble contrition and a firm purpose of amendment.

In regard to the manner in which the holy Sacrament of Penance used to be administered about fifteen hundred years ago, there is still extant a description by Alcuin, a learned and celebrated monk who was the professor of Charlemagne. He gives it as an extract from the most ancient of the penitential books of the Church. It shows that the mode then followed of reconciling a sinner to God was about the same as now, though somewhat longer.

26. The History of Extreme Unction.

"Though I should walk in the midst of the shadows of death, I will fear no evils, for thou art with me. Thou hast anointed my head with oil, and thy mercy will follow me, that I may dwell in the house of the Lord."—PSALMS xxii.

As our Saviour had directed his Apostles to anoint the sick (Mark vi. 13), and as St. James the Apostle had admonished the faithful, saying: "Is any man sick among you? Let him bring in the priests of the church, and let them pray over him, anointing him with oil in the name of the Lord" (James v. 14), both priests and faithful hastened to obey the order in the very earliest times; as we are assured by the holy fathers of the Church. Thus, for example, St. Cæsarius, who lived in the fifth century, writes as follows: "As soon as a person falls dangerously sick, he receives the body and blood of Jesus Christ. Then his body is anointed, and thus is fulfilled what stands written: 'Is any man sick among you, let him call in the priests of the church, and let them pray over him, anointing him with oil,'" etc.

On the other hand, this Sacrament was denied to excommunicated persons, as we learn from a decision pronounced by Innocent I., about the year 410. He says:

"Without doubt the words of St. James refer to the sick faithful who are anointed with the holy Chrism blessed by the bishop, and which, in time of need, is useful not only to the priests, but to all who believe in Christ. But to the penitents, who have not been reconciled to the Church, this anointing must not be administered. For it belongs to the class of Sacraments, and why should those who have refused and denied the Sacraments dare to receive them?"

From the writings of another Pope, St. Gregory the Great, we have a detailed description of the pious ceremonies then followed in the administration of Extreme Unction, and of the prayers read at the blessing of the sacramental oil for the sick.

27. The History of Matrimony.

"This is a great sacrament; but I speak in Christ and in the church."—EPHESIANS v. 32.

As our divine High-Priest had come upon earth to elevate and purify every condition of man, it behooved him of course to ennoble and sanctify marriage, which is the foundation-stone of human society. For, alas! how degraded this sacred state had become among the heathens of antiquity, and even among the Jews themselves! Christ therefore restored matrimony to its original dignity; rendering it indissoluble, forbidding polygamy, rescuing the wife from slavery and making her the equal companion of her husband, and inculcating upon married people purity of morals and mutual love and respect for each other. Moreover, he raised marriage to the dignity of a Sacrament, comparing the married state to that intimate union of charity which binds himself to his Church; and to the outward or visible signs of a nuptial contract he added all those preternatural graces which are necessary to enable the married couple to live devoutly and happily together.

St. Paul says: "Being subject one to another in the fear of Christ. Let women be subject to their husbands, as to the Lord. Because the husband is the head of the wife, as Christ is the head of the Church. He is the saviour of his body. Therefore as the Church is subject to Christ, so also let the wives be to their husbands in all things. Husbands, love your wives, as Christ also loved the Church, and delivered himself up for it, that he might sanctify it, cleansing it by the laver of water in the word of life. That he might present it to himself a glorious Church, not having spot or wrinkle, or any such thing, but that it should be holy and without blemish. So also ought men to love their wives as their own bodies. He that loveth his wife loveth himself. For no man ever hated his own flesh, but nourisheth and cherisheth it, as also Christ doth the Church, because we are members of his body, of his flesh, and of his bones. For this cause shall a man leave his father and mother, and shall cleave to his wife, and they shall be two in one flesh. This is a great sacrament; but I speak in Christ and in the Church. Nevertheless, let every one of you in particular love his wife as himself, and let the wife fear her husband."

Hence, as we learn from the testimony of St. Ignatius, himself a disciple of the Apostles, marriage in the very first years of Christianity was solemnized in the presence of bishops; while Tertullian praises this married state, "because it is ratified by the Church, fortified by the sacrifice of the mass, and sealed with Heaven's blessing." When, afterwards, during the middle ages, clandestine marriages, privately entered into without the presence of the priest or the blessing of the Church, began to multiply and to seek recognition and sanction, the Church-councils strenuously opposed and condemned them as an undignified and dangerous abuse. The Council of Trent declared positively and plainly that the Church could recognize as valid and licit among Catholics only such marriages as were performed before the parish-priest of the parties and in presence of two or three other witnesses. Marriages between Catholics on the one side and pagans, Jews, or heretics on the other were strictly forbidden in early Christian times. The significant words used by Tertullian in his admonitory efforts to dissuade a Christian young woman from marrying a pagan strike severely at the so-called mixed marriages of our own time: "If a day occur on which the people assemble for prayer, the man will pass the day at the baths; if a fast is to be observed, he will hold a banquet; and never will he find so many occupations for you at home as when you ought to go out to church or on errands of Christian charity. Where will your faith find nourishment? whence will you draw renewal of soul and the divine blessing?" In like manner St. Ambrose asks: "How can that be called a married union where the parties are not united by one belief?" And again: "How can a bond of love unite those whom their belief drives apart?"

Towards the close of the last century the so-called civic marriage took its rise in France. Matrimony was declared by the infidels to be a mere bargain, like any other business contract. This disastrous heresy undermined the well-being of the family, and sapped the foundations of the state. It is very significant that in 1792, the same year in which was passed the law concerning civic marriages, the terrible French Revolution took its rise, which brought France to the verge of destruction. The Church solemnly condemned this law, which robs the Sacrament of Matrimony and the holy state of wedlock of its moral character and religious dignity.

28. The History of Holy Orders.

"Every high-priest is taken from among men. Neither doth any man take the honor to himself, but he that is called as Aaron was."
—Ephesians v.

Holy Scripture describes plainly the institution of the Priesthood of the new dispensation. By solemnly imparting the power to offer sacrifice and to dispense the holy Sacraments, Christ himself ordained this calling, and appointed the Apostles to be the first members. The Apostles in their turn, by the Sacrament of Ordination that is, by the laying on of hands—imparted the same power and authority to deserving candidates, and made them bishops; as for instance when St. Paul laid hands on and consecrated Titus, Timothy, and others. Of the different relations existing between priests and laity, mention is made by a disciple of the Apostles, St. Clement of Rome, who says: "To the high-priest certain important charges are assigned, to the priests their position is designated, to the levites their own special duties are marked out, while the laity are bound to each other and to their clergy."

Sts. Ignatius and Polycarp, both disciples of the Apostles, term the bishop "the Head of the congregation in spiritual things." Thus it appears that bishops, even in the earliest times, governed and presided over distinct congregations or churches, and were assisted by priests and deacons. In the course of time, as the spiritual wants of the people were augmented and multiplied, the ecclesiastical offices grew in proportion, and in the year 250 we hear the holy Pope Cornelius speaking of the subdeacons appointed to assist the deacons in their many duties. He also mentions lectors who were to care for the holy books and to read from them at divine service; acolytes, as attendants on the bishops; exorcists, who had the care of possessed persons; porters, who did duty at the church-doors, allowing none to enter but those who were entitled to the privilege. The solemn introduction to these several offices, from that of porter up to the dignity of priesthood, constituted, as it does to-day, the Sacrament of Ordination. Ever and always the bishop was sole minister of this Sacrament. Originally conferred by prayer and simple imposition of hands, ordination was afterwards solemnized by the formal delivery to the candidate of all the insignia of his office, and in giving priesthood by anointing his hands with holy oil. Hence St. Augustine admonishes priests: "You must be ever mindful of your dignity, and of what took place at your ordination, when your hands were consecrated by holy anointing in order to teach you that you should not desecrate hands so sacredly blessed." In accordance with a very ancient ecclesiastical ordinance. the dignity of priesthood is usually conferred on the Saturdays of Trinity- and Ember-week before Christmas. Hence for this intention the Catholic people fasted on these days; as was done of old in Antioch, when the Christians prayed and fasted at the time that the two new apostles, Barnabas and Paul, were ordained to their sublime office by the other apostles.

29. The History of Sunday.

"Why doth one day excel another, when all come from the sun? By the knowledge of the Lord, they were distinguished. He ordered the seasons, and holidays of them, and in them they celebrated festivals at an hour. Some of them God made great and high days, and some of them he put in the number of ordinary days."— ECCLESIASTICUS xxxiii.

After having spoken of sacred places and of holy rites and ceremonies in the divine service, let the holy seasons and festivals next engage our attention.

That ancient and divine law of the Jewish dispensation

which required that one out of every seven days should be allotted to rest and prayer, and more especially dedicated to the worship of the Most High God, is still of binding force upon all nations, and for all times, past, present, and future. Hence the Apostles, by virtue of the unlimited authority and power which they had received from Jesus Christ, transferred the solemn sanctification of this day from Saturday, which was the Sabbath-day of the Jews, to the first day of the week, or Sunday. We read in the Acts of the Apostles, 20th chapter, 7th verse: "And on the first day of the week, when we were assembled to break bread, Paul discoursed with them, being to depart on the morrow, and he continued his speech until midnight." Again, St. Paul, alluding to the offerings made by the first Christians for the support of their pastors, writes in his first Epistle to the Corinthians: "On the first day of the week let every one of you put apart with himself, laying up what it shall well please him; that when I come, the collections be not then to be made" (1 Corinthians xvi. 2).

St. Justin, as early as the year 150, thus explains the meaning of the religious observance of Sunday: "We assemble together for the celebration of the Holy Sacrifice on Sunday, first because it is the day on which the eternal Father created the world and displaced the darkness for the light, and secondly because it is the day on which Jesus Christ rose from the dead." We may add the fact that on this first day of the week the Holy Spirit was imparted at Jerusalem to the Apostles, thus completing the foundation-work of the Church. So that, in truth, this day is the day of the Lord; the day of the thrice-blessed, tri-personal, triune God, of the ever-adorable Trinity, of Father, Son, and Holy Ghost. It is the day of the eternal Father, who on the first day of creation-week called heaven and earth out of nothing into existence, and summoned the light forth from the darkness of chaos. It is the day of

God the Son, who on this day sealed and stamped beyond recall, by his glorious resurrection, the great work of man's redemption. It is the day of the Holy Ghost, who revealed himself on this day to Christianity, and bestowed himself upon the Church. It is becoming to call it Sunday. For on this day, in favor of every pious congregation in God's house assembled, the Sun of truth shines in the Sermon, the Sun of divine charity burns in the Holy Mass, the Sun of divine grace warms and vivifies in the holy Sacraments. Thus the faithful observers of Sunday are enlightened, enlivened, and strengthened by the rays of this spiritual Sun, that they may be enabled to encounter the duties of the following week with courage and cheerfulness. How beautiful and appropriate in Christianity the meaning and the reality that resulted from the ignorant and thoughtless proceeding of the heathen Greeks when they dedicated the first day of the week to the sun!

30. The History of the Festivals of Our Lord.

"Seven days shalt thou celebrate feasts to the Lord thy God in the place, which the Lord shall choose: and the Lord thy God will bless thee."—DEUTERONOMY xvi. 15.

Besides the Sunday, the early Christians observed religiously certain other days. These were days commemorative of events in the life of our Lord, in the life of the Blessed Virgin, and in the lives of the Saints.

The seven most important festivals of our Lord are his Nativity, or Christmas-day; his Circumcision; his Manifestation to the Gentiles, or Epiphany; his Resurrection, or Easter-day; his Ascension into heaven; the Descent of the Holy Ghost at Pentecost or Whitsunday, and the feast of his Real Presence in the Sacrament of the Altar, or Corpus Christi. Christmas was celebrated certainly as early as the year 140, although at that time it was kept on the sixth of January, together with the festival of the three kings. Afterwards, about the year 340, the holy Pope Julius I. ordered a thorough research to be made among the records of the Roman empire, in order to ascertain the exact date of our Lord's birth; and since that time the festival has been held upon the 25th of December, and made uniform throughout the whole Church. From that time, too, the festival of Christmas, which was always celebrated with much pomp in the Church, and with sentiments of joy and gratitude by all Christians, was preceded by a season of four weeks devoted to prayer, fasting, and meditation as a preparation for the great event of the Incarnation. This season was called Advent. The festival of the Circumcision falls on the first day of the new year. Although we are not certain of the exact time when its observance began, we are sure that it was kept in the first centuries of Christianity. For in the year 567 the Council of Tours declared as follows: "With the view of eradicating pagan customs, our forefathers long since directed that on the 1st of January specified litanies should be recited and certain psalms be sung in the church, and that the mass of the Circumcision should be solemnly celebrated to the honor of our merciful Lord."

Another festival of our Lord, the Epiphany, occurring twelve days after Christmas, and sometimes called the Feast of the Kings, dates back to primitive Christian ages, and was even then of such importance that even the Emperor Julian the Apostate, during his sojourn in Gaul in 361, did not dare to absent himself from public worship on this festival. About the year 900, no manual labor could be performed during the octave of this feast, and three centuries later we find an ordinance requiring the faithful to hear at least one mass on each day of the octave. The Easter festival, together with the fast of forty days called Lent, took its rise in apostolic times, and the church-fathers of very early Christianity call it the "king of all days" and the "feast of feasts," outshining all other festive days in supernatural splendor.

In similar words, St. Augustine traces the observance of the ascension of Christ back to an apostolic ordinance, or certainly to one of the very earliest Councils of the Church. St. Chrysostom, in a sermon which he preached on Ascension-day, exclaims enthusiastically: "Our human nature, which at one time seemed unworthy to dwell even upon the earth, is to-day carried up, in Christ, to heaven, where it is ranked far above the cherubim." The feast of Pentecost, or Whitsunday, is mentioned, in what are called "The Apostolical Constitutions," as a festival which was then of time-honored memory. About the year 200, Tertullian testifies that it was "a principal festival." We have to-day several sermons preached in the fourth century on this remarkable festival, in all of which the fathers speak of it as having existed from earliest times.

One of the grandest festivals of the Church is that which she celebrates ten days after Pentecost, and which is called Corpus Christi. In this, more than any other feast of the whole year, is the actual Life of Christ as prolonged in his Church, and as manifested in a mystical manner to the eyes of faith, shown forth with practical and convincing effect. It is the feast of the life of Christ, the Church's public acknowledgment and solemn confession of his real, actual, living presence within the "Mystical Body." It is the feast of the Blessed Sacrament; a feast which in a certain sense contains and expresses the meaning of all other feasts. It preaches to the world the belief that He who was once born in a stable, who shed his first blood in the circumcision, who manifested himself to the three wise men from the east on Epiphany, who after an excruciating passion and disgraceful death ascended to heaven, whence he sent the Holy Ghost—that

He yet lives in the Church a mystic life. Corpus Christi is the feast of the Life of Christ. For our Lord and Saviour lives really and truly in the adorable Sacrament of the Blessed Eucharist on our altars. Many miracles, but especially a remarkable vision from heaven, seen by St. Juliana in Luttich, gave rise to this festival. The chief reason which induced Pope Urban the Fourth, in the year 1264, to proclaim the universal religious observance of this festival of Corpus Christi, was the firm and pious belief of the faithful in the mystery of the real presence of Jesus Christ in the Blessed Sacrament, where he treasures up for our use and benefit all the fruits of his life and death. Thus sings the royal Psalmist when, by anticipation, he meditates on the Blessed Sacrament:

"I will praise thee, O Lord, with my whole heart, in the counsel of the just and in the congregation. Great are the works of the Lord, sought out according to all his wills. His work is praise and magnificence, and his justice continueth for ever and ever. He hath made a remembrance of his wonderful works, being a merciful and gracious Lord. He hath given food to them that fear him. He will be mindful for ever of his covenant."

How admirable the beauty and power of the Catholic ritual! How gloriously, and with what pregnancy of meaning, her public worship has unfolded itself into its present solemn and majestic proportions! Our early forefathers in the faith, poor and persecuted, solemnized the Holy Mysteries in the secret gloom of subterranean caverns, and were solicitous to conceal from the scoffing and desecrating gaze of the unbelieving world the presence of the world's Redeemer in the Blessed Sacrament. To-day in Catholic lands He goes forth, as on Palm Sunday in the olden time, and is carried in triumph, surrounded by fervent and adoring hearts. He passes through the woodland, and by the field, and in the city street, blessing all with his divine presence, as he goes by in the procession of Corpus Christi.

This lovely feast-day, with its grand procession, possesses an irresistible charm. One of the most inveterate infidels of modern times was compelled to acknowledge the powerful influence wrought by the Catholic observance

The Procession on Corpus Christi.

of Corpus Christi on his own unhappy mind. He writes: "Never have I looked upon the long line of white-robed priests, nor seen the files of surpliced acolytes, nor watched the reverent crowds preceding and following the consecrated host, without being deeply moved. I have never been able to listen to the solemn chanting, by the choristers, of the grand old Latin psalms and hymns, without feeling my heart throb violently. Tears would rise to my eyes, and my whole being would become absorbed in the contemplation of this public profession of faith coming from my fellow-beings with better hearts, if not better heads, than mine. The whole ceremony contains within itself something indescribably tender, expressive, and suggestive of the loveliest sentiments of the human heart."

31. The Festivals of the Blessed Virgin.

"Behold, from henceforth all generations shall call me blessed."
—Luke i. 48.

Around the sublime festivals of the Lord as a centre, like the moon and stars about the sun, revolve the festivals of the Blessed Virgin and of all the saints. The Catholic ecclesiastical year, with its various and varied succession of feasts and fasts, its seasons of joy and seasons of penance, resembles the firmament, where the stars from their shining field of azure blue shine forth in countless rays, delighting the eye of man with their utility and beauty. In the first place, in relation to these festivals of the Blessed Virgin, it is evident to all, at a glance, that Christ lives yet in his Church, as the Son of Mary. As in the land of Judea, during his bodily life, Jesus was subject to his Virgin Mother in holy obedience and respectful love, so too should the Church of Christ continue to offer unceasingly to the Mother of her Divine Founder, a fond and willing tribute of love, admiration, and respect. The fact that the Catholic Church has at all time faithfully and enthusiastically discharged this pleasant duty: that the angel's greeting has re-echoed within her temples for centuries; that not only her simple laity, but also her most learned men, both of the laity and clergy, have rivalled each other in honoring Mary, and thereby fulfilled her own inspired prophecy, "Behold, from hence-

AVE MARIA!

forth all generations, shall call me blessed"—all this constitutes one of the most striking proofs of the truth of the Catholic Church itself.

Of the very many festival-days instituted by the Church in honor of the ever-blessed Mother of God, we can mention in this place only five.

The festival of the Immaculate Conception of the Blessed Virgin was observed in many places as early as the fifth century, and gradually the whole Church began

Procession on a Feast of the Blessed Virgin.

to adopt it. It has been kept with greater splendor, however, by the whole Church since the memorable 8th of December, 1854, when Pius the Ninth, in the midst of two hundred bishops from every part of the Catholic world, raised the time-honored and pious belief of all Catholics to the dignity of a defined article of faith.

Of equal antiquity with the feast of the Immaculate Conception of the Blessed Virgin is the festival of her Nativity on the 8th of December. Both took their rise in the Eastern Church, whence they found their way to us with the spread of Christianity towards the West. Older than either of these two festivals, having the origin of its observance probably away back in apostolic days, is the feast of the Annunciation of our Blessed Lady. On this feast we commemorate the precious moment when the Blessed Virgin received Heaven's message from the lips of the archangel Gabriel, and the Son of God took his human nature in her chaste womb.

The feast of the Purification, or Candlemas-day, had its origin in the Eastern Church, and was introduced into the West by Pope Gelasius in 494. The sad and affecting allusion of the venerable prophet Simeon to "the Light of the world," which occurs in the gospel of this feast, gave occasion to the same pope to institute the procession in which lighted tapers are held in the hands of the faithful. Gelasius introduced the observance of this procession with candles, in order to substitute a religious rite for the superstitious practice then followed by the heathens of carrying burning torches during the month of February. The Assumption of the Blessed Virgin was kept as a religious festival in the very dawn of Christianity. It was known and observed in France and Germany certainly about the year 550, and, as now, was a favorite festal day with clergy and laity. In England and Ireland it was strictly kept, and the devotional rejoicings were continued with much piety during eight days.

32. The Festivals of the Saints.

"Let us now praise men of renown. The Lord hath wrought great glory 'in them', through his magnificence from the beginning. Let the people show forth their wisdom, and the Church declare their praise."—ECCLESIASTICUS xliv.

The festivals that have been established in honor of the Saints who lived in Christ, and in whom he lived, exceed in number the days of the year. There is not a day which is not a Saint's day. At one time the feasts of the Apostles and of some other Saints were holidays of obligation, but in the present discipline of the Church only a few are kept as such, and in some countries none. Priests, however, are under the obligation of rendering to the Saints, in the name of all the faithful, the veneration to which they are entitled. This is done by reading the offices peculiar to the Saints as designated in the breviary, and in the celebration of the masses set apart in the missal to be offered to God under the invocation of these Saints. Although the Saints' days are no longer observed by the cessation of work, pious Catholics find time to honor the heroes of the Church by reading their lives, by meditating on their virtues, and by begging their intercession. They seek by good resolutions and fervent prayer to learn to imitate their ardor in the cause of Christ. The oldest Saints' days are the festivals instituted in honor of the first Christian martyrs. The primitive Christians used to assemble in the catacombs on the anniversaries of the martyrdom of their departed brethren in the faith, and there offer up sacrifice and prayer and praise, as the Acts of the disciples of the Apostles testify, such as those of St. Ignatius and St. Polycarp.

In the course of time similar honors were paid to other Saints who had been distinguished for purity of life and honored with the gift of miracles. At first only their own immediate neighbors knew their merits and honored them, but soon their virtues became known to all Christendom, and their anniversary days grew to be universally recognized and honored. The principal Saints' days, which even yet are in many places festivals of obligation, are St. Stephen's, St. Joseph's, St. John the Baptist's, Sts. Peter and Paul's, the special patron day of each country or parish, and, the chief and most favorite of all, the Feast of All Saints. This last festival was observed in very early times by the Catholics of the Eastern Church. It was placed in the Latin calendar of festivals about the year 610, during the pontificate of Pope Boniface the Fourth. There is still standing in the city of Rome an ancient and spacious pagan temple, built under the heathen emperors, and called the Pantheon, because it was the temple where all the gods of the various nations conquered by the Romans were worshipped. The emperor Phocas bestowed this building on Pope Boniface, who purified it from the last remaining traces of pagan superstition. He then had the bodies of several holy martyrs and confessors conveyed from the catacombs with great reverence and solemnly deposited in the purified church, which was then dedicated on the 13th of May as a Christian temple under the invocation of the Blessed Virgin and all the Saints. In the year 731 Pope Gregory the Third placed the commemoration of these and of all other Saints of God on the first day of November. It has ever been in the Church a glorious festival and full of deep significance; for it proclaims on its annual recurrence the triumph of the Redeemer over heathen mythology. The Saints of God have driven the false deities from the hearts and homes of men. Only God is one, single and indivisible. Yet in heaven there are beings nigh unto God, who are inebriated with divine happiness. These are the souls of those redeemed men and women who, in the battle of life here below, have persevered to the end, till they have conquered even death itself. The heavenly choirs of angels have received them with transports of delight, led them to celestial joys before the throne of the thrice-holy God, where, like the angels themselves, they will raise their voices forever in hymns of praise and exultation.

Such are the ripe, luxuriant fruits from the Vineyard of the Lord. Not untimely, then, is the commemoration just at the close of the harvest season. On this festival the faithful Christian, in joyful longing, raises the eyes of his soul to the spacious realms of heaven and contemplates the Saints in their happiness and rest. He remembers that he is closely related to the glorified elect of heaven; that he is flesh of their flesh and bone of their bone. They, like him, are also members of the one great Church of God which reaches from the recesses of purgatory to the regions of the earth, and extends aloft to the highest vaults of heaven. And if, on this festival day, he devoutly repeat that glorious prayer of the Church, the Litany of the Saints, his own comforting faith will whisper to his soul the consoling truth that the Saints in heaven above hear his cry for help, and by virtue of that charity which lives even beyond the grave, will remember him before the throne of God.

This feast is most appropriately followed by All Souls' Day. For the Church militant on earth lives in close and sacred communion with those souls, the souls of those who are asleep in the Lord, and who are atoning for their shortcomings in the fires of purgatory. When we in our necessities look aloft to our brethren in heaven, in search of relief, let us not forget to cast a glance of compassion downwards towards our suffering brethren in purgatory. Let us endeavor, by holy masses, by alms-giving, and by frequent prayer, to shorten the time of their purgation; that thus the comforting angel may the sooner come to their relief, and announce to them the glad tidings that divine justice has been satisfied in their regard, and that their hour of release has come. The observances of "All Souls' Day," including the visiting and decoration of the cemeteries, can be traced back with certainty to the year 1000. It shows forth, under the most sacred circumstances, that great article of Catholic faith, namely, that the Redeemer of the world still lives upon earth as veritable High-priest, performing the divine functions of the Church, renewing his adorable sacrifice, and thus redeeming those whom he once before, as High-priest of the cross, called to himself, selected, and purchased. To this High-priest, who is truly and efficaciously present in the Sacrament of the Altar, be honor, praise, glory, and adoration, both from the choirs of happy angels in heaven and from all the faithful on earth, now and forever.

CHAPTER IV.

THE HISTORY OF THE TEACHING-OFFICE IN THE CHURCH.

JESUS CHRIST LIVING IN HIS CHURCH AS THE TEACHER OF TRUTH AND WISDOM.

33. The Church Fathers.

"He gave some Apostles, and other some pastors and doctors, for the edifying of the Body of Christ: until we all meet into the unity of faith, and of the knowledge of the Son of God."—EPHESIANS iv. 11-13.

DURING the space of three years our Saviour preached heavenly truth in the cities, towns, and hamlets of Judea. Although the public heard his voice, yet the Apostles and disciples were the most favored witnesses of the truth and sanctity of his teachings. Much of what he taught was afterwards written by the evangelists and Apostles, and carefully preserved in the Church as Holy Scripture. Much, too, was handed down from generation to generation by mere word of mouth, and was gradually in the course of time committed to writing by the Fathers of the Church. The whole saving truth which lay enshrined in his breast our divine Teacher gave to the Church when he promised to be with her during all time, and through the instrumentality of his duly appointed teachers, and by the power of the Holy Ghost, to guide her in all truth forever. This promise is the supernatural equipment of the holy Church for her duties and office as teacher to all nations. It is the soil which has produced those giant trees whose shade and fruits have afforded life to Christian nations for centuries; namely, the Fathers of the Church. It is the miraculous power which has preserved the general Councils, as well as the successors of

Christ, our Divine Teacher.

St. Peter, the Popes, from all error in defining matters of faith.

If we go back in spirit to the first centuries of Christianity, our view rests upon a host of venerable men, who not only by their oral teachings, but also by means of their pious and learned writings, so edified and strengthened the infant Church that they have ever since been styled the Fathers of the Church.*

* In the schools a distinction is made between the Fathers and teachers of the Church and the mere writers who were not saints, and into whose writings errors sometimes crept. The people at

They are the illustrious and eminently credible witnesses of ancient Christian tradition. And the Catholic mind is inexpressibly comforted and calmed when it sees that these Church-fathers more than fifteen hundred years ago maintained, taught, and defended in their writings the self-same truths which we hold to-day. The following are a few of these most deserving men:

St. Clement of Rome, martyred about the year 100,

St. Ignatius, Bishop of Antioch.

was the friend and helper of St. Paul, and the third successor of St. Peter in the pontifical chair.

St. Ignatius was bishop of Antioch and a disciple of St. John the Evangelist. According to an old legend he was the child whom our Lord preferred to the disciples, when they were disputing about their respective titles to

large, however, include even such men as Clement of Alexandria, Origen, and Tertullian, on account of their services to Christianity, though they made some mistakes.

precedence. He was thrown a prey to the wild beasts in Rome, in the year 107.

St. Polycarp, who was bishop of Smyrna, and likewise a disciple of St. John, was condemned in the year 160, when eighty-six years of age, to be burned to death, but not being hurt by the flames, was pierced by a dagger, and so put to death.

St. Papias, bishop of Hierapolis, was a friend of St. Polycarp, and probably a disciple of St. John. He travelled about, visiting the various Christian congregations and the immediate disciples of the Apostles, taking much pains to collect all the oral traditions concerning the life and teachings of our Saviour, all of which he wrote down in five books. He died about the year 150.

St. Justin was surnamed the Philosopher, because he had passed many years in the schools of pagan philosophy, seeking in vain for that truth which he finally discovered in the Christian Church. He was beheaded at Rome in the year 166.

Athenagoras was at first a pagan, and subsequently a Christian teacher of philosophy at Athens, who, like St. Justin, wrote an excellent apology for the Christians. He died in the year 180.

St. Irenæus, of Asia Minor, disciple of the holy Fathers Polycarp and Papias, came to Gaul about the year 160, helped to found the Church at Lyons, and became its second bishop. He sealed his faith with his blood in the year 202.

Clement of Alexandria was priest and teacher in the renowned Christian academy at Alexandria, and died in the year 217.

Tertullian lived at Carthage, in Africa. First a lawyer and afterwards ordained priest, he was a man of persuasive eloquence, great ability, and varied, deep, and solid knowledge, who with talent and energy defended Christianity against the attacks of pagans, Jews, and heretics.

Unhappily, for want of true humility, this otherwise faultless man fell later into the errors of the Montanists. He died about the year 220.

Origen, called on account of his indefatigable industry Adamantius, or the man of iron, became in his eighteenth year the successor of Clement in the professor's chair at Alexandria, and notwithstanding some errors won for himself immortal fame for maintaining the purity and explaining the meaning of the holy Scriptures. His ardent zeal for Christian truth, his fund of knowledge, and his afflictions, have made him one of the most remarkable personages in Church history. He died from the effects of imprisonment and torture, under the Emperor Decius, in the year 249.

St. Cyprian was bishop of Carthage. The principal doctrine that occupied his mind, time, and writings as bishop, was the Unity of the Church. He writes: "All the life and blessings of Christianity depend on the union of all the faithful with their bishops, and the union of all the bishops with the mother Church of Rome." He was beheaded in the year 258.

St. Athanasius, patriarch of Alexandria, was the chief opponent of the heresiarch Arius, and after being exiled five times for the faith, died in the year 373.

St. Hilary, bishop of Poitiers, like St. Athanasius was an able and courageous opponent of Arianism, and its overthrow was in a great measure owing to their prudence and enlightened zeal. He died in the year 368.

St. Ephrem the Syrian, a priest of Edessa, distinguished for his opposition to the teachers of error, for his mildness towards the erring, and for his fervid eloquence, died in the year 378. In his writings are to be found the most unanswerable testimonies and proofs of antiquity in defence of those doctrines of the Catholic Church most commonly denied by Protestants.

St. Cyril, bishop of Jerusalem, was styled the Catechist, on account of his famous work, the twenty-three Catechisms, in which he defends the truths of Christian faith against heretics, and explains them for new converts. He died in the year 386.

St. Epiphanius, Archbishop of Salamis, who even in his own lifetime was honored as a saint because of his virtues, was compiler of the first history of the heresies. He died in the year 403.

St. Cyril, Patriarch of Alexandria, was the principal adversary of the heretic Nestorius, and died in 444.

Pope St. Leo I., surnamed the Great, the conqueror of the heresy of Eutyches, equally distinguished by his sagacity and activity as Prince of the Church, and by his knowledge and eloquence as teacher in the Church, died in the year 461.

St. John Damascene, priest at Jerusalem, the last of the Church fathers in the East, became renowned in the controversy concerning images, and was likewise simple, pious, and solidly learned. He died in the year 770.

34. The Four Great Fathers of the Western Church.

"You are the salt of the earth. You are the light of the world."
—MATTHEW v. 13.

Renowned as are the nineteen foregoing Fathers, and great as have been their services to the Church of God, they are completely overshadowed by the four grand and glorious Fathers of the Western Church; namely, St. Ambrose, St. Augustine, St. Jerome, and St. Gregory the Great; as well as by the four great Fathers of the Eastern Church, St. Basil, St. Gregory of Nyssa, St. Gregory Nazianzen, and St. John Chrysostom.

St. Ambrose, in early manhood a lawyer and imperial governor, became bishop of Milan in 374, and was a model of apostolic zeal, true piety, and sterling integrity, as well as a tender and faithful shepherd to his flock. His sermons, especially those on the dignity and beauty of celibacy and virginity, were very convincing. His pious hymns are to-day sung in our churches; his devotional writings still furnish an inexhaustible supply of edification and instruction to pious souls. To him, too, is the Church indebted for her greatest Doctor, St. Augustine, who was converted by the soul-stirring preaching of St. Ambrose,

St. Augustine, Doctor of the Church.

transformed from a sinner to a saint, from a reed bending before each and every breath of error to a firm pillar of the Church. In the year 395, Augustine was made bishop of Hippo in Africa, and became, from that time, by his numerous and valuable writings, by his apostolic discharge of duty, and by the sanctity of his life, the Centre, adviser, and friend of all the Christian writers of his time. He died in Dalmatia in the year 430, ten years later than his renowned and venerable friend St. Jerome of Stridon.

This latter Father of the Church prepared himself, by extended travels and a sojourn of several years in the desert, for the glorious duties assigned to him by God. From all quarters questions came to him for his decision concerning doctrine, ecclesiastical rights and relations, as well as upon perfection of Christian life. Pope Damasus entrusted to this learned Father the translation of the holy Scriptures. His profound explanations of the Bible, his unanswerable controversial writings against heretics, and his numerous valuable letters, constitute to-day one of the choicest treasures of the Church.

The last great Father of the Western Church was Pope St. Gregory the Great. Holy Scripture and the immortal works of the three last-named Fathers were the school in which this apostolic man fitted himself to become an instrument of the divine Teacher. Burning with a true shepherd's love and anxiety for the welfare and necessities of the Church universal, as well as of individual localities, this divinely inspired man occupies a front rank in the history of the Church for holy learning. And when pious legend tells us that the Holy Ghost appeared to this Pope in the form of a dove, giving him thoughts and words for his voluminous writings, we but hear an expression of the unbounded admiration with which the ancient world looked upon this resplendent Father of the Church. He died in the year 604.

35. The Four Great Fathers of the Eastern Church.

"I saw four angels standing on the four corners of the earth."— APOCALYPSE vii. 1.

The first of these four illustrious servants of God was St. Basil, Archbishop of Cæsarea in Cappadocia. His name, Basilius, signifies royal; and truly princely was he in mind and heart, in position and efficiency. He was moreover a bulwark against the Arians, and at the same time a hero of Christian charity and a mine of sacred knowledge. He was distinguished as a theologian and preacher, also as a director of souls for religious people. He drew up the first code of rules for a religious life, and was distinguished as director of Christian ceremonies, which he reduced to order and carried out with becoming grace and splendor. He died in the year 379.

His younger brother, St. Gregory, Bishop of Nyssa,* was also a glorious champion of truth against the Arians, and yet a gentle, peace-loving man, and an able writer, whose numerous works form one of the most valuable treasures of the Church. He died in 395.

With these two holy brothers was most intimately united in esteem and friendship the third of the three great Cappadocians, St. Gregory Nazianzen. He prepared himself for the service of the Church by attending the most famous schools of sacred and profane learning in Palestine, Alexandria, and Athens. The theatre of his chief triumphs was the city of Constantinople, which he purged of error with irresistible power and success. After years of hesitation, he at length accepted the episcopate of this city, but left it again in 381 in order to close his long, active, and useful life in holy solitude. He died in the year 390.

Seven years later we see St. John Chrysostom occupying the patriarchal chair of Constantinople. He was distinguished as a preacher, as an expounder of holy Scripture, as a bishop of untiring activity and charitable meekness, and also of immovable fidelity to faith and priestly independence.

A hidden life, passed in prayer, mortification, and study with the monks of the desert, had furnished him with that great power which he afterwards required in his many contests with the heretics, and with treacherous brethren,

---

* By many, St. Athanasius instead of St. Gregory of Nyssa is regarded as one of the four Fathers of the Eastern Church.

and against the vices of the imperial court. He died in banishment in the year 407.

Such are the great and glorious men whom the Church honors as her spiritual Fathers. Yet it is not to be supposed that our divine Founder and Teacher with the close of the Church's infancy ceased to raise up other chosen and eminent servants, whom he endowed with similar gifts of the Holy Ghost. Each century down to our own time has enjoyed zealous and able teachers of extraordinary power and gifts, raised up in his mercy by the divine Teacher, Jesus Christ, in order to manifest through them his living presence in his holy Church. But they are not infallible any more than the early Fathers were individually. Although chosen men, and inspired by God, they are still mortal and liable to error, and more than once has the Church been called upon to lament the sad fall of one or more of her most distinguished teachers.

36. The History of the Church Councils.

"How comely is wisdom for the aged, and understanding and council to men of honor! Much experience is the crown of old men."—ECCLESIASTICUS xxxv.

Altogether different from the individual teachers is the case in regard to Councils of the Church; those remarkable and famous assemblages of the bishops of every land, which have been called together by the Popes in times of extraordinary necessities or struggles, and over which they presided either in person or by a duly authorized representative. The General Church Conventions, or Œcumenical Councils,* constitute and compose

---

* Quite different from these are the National Councils, where the bishops of a whole nation convene together. Provincial Councils are those where the bishops of a Church province assemble under the presidency of their archbishop. Diocesan synods are those

the whole teaching Church. As this entire teaching Church has received the divine promise that the gates of hell—that is to say, error and falsehood—shall not prevail against it, the General Councils are, by a special and supernatural assistance of the Holy Ghost, infallible in all their decisions regarding faith and morals. Hence all Christendom has ever directed its most reverent and attentive gaze upon these Councils, as upon spectacles which are both important and sacred. During the period of their sessions, Catholics have always multiplied their prayers to heaven, begging for the Fathers of the Council light from heaven, peace and concord, and victory in the Holy Ghost. Whatever any single bishop may choose to utter in such a council is of course nothing more than his own personal testimony. But when, after a series of sessions protracted for months and sometimes for years, and during which the Fathers of the Councils, by study and mutual discussion, have done their best to present the truth pure and unadulterated, the General Council solemnly and formally pronounces its decision, and the Pope confirms it, then such decision is no longer a mere opinion of a human court. It is the incontrovertible doctrine of Jesus Christ himself. He who will not hear it refuses to hear Christ, and thus by his own act excludes himself from the kingdom of Christ. Hence the sentence of Anathema is naught else than the solemn declaration of the Church, that such an undutiful son has of his own choice withdrawn from her communion and family.

The first instance of such a General Council of the Church occurred in the days of the Apostles, in the year 51. Some Christians, who had been recently converted from Judaism to the Church, maintained that the converts from paganism should have themselves circumcised, and observe, even as Christians, the rites and customs pre-

where the priests of a diocese meet and discuss Church questions, under the lead of their bishop.

scribed by the Jewish law. Then the Apostles and the ancients, or priests, met together in Jerusalem to decide the points under dispute. St. Peter, the Prince of the Apostles, opened the Council. Other Apostles spoke after him, especially Barnabas, Paul, and James. Finally a unanimous decision was pronounced. It was not a human and fallible decision, but a divine definition; for the Apostles distinctly said: "It hath seemed good to the Holy Ghost and to us to lay no further burden upon you than these necessary things."—ACTS xv.

37. History of the Twenty General Councils.

"Whilst they were speaking these things, Jesus stood in the midst of them and saith to them: Peace be to you; it is I, fear not."—LUKE xxiv. 36.

Adopting this first Council for its model and guide, the Church has held during the lapse of eighteen centuries twenty Œcumenical Councils. At the first, held at Nice, in the year 325, the errors broached by Arius in opposition to the Divinity of Jesus Christ were condemned. At the second, which convened at Constantinople, in the year 381, the errors of Macedonius against the Divinity of the Holy Ghost were condemned. The third Council, held at Ephesus, in the year 431, declared, in opposition to Nestorius, the revealed truth that there is but one person in Christ, and not two separate persons; it defined that this person is divine, and consequently it established and confirmed, against the blasphemies of the same heretic, the honor and dignity of Mary as Mother of God. The fourth Council, held at Chalcedon, in the year 451, declared against the heretic Eutyches, and defined the revealed teaching of faith, that in Christ there are two distinct natures, the divine and the human, hypostatically united in one divine person. Similar contested points were settled in the fifth and sixth General Councils at Constantinople, in the years 553 and 680. The seventh Council, held at Nice, in the year 787, sustained and confirmed the time-honored and pious veneration of images. In the eighth General Council, held at Constantinople, in the year 869, the wickedness of Photius, who was seeking to separate the Oriental from the Western Church, was exposed and condemned. Unhappily the sad disruption was soon after effected, and hence this was the last General Council ever held in the Eastern Church.

The four following were held at the Lateran Basilica in Rome. In the year 1123, the independence and freedom of the Church from the civil power of the emperor were declared and maintained. In 1139, the evil effects of the attempted dismemberment which Peter Leonis had in vain essayed were effectively remedied, and the baneful doctrines of the fanatical Arnold of Brescia were rejected and condemned. In the year 1179, the errors of the Albigenses and Waldenses were condemned. Finally, in 1215, in the twelfth General Council, called also the fourth Lateran, an effort was made to reunite the Greek Church with the Latin. The errors of Berengarius, which had been already refuted in previous years, and which denied the Real Presence of Christ in the Blessed Sacrament, were again rejected, and the true Catholic doctrine regarding that sacred mystery was more firmly established and elucidated by the adoption of the term transubstantiation—a theological word used to express the change of one substance into another. At the same Council, the dogmas of the Blessed Trinity, and of the Incarnation of the Son of God, both of which had ever been taught and believed in the Church, were reaffirmed, and clearly and briefly formulated. Many other heresies were condemned in this Council.

The thirteenth and fourteenth Councils were held in 1245 and 1274, at Lyons; the fifteenth at Vienna, in 1311.

In the first of these, all Christendom was exhorted to take up arms and to defend themselves against the incursions of the Saracens. In the Council held in 1274, the ancient doctrine of the Procession of the Holy Ghost from the Father and the Son was renewed and confirmed, and the union of the Greek and Roman Churches was established, to be severed again after a very brief duration. In the fifteenth Council, the excesses and errors of several associations were condemned, and the order of the Knight Templars was suppressed.

The next four Councils have been termed Reformation Councils, because in them laws and regulations were established with a view of putting an end to many abuses that had crept into the public administration, and into the lives of people and clergy. These Councils were held as follows: the sixteenth at Constance, from 1414 to 1418; the seventeenth at Basel, and afterwards at Ferrara and Florence, from 1431 to 1447; the eighteenth in the Lateran at Rome, in 1512. The nineteenth Council was assembled at Trent, and, with some intermissions, lasted from 1545 to 1563. At Constance the dismal divisions caused by the schismatical antipopes were healed, and the errors of Huss and Wickliffe were condemned. In Florence was again effected a short-lived reunion between the Churches of the East and the West. At Trent the disastrous errors of the so-called Reformers were rejected and condemned.

The twentieth General Council of the Church was called together by the great and glorious Pius the Ninth, in the twenty-fourth year of his pontificate. The first session was held at the Vatican in Rome, on the festival of the Immaculate Conception of the Blessed Virgin Mary, the eighth day of December, 1869. Nearly eight hundred prelates of the Church responded personally to the call of the Vicar of Christ. Although the enemies of the Church, on all sides, used every effort, both by threats, falsehood, and calumny, to disturb the peaceful proceedings of the

Council, their poisoned arrows fell harmless against the Rock of Peter. The wonderful tranquillity of soul, the unshaken confidence in God, the unconquerable fortitude, all so plainly shown in every word, in every act, look, and gesture of the venerable Pontiff, were not in vain. The grand and imposing Council was opened, and entered upon its duties, regardless of the insane opposition of unbelievers. The prevailing errors of our age were mercilessly condemned. The Fathers lifted the veil from the hypocritical face of that false science of our day which would fain build its proud throne upon the ruins of divine faith. The independence, rights, and privileges of God's Church were asserted. On the 18th of July, 1870, the ancient belief in the Infallibility of the Pope when defining matters of faith was formulated into a fixed dogma, and solemnly and officially promulgated as such.

38. The Infallibility of the Pope.

"In Christ Jesus, I am appointed a preacher and an apostle. I say the truth, I lie not: a doctor of the Gentiles in faith and truth."
—I. TIMOTHY, ii. 7.

By the inspired action of the Vatican Council, the sublime teaching-office of the Successor of Peter was solemnly set up in its proper place, before the eyes of the whole astonished world. There were not wanting silly and wicked men, who endeavored by misrepresentation and idle threats to undermine the strength and lessen the dignity of this grand and bold movement on the part of the Fathers of the Council. They would fain make the world believe that the Vatican Council had made a god of a sinful, fallible, mortal man. What folly! The Pope is, in very deed and truth, infallible. But this does not mean that he is impeccable; that is to say, incapable of being a sinner personally. Nor does it mean that he cannot err in his own person. He is, of course, a man, and will be such till death. He can err in his unofficial teachings. He can err even when deciding as a learned and experienced man on questions of profane and sacred knowledge, or even in ordaining matters of Church discipline. It is only when, in virtue of his sacred office and position, as Shepherd of Christ's fold and as authorized teacher of all Christians, and by virtue of his supreme apostolical authority, and by virtue of the assistance that our divine Saviour has promised to St. Peter and his successors, he decides and defines a question of faith and morals as binding upon the whole Church, that the Pope of Rome is infallible. Such was the teaching of the Vatican Council on the question of the Infallibility of the Pope. And, in truth, it was not a new doctrine, but an ancient, time-honored belief, that was defined and promulgated on the 18th of July, 1870, by the Fathers in Council assembled. Our Lord himself, Jesus Christ, proclaimed this doctrine to the world more than eighteen centuries ago, when he said to Peter: "Thou art Peter, and on this rock I will build my Church, and the gates of hell shall not prevail against it. I have prayed for thee that thy faith fail not."

Though in former times, before this doctrine was defined dogmatically, some eminent persons held other opinions on this subject, yet the great body of the doctors of the Church have in all ages expressed themselves clearly on Infallibility, whilst the whole universal Church has at all times accepted as matters of faith all decisions of the Popes, and with that complete submission and docility which indicate a firm belief in the infallibility of the highest authority on earth.

It could not be otherwise. Our divine Saviour has set up firmly and permanently, within his Church, a supreme, unfailing teaching authority, to which the faithful in every age, when differences arise among them regarding questions of faith, can have recourse, and receive, with unqualified confidence, a positive and infallible decision. But centuries may elapse, and have elapsed, without its being practicable to assemble a General Council. Now the faithful must necessarily be assured of their faith without delay. Hence there must always be some power to pronounce at once on disputed points. To whom does this office and authority to decide more properly and justly belong than to the lawful successor of him whom Christ appointed to be the foundation-stone of his Church, and to whom he entrusted the keys of his kingdom on earth, the Pope? How can the Pope pronounce a decision, safe and sure and certain to the doubting, and consoling to the believing, unless he possess, through supernatural assistance granted for the purpose, the prerogative of infallibility?

Hence all Christendom returns to its divine Lord and Master, Jesus Christ, its heartfelt thanks for this sublime and unfailing teaching authority, which he himself has constantly exercised throughout all ages, in the person of the Pope, his visible representative before mankind. When we see how, on every side of us, those who dwell beyond the pale of the Church are constantly changing from one opinion to another, how each individual interprets according to his own private notions, and differently from everybody else, the sacred pages of Holy Writ, we congratulate ourselves upon the bright and shining light vouchsafed by Christ to our Church; we appreciate more and more the priceless blessings of unity and security granted through infallibility; we cling more closely, and with renewed confidence and hope, to the immovable rock sustaining our Church. We unite our voices to St. Ambrose, and repeat with gladness and triumph, " *Ubi Petrus, ibi Ecclesia*"— " Where Peter is, there is the Church." We make a comforting act of faith in the decision rendered by the Fathers of the Council of Florence, in 1439: "The Roman Pontiff is really and truly the successor of Peter, the Prince of the Apostles and the Vicar of Christ, the Head of the Universal Church; and, in quality of Father, also the teacher of all Christians; receiving through St. Peter the power and authority of Jesus Christ our Lord."

Now, if the Council of Florence, nearly five hundred years ago, thus clearly defined the ample powers of the Chief Pastor of all Christendom, and if, as is really the case, three œcumenical synods have been held since that time, the objection, made by some, that, since the definition of the Infallibility of the Pope, all General Councils are unnecessary, falls to the ground at once. Such objection, in any case, would be groundless. As in the past, so will it be in the future. Every question of faith and morals to be decided will be subjected to a rigid and searching examination, which will be best conducted amid an assembly of all the bishops, if the circumstances of the times will permit such meeting.

CHAPTER V.

THE HISTORY OF THE HIERARCHY, OF CHURCH RIGHTS, AND OF CHURCH PENALTIES.

CHRIST LIVES IN HIS CHURCH AS KING AND LEGISLATOR.

39. The Kingly Office in the Church.

"We see Jesus, for the suffering of death, crowned with glory and honor. For in that God hath subjected all things to him, he left nothing not subject to him."—HEBREWS ii. 8, 9.

WHEN Pontius Pilate, the Roman governor, addressed to our beloved Lord the question, "Art thou a king?" Christ answered decidedly, "Thou sayest it, I am a king: for such I was born, and for such came I into the world." Oftentimes, too, he styled his Church his "kingdom." As this Lord and Saviour still lives in his Church, and shall live forever, so, too, must the kingly office still exist visibly within her, and for all time; that is to say, as the Church is a visible kingdom, and, indeed, the kingdom of Christ, who is himself a king, she must have a visible government. To this system of government appertain not only the duly appointed and lawfully commissioned officials, but also the justly and legally enacted laws, according to which these officers must govern themselves and the general Church. But the Founder of the Church has said expressly, "My kingdom is not of this world." That is to say, it has not for its object the acquisition of worldly goods; it is not dependent on earthly power or authority; nor does it seek to oversee or to administer civil governments, yet it cannot permit itself to be controlled or enslaved by the laws of the civil power. The Church and the State are two distinct powers which work harmoniously together, and side by side, for the welfare of the people collectively and individually. Both emanate from God, and both are founded on God's sacred ordinance. Hence the authority of the civil functionary is not dependent on the Church, any more than the authority of ecclesiastics depends on the civil power. The power and authority with which the Heads of the Church are clothed, are altogether spiritual, and are derived from heaven itself. The several grades of orders and of dignity among the clergy, when taken together, are termed the hierarchy, whilst the laws and ordinances in accordance with which these administer their respective offices, are called canon law and Church discipline.

40. History of the Grades, or Order of Dignity, among the Clergy of the Church.

THE HIERARCHY.

"Behold, I will lay thy stones in order. All thy children shall be taught of the Lord."—Isaiah liv. 11.

The "living stones laid in order," with which the Jerusalem of the New Law, namely the teaching Church, is built, are the clergy of the different ranks or grades.

We find, even in apostolic times, sufficient evidence to enable us to conclude with positive certainty that the hierarchy existed then, with its grades and dignities, and that therefore it must rest upon divine appointment. At the head and front of the clergy we find St. Peter and his lawful successors, the bishops of Rome, afterwards called

Popes. We know that Pope Clement, who was only the third in succession after St. Peter, wrote from the city of Rome a pastoral letter to the people at Corinth, in which he authoritatively counsels them concerning their strifes and contentions, and plainly says that he "dare not depose their priests who had been correct and faithful in the discharge of their duties." And at the very time that Clement sent, from so great a distance, this letter to the Corinthians, the holy Evangelist St. John was still alive and in their immediate vicinity. How, then, could St. Clement have presumed to interfere in the Church affairs of so remote a congregation, and during the lifetime of an Apostle, if Christendom did not recognize the bishop of Rome as the general head of the Church? Hence, St. Ignatius, who was himself a disciple of the Apostles, styles the Church of Rome "the Mistress of the Covenant of love," that is, of Christianity. Other Fathers of the ancient Church assert the same truth. St. Irenæus declares: "On account of her mighty pre-eminence, all believers must agree with the Church of Rome." And Tertullian, even after he had fallen into error, testified that the bishop of Rome "is the bishop of bishops." St. Cyprian, too, styles the episcopal see of Rome, "the chair of Peter, the centre of ecclesiastical unity, with which all bishops must be in communion." We see, therefore, how far out of the way these people are, who imagine that they utter a reproach against our good sense when they call us papists or ultramontanes.* The disgrace is not ours, but they themselves are to be pitied; for they are but little conversant with holy Scripture and the history of early Christianity, and they give the lie to their own fathers, who but a couple of centuries ago were truly loyal to the Popes.

* *Ultramontane* is a term applied to those Catholics who are in faithful communion with the Pope. The word itself means "over the mountain;" that is, beyond the Alps.

HISTORY OF THE HIERARCHY. 135

As the Popes are the lawful successors of St. Peter, so the bishops are the lawful successors of the other apostles. Even in the apostolic age the prelates maintained their superiority over the other ministers of the Church. Thus, although in the island of Crete, at Ephesus, and in the seven churches to whom St. John in his Apocalypse addresses himself, there were several ministers of the Church, yet the apostles Paul and John, in their epistles, address but one person, who appears to have been a bishop intrusted with the spiritual charge of the entire Christian commu-

The Catholic Hierarchy.

nity. We have from Tertullian a very remarkable decision on this question: "The right," he says, "to baptize belongs to the higher or superior priest, who is the bishop; and after him to the priests and deacons, who, however, must be authorized by the bishop."

At a very early period the individual bishops of a neighborhood conceived the idea of uniting themselves in a common union, giving the precedence to the bishop who dwelt in the metropolis, or mother city, or chief town of the province. Thus Jerusalem (afterwards Cæsarea), Antioch, Alexandria, and later Constantinople, and other cities were considered as metropolitan or mother-churches of their surrounding districts respectively. Among these metropolitan dioceses, after the Church had begun to spread wider and more rapidly, another order or office was soon established; for the prelates in the most important cities were styled patriarchs, by virtue of which title they enjoyed in many points a superiority over the archbishops, as these did over their suffragan bishops.

At a very early period the bishops had ministers to assist them, who, although by virtue of their ordination enjoyed full sacerdotal powers, yet were permitted to exercise them only when commissioned by their respective bishops. These were the simple priests, whose duty it was to assist the bishops in their functions in the principal congregation, or in the surrounding districts of the neighborhood, as well also to act in their places in case of necessity. In the fourth century, after the conversion of the Emperor Constantine, the Church grew so very rapidly, that besides the bishop's church in the chief city, many other congregations were formed both in the city and in the surrounding country, and intrusted to the care of these priests, who then became pastors. That is to say, they were assigned permanently to separate churches, with full power to conduct divine service and to exercise the care of souls, but always in the name of the bishop. St. Athanasius describes the existence of several parishes in the vicinity of Alexandria. At the time of the Council of Chalcedon, in the year 450, such parishes existed everywhere.

Besides the priest, we meet with other spiritual assistants of the bishops, as was explained previously in the discourse on priestly ordination. The deacons, the institution of whose office is mentioned in the sixth chapter of the "Acts of the Apostles," occupied the first place among these last. Besides having charge of the poor, sick, and needy, they were expected to care of, and take part in spiritual functions, such as preaching, baptizing, and assisting the bishop at the sacrifice of the mass.

All these spiritual assistants, priests, and deacons, when permanently attached to a bishop's church, were called cardinals in the early times, from the fact that a bishop's church was looked upon as a centre or middle-point (*cardo*) on which all the surrounding churches hinged. We may easily suppose, as was indeed the case, these ecclesiastics were very numerous in the ancient and mother Church at Rome; and as this Church advanced in numbers and importance, it gradually became customary to limit the title of cardinal to the immediate assistants of the Popes. According to a decision of Pope Sixtus V., their number was not to exceed seventy: six cardinal bishops, fifty cardinal priests, and fourteen cardinal deacons. These compose the high senate of Christendom, the Council of the Pope; and to them belongs, especially since the pontificate of Pope Nicholas II. in 1059, the right of electing the Popes

41. The History of Church Rights.

"Stand fast, and hold the traditions which you have learned, whether by word, or in our epistle."—THESSALONIANS ii. 14.

The dignitaries of the Church, or ecclesiastical authorities, do not own the Church, nor its inferior ministers, nor the faithful. Neither have they the right to govern the Church of God according to their own whims and fancies. For the divine-human King, whose subordinates they are, is a Prince of peace. He himself brought us this peace, and it is his wish that this peace of his should ever prevail in his kingdom upon earth. Now peace can exist only where there are wise ordinances and judicious laws, and both of these have existed in the Church from the very beginning. Both clergy and laity are bound by these laws and regulations, and thus the whole Church is grounded in holy discipline and maintained in peace and harmony, as Christ intended. Ecclesiastical ordinances, also called Church-laws, were not enacted all at once, and centuries elapsed before they reached the completeness in which we now possess them, as contained in that law code which theologians call *corpus juris canonici*—the embodiment of canon law. They grew gradually from the decisions of Church-councils, from the decrees of popes, and the opinions of learned Doctors and Fathers of the Church. Although many of these laws, unlike divine faith, are liable to and susceptible of change, according to the circumstances of time and place, yet they are founded upon unchangeable and undying principles established in the Church by Christ himself or by his immediate Apostles. A few of the most important of these everlasting principles may be here adduced for the instruction and edification of the Christian reader.

1. The Catholic Church is the sole and sacred spouse of Jesus Christ. Hence, those persons who wilfully and obstinately repudiate the faith of this universal Church, or who, by great scandals and wickedness of life, cast dishonor upon her, must be excommunicated or banished from her bosom, till such time as they repent and seek readmission with a full and sincere determination to make ample satisfaction. Our Lord himself decreed this law when he said : "He who will not hear the Church, let him be to thee as a heathen ;" that is, let him be considered as outside of the pale of the Church. The holy Apostles themselves acted in accordance with this decree. St. Paul, for example, writes to Timothy : "This precept I commend to thee, O son Timothy, according to the prophecies going before on thee, that thou war in them a good warfare. Having faith and a good conscience, which some

rejecting have made shipwreck concerning the faith, of whom is Hymeneus and Alexander, whom I have delivered up to Satan, that they may learn not to blaspheme."

Indeed, the Apostles looked upon a strictness of faith and a concurrence in Christian teaching as of so much importance, that St. Paul does not hesitate to declare that if an angel from heaven should come and teach any other doctrine, he should be anathema. In the same way, too, they treated other vices; for St. Paul, in the name of our Lord Jesus Christ, delivered the blasphemer at Corinth to Satan, to the destruction of the flesh, that his soul might be saved. And this power of excommunication existed during all ages in the Church down to our own time, as a sad but necessary means of preserving purity of faith and of maintaining holy discipline in the Church of God. Should the transgressor enter into himself, he would, after longer or shorter penance, be absolved from the sentence of excommunication and readmitted to the pale of that Church from which he had of his own choice gone forth.

2. It is of extreme advantage to the Christian to follow the example of Christ and his chosen followers, and to crucify the lusts of the flesh by fasting and abstinence from certain kinds of food. The Church has always claimed and exercised the right to appoint common days and general seasons of fasting. She preached and practised bodily mortification, from the very earliest days of her existence; for we find mention made, in the first General Council of Nice, of the precept of fasting, as of a very ancient, well understood, and universally admitted matter of discipline. And although the prescribed time of fasting, and its ancient severity, have in the course of ages been very much modified and moderated, yet at no time did the precept itself cease to exist, or to have binding power.

3. Matrimony having been elevated by Christ to the dignity of a great sacrament in his Church, to that Church

necessarily belong the right and the duty to establish the conditions under which, and the mode in which, it is to be administered. She has always maintained, as an article of faith, that a lawfully contracted and fully consummated marriage between two Christians is indissoluble. On the same grounds, she has, in accordance with the will of God, appointed certain impediments to marriage; such as near relationship, affinity, and others. From the beginning, she ordained that matrimony should be administered publicly, that is, before the face of the Church. With this view, the Council of Lateran decreed that every betrothment (*sponsalia*) should be made known; while the Council of Trent requires the publication of the banns three separate times at the parish-mass on Sundays or holy days of obligation. The Church has always looked upon mixed marriages as a great misfortune and as threatening danger; permitting them merely in order to avoid greater evils, and always on condition that the offspring shall receive Catholic education and training. The Church has never admitted as true and real marriages the so-called civil marriages, that is, those pretended marriages performed before a politician, with intended contempt for the principles and blessing of the Church.* Moreover, she looks with a shudder upon the so-called married life of such parties, and considers such wedlock a continued protest and sin against the most sacred laws of God. (See page 97).

4. The celibacy of the clergy is in keeping both with their sublime calling and with the sacred duties of their office. Jesus Christ, the first and greatest high-priest, chose to observe in his own life perpetual continency. And according as the Church became more vividly impressed with the dignity and sacredness of the holy mass,

---

* Where the Council of Trent has not been officially promulgated, these marriages before politicians, though clandestine, escape nullity.

the more ardently she must have desired to see these holy mysteries performed by a pure and virgin priesthood. The priest is the bridegroom of the congregation of souls intrusted to his care. He must love each and every soul with a supernatural love; be willing to share his income with the poor; must be indefatigable in the discharge of the duties of his office night and day, and employ his leisure moments in study and prayer. Even in time of pestilence and contagious epidemic, he must not hesitate to risk his health and even his life for his flock. It is his happy privilege and sacred duty to defend, regardless of human respect, the truth and the law of Christ, and the rights of His Church, even if such defence bring upon him enmities, ridicule, worldly losses, imprisonment, death itself. How could the priest comply faithfully with all these inexorable obligations, if entrammelled with the duties of a husband and of a father of children? Hence the apostles renounced all things, even their wives, in order the more freely and exclusively to devote themselves to the service of Christ; and from their time we may date the custom which generally prevailed, of all those who served in the ministry living unmarried lives. As this edifying custom was threatened with lapsing into disuse, it was made a fixed law by the bishops assembled in 305 at the synod of Elvira. They decreed that married men, desirous of entering the ministry, should renounce the cares of married life. In a like manner, the Fathers of the Church, assembled at Neo Cæsarea in the year 314, declared: "Any priest who contracts matrimony shall be deprived of his office." When, now and then, in the stormy and unsettled condition of society in the earlier years of the middle ages, corruption threatened to invade the ranks of the clergy, there were always great and good men, such, for example, as Gregory VII., Innocent III., and many others, who rose up and renewed and enforced the law of celibacy. And if, from time to time, unhappy ecclesiastics have fallen, and thereby plunged the Church into grief, she has not forgotten that similar misfortunes have befallen even married men and married preachers of heterodox churches, all too often ; and that the Catholic priest, if he will but avail himself of the superabundant means of grace placed at his disposal, and be mindful of his heaven-like dignity, may readily and successfully maintain his purity intact, and thereby gain for himself not only the brightest of crowns in the next world, but even here below secure the unbounded confidence and tenderest respect on the part of those intrusted to his charge.

42. Selection and Appointment of the Clergy.— Their Maintenance.

"For this cause I left thee in Crete, that thou shouldst ordain priests in every city, as I also appointed thee."—Titus i. 5.

The right of appointing ecclesiastics to any special office of the Church must be confined to those only whose lawful position and relation to the office in question, or whose long and faithful services to the Church, are a guarantee that they will make a suitable and useful and disinterested choice. Hence, in the beginning, the first bishops were appointed by the Apostles themselves. Later, the bishops were chosen by the assembled ecclesiastics of the vacant episcopal sees, respectively; but under the direction of the neighboring bishops, and in presence of and with the consent of the faithful. But afterwards, when the Cross had gained complete victory over paganism, and kings and governments had become Christian, this right of a voice in elections, which formerly was exercised by the people, was gradually and imperceptibly wrested from them by the more cunning, or more able leaders and princes and politicians. And as some subsequent bishops were also princes, the German emperors especially claimed, and for a short time exercised, a right of appointment, by means of which many of their unworthy favorites were thrust into vacant episcopal sees. Gregory VII., however, combated vigorously this dangerous abuse, but it was not till after many struggles, that at last a settlement was agreed upon, in the year 1122, between Pope Calixtus II. and the emperor Henry V. of Germany, by virtue of which the free election of bishops was guaranteed to the chapters of the respective cathedrals. However, in order to show a becoming respect to the princes of the different countries, who were, or at least ought to be, the proper representatives of the people, a very important part in the election of bishops was, in the course of time, granted to these lay representatives. In order to guard against the appointment or election of unworthy persons to so sublime and sacred an office as that of the episcopacy, the Pope always reserved to himself the right of confirming or rejecting the choice made by the electors.

The choice of the other ecclesiastics in a diocese belonged, in the beginning, by common consent, to the bishop. Of this fact, St. Jerome assures us, when he says: "The bishops have the right, in their own districts, to appoint the priests." Yet, in very early times, many bishops used to call to their aid and counsel, in making an appointment, the other priests of their dioceses, and even the laity. Again, in later times, the bishops granted to such princes, monasteries, and communities as were generous enough to support a parish with their own means, the privilege of designating their clergyman, whom he himself then confirmed, if a proper person, or rejected if unfit for the office. The bishop's approbation was necessary to entitle the candidate to receive the revenues of the parish.

As the priest must serve the altar, so too he must live by the altar, and be provided with the necessary means of subsistence. The primitive Christians attended to this important matter without any fixed law. As under the old dispensation, the priests and Levites received a tenth part for their subsistence, so the early Christians took pleasure in offering the best of their substance to those who had care of their souls. These offerings were made sometimes monthly, sometimes weekly, and again during the offertory at public service, when bread, wine, corn, oil, and other gifts were presented in the churches. At a very early period the aggregate income of a church was divided into four parts. Of these, one was for the maintenance of the bishop, one for the proper and decent support of the clergy of the church, a third part was employed in repairing the edifice and keeping up divine service, and the fourth part was invariably given to the poor.

As in the course of centuries, the Church obtained many bequests, and even very considerable emoluments from the emperors who embraced Christianity, and as different Church Councils, as that of Tours in 560, and that of Macon in 586, enforced the offering of tithes, the system of benefices gradually arose. Certain parcels of land were attached to every ecclesiastical office, and out of the income yielded, the clergy appointed to such office were to live. About the year 850, this system had become universal in the Church. At the same time, the clergy were required by law not to consider these revenues as exclusively their own property. They were permitted to use what was necessary for a comfortable sustenance, and to employ the remainder for God's honor and glory, for the advancement of religion and education, and for the relief of the poor.

In later years, several of the state governments have appropriated to themselves the revenues and ancient endowments of the Church, and pretended to assume by law the duty of paying out of these moneys an annual salary to bishops and priests. As these salaries are the product of the ancient Church property, and as a large part of the ecclesiastical wealth of former times is still in the hands of politicians, and used for political purposes, it were unkind and unjust to boast of the "alms" which these governments extend "in charity" to the clergy.

43. The History of Church Temporalities.

"I have given to the sons of Levi all the tithes of Israel in possession, for the ministry wherewith they serve me in the tabernacle of the covenant."—NUMBERS xviii. 21.

Although the kingdom of God is not of this world, yet as it exists in this world, and is to a certain extent dependent upon human means and earthly resources in order to attain its aims and objects, the Church may accept endowments, tithes, bequests, and other donations. These are to be considered as inviolable ecclesiastical property, and must not be diverted from the sacred purposes of the Church. On the other hand, several fanatical persons arose at various periods, who condemned the holding of goods by the Church as unchristian. They inveighed bitterly against the wealth of the monasteries and the income of the bishops; seeming to forget that these moneys were used for the most part in good works, such as the beautifying of divine worship, the education of the young in convents and parish schools, and for the support of the needy, and hence contributed much to the free action and usefulness of the Church in the spirit of Jesus Christ. It is remarkable that those bishops who used the least of their revenues for themselves, and who led the most abstemious and mortified lives, were those who fought most strenuously in defence of the rights and property of the Church.

Among the countless instances that have occurred throughout the history of Christianity, showing the fidelity with which the Church revenues were applied by the bishops to the purposes intended, and also the disinterestedness of the prelates, may be mentioned the case of Bishop Caulet, of Pamiers. This saintly prelate was condemned by Louis XIV., of France, in 1678, to lose the temporalities of his diocese, because he was bold enough to rebuke the unjust and despotic actions of that king in his dealings with the Church. The bishop, on hearing his sentence, sent to the king a letter, in which he wrote: "I cannot be denied permission to ask your royal majesty a just request. If I have been guilty of any wrong, and have been so adjudged, please to take from me only that portion of my episcopal revenues which I have hitherto employed for my own personal maintenance. I am not ashamed to appeal to the generosity and charity of my flock, who will not see me in want of the necessaries of life, without offering abundant alms. But do not compel others, who are innocent of any wrong-doing, to share my disgrace and punishment. For I must inform your majesty that those incomes, just taken away from me by judicial proceedings, were to be devoted to the support of two seminaries in which young ecclesiastics are being trained for the direction and instruction of the souls of your subjects; to the renovation of the Cathedral, almost ruined by the excesses of the heretics; to the restoration and beautifying of other churches in my diocese; to the support of many poor persons, who if deprived of this support will be reduced to extreme suffering; and finally, to the liquidation of the debts that I have contracted for all the above purposes. In regard to my own person, and my private necessities, I shall bear with fullest resignation whatever divine Providence may be pleased to inflict upon me."

44. The Temporal Power of the Popes. Rome and the States of the Church.

"And the angel said: O Lord of Hosts, how long wilt thou not have mercy on Jerusalem and on the cities of Juda, with which thou hast been angry? This is now the seventieth year. And the Lord answered the angel comfortable words."—ZACHARIAS i. 12.

The Church of Rome, being the centre of Christianity, surpassed at a very early period all other churches in the amount of her money, and in the value of gold and silver vessels, and of houses and lands. The aggregate of this wealth was called the Patrimony of St. Peter. Nowhere on earth could there be found a more honestly-earned property, or more honorable and lawful possession. Many of the descendants of ancient and renowned Roman families, heroic and senatorial families, became Catholics during the first three hundred years of Christianity, and from time to time they consecrated the whole or a part of their immense fortunes to the service of Jesus Christ, in the person of his Vicars on earth, the Popes. Constantine the Great and his successors, as representatives of the law of the land, subsequently confirmed and augmented these endowments. Hence the Popes of the fifth and sixth centuries, even before they became temporal rulers, were the largest technical real-estate holders in Europe: all of course in trust for the benefit of the Church. The magnitude of these possessions; the judicious management of the same; the truly Christian fidelity with which the revenues were applied to promote the honor of God, the advancement of the Church, and the welfare of the people; more especially the poor widows and orphans; all tended to so augment the power and influence, and heighten the character of the Popes in the estimation of the people, that the Chief Pastors enjoyed, even then, almost princely recognition as wise and faithful temporal rulers. Let any one acquainted with the history of governments examine the title-deeds of the several reigning dynasties in Europe and America, whether monarchical or republican, and he will find that sovereignty was acquired in many, if not most instances, by the founder of each royal house or commonwealth, through the means of falsehood, perjury, usurpation, oppression, bloodshed, and oftentimes by the violent casting aside of those who had a better claim to the sceptre, the crown, or chair of supreme authority. There are dark blotches on the parchment which records their acquisition of authority, and if submitted to chemical tests by experts in chemistry, it would be found that these are spots of human blood. Not one of these dynasties, however, goes so far back into antiquity as that of the Popes. Their title, whatever else may be said of it, is as pure and stainless as the ermine which borders their robes of office.

The Emperor Constantine, after having overcome his adversaries in battle, resolved to build the city of Constantinople far away in the East, and establish there the seat of empire, which had hitherto been at Rome. From that period there was no little confusion in the mode of administering temporal authority within the states that have since been called the Patrimony of St. Peter. The interval was nearly five hundred years. For some time the Roman emperors kept their representatives in Italy, but these almost without exception proved inefficient and insincere. They could not protect the people of Italy against the successive incursions of the Herules, Goths, and Lombards. The people became a defenceless prey to the avarice and cruelty of these barbarous marauders. Again and again the Popes, as chief pastors of these suffering people, appealed to the emperor in Constantinople, beseeching him to send troops for the protection of the Italian States. But their efforts were in vain, their appeals disregarded; for the eastern portion of the Empire was itself threatened from similar sources. It was even discovered that the emperor had made secret treaties with the marauders, to the effect that if they spared the eastern portion, their incursions into Italy would not be interfered with by the presence of the imperial troops. In the meantime, the people of Central Italy threw themselves into the arms of the Sovereign Pontiffs for the protection which they could not longer expect from any other source. The Popes left nothing undone to correspond with their

Pope Leo the Great and Attila.

wishes; in famine, in pestilence, amid the desolations of carnage, they were, if not the protectors of the people, at least their fathers and their comforters. In his solicitude for his flocks, the Chief Pastor at Rome even risked his life to defend them. His heart bled with theirs in the contemplation of the ruins surrounding them on all sides.

As early as 449, when Attila, king of the Goths, after laying waste a great part of Italy, was about to attack and destroy the city of Rome, Pope Leo the Great went forth as the temporal Representative of the people, as well as the spiritual and temporal Representative of Christ, to meet and check the ruthless invader. By the impressive dignity of his presence, but more especially by the wisdom and miraculous power of his words, the Pope touched the heart of Attila, who at once retraced his steps and left Italy. An old tradition has it, that during the Pope's address to the devastating commander, the latter saw in the air the figures of the twin Apostles Peter and Paul, both with drawn swords, and threatening instant destruction of himself and army, should he venture to enter the Eternal City. Again, a few years later, Genseric, the ruthless king of the terrible Vandals, was advancing towards Rome, spreading death and desolation on all sides. The same Pope, Leo the Great, went out unprotected to meet the barbarian, and although not succeeding in preventing the capture of the city, he dissuaded the enemy from destroying it, and from murdering its inhabitants. Like Pope Leo, all the subsequent pontiffs continued to shield and assist the people of Italy. They employed their incomes in rebuilding the defences of the Capital, in raising the temples of God, and the homes of man from the ruin caused by time and war. They sent into the plundered districts whole fleets laden with grain, and lent their aid, both by word and work, where no other aid or encouragement could be found.

Thus the Popes became *de facto,* if not *de jure,* temporal sovereigns of that portion of Italy which had been abandoned by the Eastern emperor, and which, until the recent robberies of the late Victor Emmanuel, constituted the States of the Church. During the eighth century, a succession of conflicts arose between the Lombards on one side, and the few feeble forces of the Empire still in Italy on the other. The Popes interfered in behalf of peace and humanity. The Lombards were victorious, and captured many towns, among them Ravenna, the seat of the last vestige of imperial power. King Luitprand, in 742, gave to Pope Zachary the city and province of Sutri, as *"being the lawful property of St. Peter."* This was the first formal bestowal of a city to the Church, and really the nucleus of the "Temporal Power."

It was not long, however, till the Lombards renewed hostilities against Rome and Lower Italy. Pope Stephen III. appealed earnestly once more to the emperor in Constantinople, beseeching him to protect his subjects' lives and property. In vain. The Eastern Empire now completely abandoned the ancient capital of the world, and thus forfeited all claim to the allegiance of its inhabitants. A visit, made in person by the Pope to the Lombard king Astolphus, was equally barren of any good results. In this emergency, Pope Stephen, in his solicitude for the safety of his flocks, resolved to go himself to Pepin, king of France. The visit took place in November of the memorable year 753. At the convent of St. Maurice, in Switzerland, the Pope was met by the French ambassadors, who, with all possible respect, accompanied the Head of the Christian Church to the royal palace of Pontignon, north of Paris. Pepin readily acceded to the Pontiff's request, namely, to deliver the Romans from the attacks of Astolphus. So well were the temporal rights of the Pope recognized, that Pepin first sent ambassadors to Astolphus, king of the Lombards, entreating him to make *restitution* of the territory belonging to the holy Church of God. The Pope also wrote to him in the same spirit. Deaf to these entreaties, he still persevered in his encroachments upon the Papal territory. Pepin came at the head of his army, chastised the barbarian, compelled him to restore the territory which he had usurped, and bound him by treaty not to invade it again. This treaty, however, was not observed, and it soon became necessary for Pepin's son Charlemagne to make war again on the Lombards, and wrest from them, once for all, the property of the Church, which he gave to the Popes as the patrimony of the holy

Apostles and of the Roman Church. He also confirmed the Pontiff in the temporal sovereignty, which he had exercised already for many years. The emperor Copronymus sent, from Constantinople, ambassadors to the French conqueror, claiming the territory from which the Lombards had been driven; but, as may be supposed, the petition was refused with contempt and disdain. The Eastern emperor had allowed the barbarians to invade the States of the Church, which he should have protected, and then when these barbarians had been expelled by French valor and chivalry, under the command of their sovereign, it was too late for Constantinople to make the petition. Pepin and Charlemagne were at liberty to dispose of the conquered territory as they thought proper, and they conferred it upon the See of St. Peter.

It is true that amid the incessant storms of persecution that have raged about and against the Bark of Peter, these temporalities have frequently been unjustly torn from the faithful and protecting hands of the Head of the Church. Often, too, has he himself been driven into exile, and sometimes held as a prisoner. Yet always, in his own good time, the Providence of God has conducted the Sovereign Pontiff, in triumph over his enemies, back to the Eternal City, and placed him again custodian of those possessions which have been consecrated to the maintenance, dignity, and independence of the Church.

To-day, all Christendom is awaiting with patient confidence the time when that same God will restore to his venerable and Saintly Representative, Leo the Thirteenth, those temporal possessions which a sacrilegious and avaricious government wrested from his predecessor, amid bloodshed and carnage, in September, 1870.* Although

---

* At the "Congress of Paris," during the year 1856, the Italian Minister of State, the infamous Cavour, aided and abetted by English perfidy, declared against the temporal power of the Pope. His objections were triumphantly refuted by Count Rayneval, French during the first three centuries of Christianity, when the Church was bathed in the blood of her children, the Sovereign Pontiff was not a Temporal Ruler, and although the Temporal Power may not be absolutely necessary to the Church, yet the Catholics of all tongues and climes have spoken out on the subject with marvellous unanimity: declaring it to be their irrevocable desire that the lawful bishop of Rome shall be the sole guardian of the accumulated offerings of their generous and self-sacrificing forefathers in the faith. All Catholics believe that the Temporal Power is necessary in order to insure the independence of their Chief Pastor, and to secure the untrammelled liberty of the Church. They demand and will accept nothing less than the recognition by all men of the ancient rights and privileges of the Holy See.

ambassador to Rome. After the defeat of Austria at Magenta, by Napoleon III., in 1859, the Romagna and the Legations were wrested from the government of Pius IX. Again, after the engagement at Castelfidardo, in October, 1860, the Marches and Umbria were stolen. On the 3d of November, 1867, the Papal troops, with the aid of the French soldiers, repelled successfully an assault made by the Garibaldians at Mentana. But, as soon as Rome was vacated by the French troops, the late king, Victor Emmanuel, besieged the city, and finally wrested from the Church the last of her possessions.

CHAPTER VI.

THE HISTORY OF RELIGIOUS ORDERS. CHRIST LIVES IN HIS CHURCH AS THE HOLY ONE.

45. Holiness in the Catholic Church.

"Christ also loved the Church and delivered himself up for it, that he might sanctify it, a glorious Church, not having spot or wrinkle, holy and without blemish."—EPHESIANS v. 25 *et al.*

WELL and truly does St. Luke describe the happy effect of close union with Christ, when he tells us, in "The Acts of the Apostles," "The multitude of believers had but one heart and one soul." Our Blessed Lord and Saviour has himself explained to us, by means of a beautiful parable, his very close union with the living members of his Church, and his undying life in that Church. He tells us, "I am the vine, you are the branches." The branch shoots forth from the main trunk, and must be connected with it in order to preserve its own life. For only one life exists in both. All those saps or vital forces circulating in the branch and producing leaves, blossoms, and fruit, flow from the vine into every healthy limb. Christ is the true vine, and in him dwelleth, in the greatest fullness and completeness, all holiness of life; for the eternal Father hath declared: "This is my beloved Son in whom I am well pleased." Now, as the vital power of the main vine-tree circulates through the branch, so does holiness of life flow from Christ into each individual believer in particular, and into the Church of God in general.

As Christ, who is holiness itself and the source of all sanctity, lives in his Church, that Church must necessarily be holy, and holy men must likewise necessarily exist within her pale at all times. Christ, the all-holy one,

A Monk at Prayer.

manifests himself in their virtuous lives. They are the certain, living witnesses of the true and real existence and life of Christ in his Church; for each one of them practically says, by the holiness of his life: "I live, now not I; but Christ liveth in me." Yes, Christ lives in his saints, first by his example: for the faithful Christian who cherishes in his heart the image of the lowly, obedient, chaste, and loving Saviour, feels himself inspired and drawn to become like unto him. Christ lives in his saints by virtue of his promises; for the superabundant joy of heaven in the future sweetens the bitter struggles of the present life; and he lives, thirdly, by virtue of his mysterious grace, which flows through the faithful soul with supernatural life-power, and helps it to overcome the flesh, the world, and even hell itself.

But the outgrowth of holiness from Christ, the all-holy One, was not limited merely to the myriads of holy souls who have adorned the Church in all ages, and who will adorn her till the end of time. It animated and vivified, moreover, the very institutions in which and through which these souls obtained the means of holiness; such as holy practices, popular pious customs, devout associations and confraternities, the two-edged sword of the eloquent preacher and expounder of Scripture, missions, and other devotions. For, although all these means of holiness may come through the agency of men, yet it cannot be denied but that the Spirit of Jesus Christ is acting, in these men and their works, to the sanctification of his elect.

46. History of Monastic Life in General.

"Jesus saith to him: If thou wilt be perfect, go sell what thou hast, and give to the poor, and thou shalt have treasure in heaven: and come follow me."—MATTHEW xix. 21.

Among all these means of holiness, outside of grace and the sacraments, the monastic life is the most magnificent; resembling a glorious old tree whose widespreading branches overshadow the earth. This tree has its triple-root in Jesus Christ, namely, in his voluntary poverty, holy obedience, and virgin chastity. In the splendor of this three-fold beauty, Christ wishes to live here below through all ages, and hence he has ever drawn to himself by mysterious bonds magnanimous and noble souls, and inspired them with pious and steadfast resolution, to live like Christ in voluntary poverty, unlimited obedience, and virginal purity.

And what do these souls seek, who come in such vast crowds, decked with the harsh thorny crown of voluntary poverty, laden with the chains of holy obedience, and bearing in their hands the lily of chastity? They wish to be released, and to remain forever free from the poor, passing world; from the desire of wealth, and from sensuality, pride, and self-will. They wish to be so free from the world, and to belong so exclusively to Christ, that they may in truth cry out with him, "Our kingdom is not of this world." But although Jesus Christ was not *of* this world, yet he was altogether *for* this world, and gave himself up for the life of the world. So, too, these holy souls, though not of this world, yet wish to sacrifice themselves entirely for the world, partly by effecting in the quiet cloister life, and by prayer, meditation, and rigorous mortification, a never-ending sacrifice of atonement and propitiation; rendering to divine majesty that adoration and thanksgiving which the world owes, but which it commonly neglects to pay. These constitute the contemplative orders.

Others sacrifice themselves for the world, by benefiting it through much manual labor, by imparting knowledge to the ignorant, and by rendering assistance to the sick and afflicted. These are the active orders.

The monastic life is as old as the Church itself, and will endure, as the fairest flower of Christian life, as long as the Church shall live. Originally, those chosen to serve God in religion remained in their families and parishes, and there practised faithfully the works of Christian perfection. During the persecution under the emperor Decius, about the year of Christ 250, many of these religious fled into the deserts, where they led the lives of hermits. The very deserts, especially in Egypt, blossomed with the holy lives of countless servants of God. When some pious and truly spiritual man of extraordinary gifts would retire into the solitude, multitudes would gather around him and linger in his neighborhood, in order to be guided by his holiness, wisdom, and experience, on the way of Christian perfection. Thus, hundreds of cells would rise around his hermitage, and here his disciples would dwell and lead lives in conformity with his directions.

St. Antony.

The first of these "Fathers of the Desert" mentioned in history was St. Antony, born in 251, and who was the founder of solitary monastic life. The first Father who withdrew the monks from their separate cells and assembled them into one monastery was St. Pachomius, about the year 325. In a similar manner the sister of St. Antony established a convent for the virgins. Monastic life, founded as it was upon the three vows of poverty, chastity, and obedience, grew and flourished in the East, under the guidance of such great and holy men as St. Basil of Cæsarea and others, who cherished and cultivated this fair young plant with extreme tenderness and skill.

In the West, monasticism honors as its father and patriarch the great St. Benedict. Here too the religious life grew and developed in a variety of forms, spreading over

HISTORY OF MONASTIC LIFE IN GENERAL. 159

all the earth, so that to-day, in spite of persecution and confiscation, countless monasteries and convents exist in every quarter of the globe, with more than two hundred thousand religious of both sexes.

Among the numerous orders instituted in the West, and which, with the exception of the spiritual knights, still

St. Dominick.   St. Francis.   St. Alphonsus.   St. Benedict.   St. Ignatius.
The Founders of the Five Religious Orders.

live and persevere in the active pursuit of their respective vocations, the Benedictines, Augustinians, Franciscans, Dominicans, Jesuits, Redemptorists, and other male and female orders established for education, for the care of the poor, sick, and orphans, deserve our attention.

47. History of the Benedictines.

"The manifold wisdom and glory of God may be made known to all the principalities and powers through the Church."—EPHESIANS iii. 10.

St. Benedict of Nursia was the founder of the Benedictine order, and the patriarch of the monks of the West. Born in the year 480, he attended the public schools in Rome, and in early life conceived a horror for the world and its excesses. He therefore retired into the solitude of

St. Benedict Destroys the Idols on Monte Casino.

Subiaco, where he led the life of a hermit. The fame of his sanctity spread far and wide, so that the monks of Vicovaro chose him for their abbot. But his rigorous discipline soon displeased a small portion of these monks, and they concocted a plan to poison him. But Benedict, according to custom, having made the sign of the cross over the proffered wine before tasting, the vessel burst in pieces, and the wicked men acknowledged their guilty design and repented. The saint forgave them, but returned to Subiaco, where he soon gathered about him a multitude of disciples. From this place he went to Monte Casino, where he founded the mother-house of his order, and compiled that renowned rule of monastic life in which Christian rigor is mingled with paternal mildness, zeal for the glory of God combined with tender solicitude for the welfare of our neighbor, and profound wisdom of life tempered with child-like simplicity. When this holy man of God felt his end approaching, he asked to be carried into the church

Monks at Work.

for the reception of the last sacraments, took an affecting farewell of his disciples, prayed with clasped hands, and died while in a standing position, leaning on the arm of a monk, on the 21st of March, 543.

But his work, the glorious Benedictine order, continued to live through all successive ages. Its humble and indefatigable monks became, in the hand of God, the chosen instruments who rebuilt Europe upon the ruins which the barbarous invaders from the North had spread around on all sides. They effected this work successfully by science, education, and industry. The Benedictine monk had preserved in his cell the treasures of pagan wisdom and the sacred learning of Christian antiquity. It was to the Benedictine monk that the citizen, the knight, and the prince intrusted their sons for education of mind and heart. It was Benedictine monks who cleared the primeval forests of Europe, dug canals, laid out roads, built bridges, and transformed barren solitudes into blooming gardens. Their monasteries became the beginnings of flourishing settlements, the nucleus of prosperous and wealthy cities; so that they contradicted the oft-repeated assertion, that religion and piety are useless and of no avail, even to the earthly welfare of nations. Hence these monks commanded the respect of the people, who loved them as fathers, while kings and princes honored them for their prudent counsels and great learning. Owing to their own industry and the liberality of a grateful people, their possessions grew to vast proportions and became of enormous value. This order has had thirty-seven thousand monasteries or institutions, out of which have come forth, during the course of centuries, twenty-four Popes, and fifty thousand canonized saints.

48. History of the Crusades.

' God forbid that I should glory, save in the cross of our Lord Jesus Christ."—GALATIANS vi. 14.

In the Benedictine order our divine Redeemer manifests himself as sanctifier of the works of peace, while in the military orders we recognize him as animating the heroes of war with supernatural life, and as conferring blessings even on the sanguinary profession of arms. These remarkable orders owed their beginnings partly, and their confirmation, permanent establishment, and wide extensive growth wholly and specially to the Crusades. There were six holy wars prosecuted by the Christians from the eleventh to the thirteenth centuries, and directed against the Saracens in the East. These Crusades were undertaken, first, with a view of protecting the devout Christian pilgrims who were in the habit of frequenting the venerable places where our Saviour had lived, taught, suffered, and triumphed, from the fury and avarice of the heathens; and secondly, with a view to get possession of the Holy Land itself, and annex it to Christendom; and thirdly, to break down the power of the Crescent,* and to elevate the Cross in triumph and victory in Palestine.

We behold kings, emperors, and brave heroes of every degree taking the lead in these Crusades, two of whom in particular, and whose names are inseparably connected with these holy wars, deserve our special attention. These are St. Bernard of Clairvaux, in 1153, and St. Louis IX., King of France.

The holy monk of Clairvaux traversed Germany and

---

* The Crescent, or half-moon, is the standard of Mohammedanism.

The first Crusade was preached by Peter the Hermit, and was led by Godfrey de Bouillon, in 1099, during the pontificate of Pope Urban II.

The second Crusade, from A.D. 1147 to 1149, was preached by St. Bernard, and was prosecuted chiefly by the German emperor, Conrad III., and by the French king, Louis VII.

The third Crusade was jointly led by the Emperor Frederic Barbarossa, King Philip Augustus of France, and Richard the Lionhearted of England, from 1189 to 1192.

The fourth Crusade took place under Baldwin of Flanders and Boniface of Montserrat, in 1204, during the reign of Pope Innocent III.

The fifth Crusade, under the Emperor Frederic II., lasted from 1219 to 1229.

The sixth and seventh Crusades were conducted by St. Louis IX., King of France, respectively in 1248 and 1270.

France, preaching the Crusades. He proclaimed, in glowing and eloquent language, the duty of Christendom to save from dishonor by the unbelievers, the land of our Redemption; and to sacrifice for the attainment of this grand design, power, money, blood, and life. The words of the man of God penetrated like fiery arrows the hearts of all. "God wills it," shouted the multitude; and kings and noble knights, and the people from city and country pressed in eager throngs about the inspired

St. Bernard preaching the Crusades.

preacher, to receive the cross from his own hands, and thus enroll themselves in the grand army of the cross of Christ. But neither this first Crusade, nor the several successive ones, effected the end proposed or the wished-for result. Jerusalem, although captured by the Christians in July, 1099, and transformed into a Catholic kingdom, fell again into the hands of the infidels; and in May, 1291, Ptolemæus, the last stronghold of the Christians in Palestine was wrested from their hands by the Mohammedans.

The want of success in these wars was attributed partly to the treachery of the Greeks, partly to the disloyalty of some of the Crusaders themselves, but chiefly to the many abuses and scandalous excesses which crept into the prosecution even of this sacred cause. King Louis of France became the innocent victim of atonement for the sins of the less sincere Crusaders. This pious prince, though he had organized and sent out a Crusade in 1248, undertook in 1270, when quite advanced in years, another expedition in which he intended to give battle to the Saracens in Tunis. But a dreadful pestilence broke out in the ranks of the army, and attacked the king himself in its most malignant form. Amid this calamity, the king displayed the magnanimity of a true Christian hero, not permitting one word of complaint to fall from his lips. "Grant, O Lord," he prayed constantly, "that we may learn to despise worldly success and to embrace cheerfully the trials sent to us by heaven." When the priest was reaching to him the Body of the Lord, the face of the dying king lit up with holy rapture, and he exclaimed: "I am going into thy house, O Lord. In thy own holy temple I shall adore thee and rejoice in thy blessed name." Having uttered these words, he fell asleep in the Lord, on the 25th of August, 1270.

Although the Crusades did not accomplish the great object intended, yet they became, in the hands of God, the means of much good. The increased liberty and improvement of the middle classes, the founding of new states and governments, great advancement in the several departments of knowledge, an unprecedented extension of European commerce, were some of the results of the Crusades. But the most precious fruit of all, was that interior awakening of the soul towards Christ and his kingdom, which during those two centuries took permanent hold on Christians and their leaders; familiarizing the nobility and the multitude with the history of Christ, elevating and refining all classes, and giving birth to the three great religious orders of knighthood in the Church.

The glorious spirit which animated these "monks in armor," may be best understood by means of the questions put to each candidate at the time of his admission to the brotherhood: "Do you solemnly promise, beloved brother, in the name of God and the Blessed Virgin, to practice faithfully a life-long obedience to each of your superiors? Do you solemnly promise, in the name of God and his Virgin Mother Mary, perpetual celibacy and perfect purity of soul and body? Do you solemnly pledge yourself to renounce forever all your worldly goods, and to serve the Order in poverty and submission, and to risk your life for the deliverance of the Holy Land? As you promise each and all of these things, we receive you into the holy brotherhood, and promise you bread and water, the simple garb of our monastery, and labor and trials in abundance."

The first of these Orders, in point of time, were the Knights of St. John, afterwards termed the Knights of Rhodes, or of Malta. These owed their origin to some Italian traders, who in the year 1048 founded at Jerusalem a hospital for the use of sick pilgrims. During the Crusades, this hospital obtained numerous endowments and privileges, and many knights requested admission to the community in charge of the institution. Finally, in the year 1120, this Order became, under the lead of its head, Raymond of Puy, an Order of knights, having for their main object the overthrow of the Saracens. Afterwards, when Palestine was wrested from the hands of the Christians, these Knight-Hospitallers moved their headquarters to the island of Cyprus, thence to Rhodes, and again, in 1530, to Malta. The Order diffused itself over all Europe, and its members acquired undying fame for the faithful and efficient services that they rendered in the wars against the Turks and the Corsairs from Tunis, Tripoli, and Algiers.

The Order of Knight-Templars was founded by Hugh of Paganis in the year 1118, at Jerusalem; in which city they had their chief monastery, in the immediate vicinity of the so-called Solomon's Temple. They soon became the most dreaded enemies of the infidels. After the close of the Crusades, the chief houses of their Order were in France, where it owned large possessions. Their wealth aroused the avarice of the unprincipled king of that country, Louis the Fair, who put into circulation the most shocking reports against the character of the Templars, and at last succeeded, in 1312, in compelling Pope Clement V., whom he held in his power at Avignon, to proclaim the suppression of the Order.

The origin of the German Order was very similar to those of the two just described. It took its rise, about the year 1190, from a certain hospital called "the German House of our Blessed Lady at Jerusalem." After their return from the East, the members of this German knighthood were sent against the pagan Prussians, whose forces they conquered. These martial monks displayed so much judgment, and worked with such diligence, that this hitherto heathen people were brought into the fold of Christ. In the year 1525, Count Albert of Brandenburg, Grand Master of the Order, proved untrue to his brotherhood and to the Catholic religion, and converted the lands of the Order, in Prussia, into a civic province. However, the rest of the communities in other German countries continued loyal to the Church and the emperor, rendering invaluable services in the wars of the Reformation and against the Turks.

49. The History of the Franciscans.

CAPUCINS.

"Come to me, all you that labor and are burdened, and I will refresh you. Learn of me, because I am meek and humble of heart."—MATTHEW xi. 28, 29.

As the motto of the foregoing Orders was "Christian Warrior," and their aim Christian courage and chivalric self-sacrifice on the field of battle, so in the Order founded by St. Francis of Assisi, in the year 1212, the predominant traits were Christian humility and quiet self-sacrifice. The fondness entertained for sports and tournaments in his youth by this man of God, suddenly gave place to the most perfect contempt for things of earth, and was replaced by an ardent zeal for the glory of God's kingdom. Having given all his possessions to the poor, he was disinherited by his father, and looked upon by the world as a fanatic. He, however, took refuge in a half-ruined church, called "Our Lady of Angels," which had been placed at his disposal by a Benedictine abbot. This edifice he restored by means of the alms contributed by generous admirers, calling it his little Legacy (*Portiuncula*). His severe spirit of penance, joined with a childlike cheerfulness and humble disposition of mind, attracted many companions about him, with whom he made pilgrimages through the country, preaching penance, not indeed by sublime and learned eloquence, but in plain and simple language, intelligible to the least cultivated minds and hearts.

But their most effective sermon was the example of their holy poverty and self-denial. Although the individual members of the old Benedictine order were required to observe strict poverty, yet their monasteries, as such, were permitted to own money and lands. But this last privilege was denied even to his monasteries by St.

Francis. The communities were to live on the daily alms of the faithful people, the monasteries should possess no wealth, and all over above their wants was to be given to the poor.

This severe voluntary poverty was to be the foundation-stone of the Order. St. Francis called it the "Bride of Christ," the source and foundation, the very queen, of all other virtues.

His rule of life was approved by Pope Honorius in

Death of St. Francis of Assisi.

1223. When the holy Founder died, only three years later, the members of his Order could be counted by thousands. Our divine Lord, in order to give supernatural proof before all men that he still lived in his saints and in their establishments, but more especially in St. Francis, was pleased to imprint in a most miraculous manner the marks of his five wounds in the hands, feet, and side of the Saint, about two years before his death.

Thirty-eight years after his death, the Order possessed

nearly eight thousand monasteries, with two hundred thousand members. On account of the excessive charity of their founder, they were called the Seraphic Brethren, and on account of their humility, the Little Brethren, or the Friars Minor. Soon many pious virgins, under the direction of St. Clare, subjected themselves to the rule of St. Francis, and were known by different names in different localities. Moreover, in course of time, another branch was established for persons who, though living in the world, followed the rule, and put themselves under the direction of the Franciscans. These are called "The Third Order."

Among the spiritual sons of St. Francis many were distinguished for their learning and piety. For example, the renowned miracle-worker, St. Antony of Padua, who died in 1231; the profoundly learned Alexander of Hales, who died in 1245; the seraphic doctor, St. Bonaventure, who died in 1274; the intellectual Roger Bacon, who died in 1292; and John Duns Scotus, the celebrated defender of the mystery of the Immaculate Conception of the Blessed Virgin Mary. He died in the year 1308.

As in the course of time, the spirit of the world invaded some monasteries of this Order, bringing with it a relaxation of ancient discipline, several new branches were formed by holy persons, who made it the object of their lives to preserve sacredly the spirit of St. Francis in its original purity and severity. The most important of these branches was the society of the Capuchins, founded about the year 1526 by Matthew Bassi. The untiring activity of these truly apostolic friars, and their close observance of rule, have secured to their branch of the Franciscan Order great prosperity, and made it an object of the affection and admiration of all good men.

50. History of the Dominicans, or the Order of Preachers.

"The word of God is living and effectual, and more piercing than any two-edged sword: and reaching unto the soul and is a discerner of the thoughts and intents of the heart."—HEBREWS iv. 12.

Our Blessed Lord has in every instance assigned to each Order, at the time of its origin, its own special mission. Thus it became the duty and happy privilege of the Benedictines to rescue Europe from the destruction threatened and partly effected by the incursions of the barbarous Northmen. The Orders of knighthood were established to save Europe from the inroads of the Saracens; the Franciscans were chosen to kindle among the people the seraphic fires of divine love; and the Dominicans were sent to keep alive and burning, amid the impending darkness of error in the middle ages, the light of divine faith.

Just about 1170, the year in which St. Dominic was born in Spain, the Albigensian heretics were afflicting the Church of God in that country, in England, Germany, Italy, and especially in the south of France. St. Dominic having received holy orders, and animated with a burning zeal and earnest enthusiasm for the purity of the faith in the Church, traversed all the districts affected by the heresy, and preached in defence of the true faith. Worthy and zealous men soon joined him, and the results of their preaching were marvellous. The devotion of the holy Rosary, which St. Dominic always combined with his sermons, imparted a wonderful efficacy to his words. And thus was established the Order of Preachers, otherwise called, after their founder, Dominicans. Their rule was approved and confirmed by Pope Honorius simultaneously with the approval of the Franciscan Order. Like these latter, the Dominicans soon established a female branch, and also a Third Order, of persons living in the world. St. Dominic died on the 4th of August, 1221, five years earlier than his beloved friend St. Francis. His Order continued to be a pillar and bulwark of strength in the Church. To it the Church is indebted for one of the greatest and profoundest of her modern doctors, the grand-master of the schools, St. Thomas Aquinas, who died in 1274; and also for the holy Albertus Magnus, who was completely conversant with every branch of human knowledge, and who died in the year 1280. The members of this Order were usually intrusted by the Popes with the care of the Inquisition; that is, with the important duty of seriously and attentively watching over the faith of the Church, lest the germs of error should take root in some regions, spring up and produce unhappy fruits of dissent, and disunion, and loss of souls. This was the ecclesiastical Inquisition, and is in no way to be confounded with the Spanish Inquisition, which was chiefly a political institution, and used more for political than religious purposes, and against the excesses of which the Popes frequently protested.

51. The Jesuits.

"If the world hate you, know ye that it hath hated me before you. Remember my word. If they have persecuted me, they will also persecute you."—John xv. 18 and 20.

As the Church was called upon, in the twelfth and thirteenth centuries, to combat the errors of the Albigenses, she was again, in the sixteenth century, obliged to enter the lists of spiritual warfare against the hosts of so-called reformers. But as in the first instance Christ proved himself, through the person of St. Dominic, to be still living in the Church, so will he now show that he yet abides in his Church, and Ignatius and his companions will furnish ample proof of this truth.

The much-abused, cordially-detested, and severely-persecuted order of Jesuits was founded in 1535, and its constitution was confirmed by Pope Paul III. in 1540. It had for its original object missionary work among the heathens, and among those Christians who had been blinded and led astray by error. To this worthy object was afterwards added that of educating youth. St. Ignatius, born in 1491 in the Spanish castle of Loyola, abandoned in 1522, at the age of thirty-one, the army of the world to enroll himself among the soldiers of the cross, and soon after established his glorious and world-renowned Order of the "Society of Jesus;" with his chosen friends, Francis Xavier, Peter Lefevre, James Lainez, Alphonsus Salmeron, Nicholas Bobadilla, and Alphonsus Rodriguez as his first companions. To this order of Jesuits, the Catholic countries of Europe, especially Southern Germany, are indebted for their preservation or deliverance from the errors and miseries of Protestantism. The whole Catholic world has to thank this Order for their greatest missionaries; the educated classes of Europe for their most learned professors; the Church recognizes its members as her stoutest and ablest defenders, and countless sinners owe to them their salvation; pious souls regard them as their surest and most enlightened guides on the road to Christian perfection. St. Ignatius died on the 31st of July, 1556.

If we inquire by what magical means the Fathers of the Society of Jesus effected such wonders, we will learn that there are three principal agencies:

1. A rigorous and unrestricted obedience to all ecclesiastical superiors, in all that is not sinful. The most obedient of obedient religious also exacts implicit obedience from those under his charge.

2. The long and thorough course of studies pursued

by the Jesuits. The true disciple of St. Ignatius considers a course of studies consuming twenty years as barely long enough to fit him for a successful active life; and if he spend but ten or even five years in actual service, he deems it better and more profitable, and hopes to gather more abundant and precious fruit, than if he labored for forty years with a mind and soul only imperfectly prepared for the work.

3. The spiritual exercises of St. Ignatius. While the founder of the Jesuits was preparing himself in solitude in the cave at Manresa, for the grand and difficult work of founding an Order, the divine Spirit supplied him with a most efficient means of success in the "Spiritual Exercises." The Christian who avails himself of this great work, spends several days in a well-ordered meditation on eternal truths, alternated with prayer and spiritual reading; learning thus to amend his mode of spiritual life, and advancing by a judicious, skilful, and very attractive gradation of interior improvement, and a cleansing and enlightenment of soul, to a most intimate and permanent union with God. The application of this truly heavenly means to their own lives and to the lives of others, has secured to the Jesuits that extraordinary power over the minds of men, which has filled the envious hearts of the enemies of God and of his Church with absurd concern and burning hate.

These enemies did succeed, through the combined influence of the kings of Portugal, Spain, Naples, and France, in inducing Pope Clement XIV., not indeed to condemn, but to suppress this Order in 1773. It was re-established in 1814 by Pope Pius VII., who restored to it all its ancients rights and privileges.

52. The Redemptorists.

"The Spirit of the Lord is upon me, wherefore he hath anointed me, to preach the Gospel to the poor he hath sent me, to heal the contrite of heart."—LUKE iv. 18.

St. Alphonsus Mary Liguori was the founder of the Society of the Most Holy Redeemer, sometimes called the Liguorians, but generally known as the Redemptorists. He began to form his Society at Naples in 1732, but it was not until 1759, twenty-seven years later, that Pope Benedict XIV. confirmed its constitution. As it had been for many long years the freely and cheerfully self-imposed duty of Alphonsus to go in search of poor neglected persons, in order to afford them relief both for soul and body, so too it was his ardent desire that his disciples should serve as "missionaries for the poorest and most neglected sheep" of Christ's flock. He was compelled, much against his will, to accept in 1762 the episcopal chair of St. Agatha of the Goths. He still continued to live in closest communion with his Society, acting as their chief director and adviser. He enriched the Church with copious, profound, and edifying writings, and died on the 1st of August, 1787, at the advanced age of ninety-one years. The members of his Congregation spread throughout Europe; preaching in Poland, Austria, Germany, Switzerland, France, and in America; everywhere rendering incalculable service to our holy Church, by their arduous and well-attended missions, by defending ably and valiantly the morality of Jesus Christ, by encouraging and strengthening myriads of flocks, and even their pastors, in zeal and piety, as well as by training young men for the sublime work of the ministry.

53. History of the Religious Bodies dedicated to Schools, or to the Care of the Sick and Destitute.

"Jesus saith: Suffer the little children to come unto me. And embracing them, and laying his hands upon them, he blessed them."—MARK x. 14 and 16.

Our blessed Lord and Saviour Jesus Christ, during his brief sojourn on earth, always manifested his infinite per-

Christian Charity.

fection and holiness, not only by his zeal for the honor of his heavenly Father, but also by his unbounded mercy and love towards poor and needy men. This same holiness of Jesus Christ is still made practically manifest in the Church, and especially in the religious life; not only by the mere dedication to God, but also in the compassionate devotion, for God's sake, to humanity and its earthly wants. This devotion is the source and origin of all those numerous male and female Orders who consecrate themselves to the instruction of the people, and to the care of orphans, the sick, and the poor.

Both of these works, namely, the Christian education of youth and the care of the poor, have ever been cherished duties dear to the heart of the Church. And our holy mother looks on with deep anguish of soul, as she sees the politicians of the present day tearing the young and the poor away from her motherly protection, and by means of tax-schools and political poor-houses, making a pretence to discharge duties which she alone is entitled to discharge, and which for centuries she has discharged, enlightened as she was by the wisdom of Christ, and filled with his holy and disinterested charity. The enemies of the Church know well what they are doing. They would sever education and the care of the poor from the Church, in the hope of dragging her into contempt with the people; they would point at her the finger of scorn, and say to the unthinking masses: "See how idle, slow, and useless to society your Church is." But when this measure of folly, that is now filling up from day to day, shall have reached the brim and begins to overflow; when once those children who are now being taught learning devoid of religion, shall have grown to manhood and womanhood, and shall give evidence of their lack of principle, of all belief in God, of honesty, justice, of submission to God's will; when, believing as they have been taught to believe, that success in life is to be the great aim of their efforts, the disastrous system of godless education shall have borne its legitimate fruits. Already we see social disorder, financial distress and confusion, absence of confidence between man and man, poverty and suffering among the lowly, mental agony among the wealthy, all because each man knows that his neighbor is striving, regardless of religion, to become richer than he. Even the poor, who from time immemorial were content to receive the voluntary offerings of the Church, now begin to understand that the present system of aiding them is altogether a political machine. They claim a right to be supported from the abundance of taxes extorted from the industrial classes, and as taxes are increased for the support of the poor, the industrious are thus made poor themselves, and soon begin to demand that they shall have a share in what they have already paid to the tax-gatherer. Thus pauperism is frightfully on the increase, and becoming every day more odious and intolerable. The charge of assisting God's poor was delivered to God's Church, and not to salaried politicians. The time must certainly come when thoughtful men will discover these evils that are undermining society, and will be glad to have recourse to the wisdom, and experience, and supernatural excellence of the Church; beseeching her to bring the power of the Gospel and of the Sacraments to the restoration of contentment among all classes, and to the re-establishment of security in the very important affairs of life and property.

As already stated, both the children and the poor were placed by Christ and his Apostles under the guardianship of the Church. During centuries, she took unexceptionably good care of both. Her free schools bear witness to her fidelity towards her children. In remote antiquity and in the middle ages, these schools were to be found in the palaces of her bishops, in the halls of her hallowed cloisters, and even under the roofs of her humble but learned country parish-priests. Hence a learned Protestant historian, Raumer, asserts that "the merit of establishing and maintaining schools in the dark ages belongs exclusively to the priests and other ecclesiastics."

The Church never neglected the needy. All through the first ages of Christianity and in mediæval times, she kept her voice raised in behalf of God's poor. Decrees of Popes and Councils, mandates of bishops and other ecclesiastical authorities, have constantly warned those in charge of souls, that the revenue of the churches were the property of the poor and the infirm, of the widow and the orphan. Bishops were required to exercise in their dioceses a very special solicitude for the helpless, and destitute; the pastors of souls were also required to know the poor in their parishes, and to take measures for their relief; using for that purpose the revenues of the Church and the special offerings of the benevolent. In fact it was

Christian Schools.

a general law of the Church, and a law in most part scrupulously observed, that the Church revenues were to be divided into three parts: one third to be used for the decent support of the clergy, one third for the keeping of the Church and the maintenance of religious worship, and one third invariably for the poor. Thus we see that at all times and in all circumstances the Catholic Church has devoted her time and attention, all her energies, and much of her means in educating her children, and in comforting her poor.

Where could the Church find safer hands in which to place both her poor and her little children, than among various religious associations of brothers and of sisters. The members of these communities being free from family cares and ties, from the distractions of the world, being devoid of selfishness and regardless of worldly gain, having their souls constantly invigorated by prayer and meditation to renewed sacrifices, watched over and guided by wise and experienced directors, animated by the examples of fellow religious, devoted to Jesus Christ, and well versed in all spiritual things and in all human weaknesses, it is not possible that their efforts in doing good should prove barren of the most gratifying results. It is next to impossible that a pupil at school, a patient in a hospital, or a poor person under the care of such devoted guardians, should not be carefully and tenderly treated in these veritable sanctuaries of the Church. Hence at every period of the Church's existence, since the close of the pagan persecutions, the religious Orders of monks and nuns have sedulously and fondly devoted themselves to the support and education both of the orphan child and the aged invalid. In modern times these self-sacrificing associations have become almost innumerable.

To superintend the education of youth, St. Jerome Emiliani founded, in 1528, the Congregation of the Clerks Regular of Somascha; and St. Joseph Calasanctius, the Society of the Piarists, or Fathers of the Pious Schools, in 1597. The Society of the Brothers of the Christian Schools, was founded, at Rheims, in 1681, by the Venerable John Baptist De La Salle. The Marian brothers took their rise in the diocese of Lyons in 1816. The Ursulines were established in 1544 by St. Angela of Brescia. The Visitation Nuns, by St. Francis of Chantal in the year 1610. Countless other orders in all countries and in all circumstances have been set on foot to meet the wants of their respective localities and times. We may form some notion, though an imperfect one, of the efficiency of these religious societies, by referring to France alone, which counts more than sixteen thousand schools, containing more than a million of children under the guidance and tutorship of educational communities of monks and nuns.*

St. Vincent of Paul.

Of the many religious communities founded by holy and benevolent persons for the protection and care of the sick, the blind, the crippled, and the destitute members of society, mention may simply be made of the Brothers of Charity, established in the year 1540 by St. John of God, and the Sisters of Charity established in France, in

* Since the above was written, many of the religious communities have been banished by the Government, and many schools are thus broken up.

1633, by St. Vincent of Paul. All the good accomplished by these self-sacrificing religious orders since their establishment, is known only to God. Though men have seen them at their incessant labors in hospitals, refuges, reformatories, and prisons; in the cabins of the poor and the wretched, assuaging and alleviating pain and misery and poverty, yet no one but God can fully estimate the value and merit of their labors. We may approximate an idea of their good works when we learn that in one country alone, Austria, the Brothers of Charity, during a single year, received into their institutions, and treated gratuitously, more than twenty-four thousand patients of all religions and nationalities.

In America, as in the older nations of the Church, the religious Orders have given every possible evidence of fulfilling in their daily conduct the saying of the Apostle Paul: "This is the will of God, your sanctification" (1 Thessalonians iv. 3). "If thou wilt be perfect, go, sell what thou hast and give to the poor, and come, follow me" (Matthew xix. 21). The missionaries of the New World distinguished themselves by their zeal and self-sacrifice to a degree little less than that of the Apostles themselves. The Fathers of the Society of Jesus and of other Orders first planted the Church, and then set to work with ability and zeal to educate not only the children of the forest, but also the sons of the hardy pioneers who came with their faith from Europe. Next followed the Christian Brothers, who soon became the admiration of all friends of education. With wonderful rapidity they multiplied their admirable parish-schools, where, besides a thorough training of the mind, they imparted to their pupils a correct knowledge of their duties to God. The Sisters of Charity, the Ladies of the Sacred Heart, the Sisters of Notre Dame, the Sisters of St. Joseph, and many other communities of gentle, pious, and educated ladies, have devoted their lives and talents to the infusing of the

Spirit of Christ and of his Church into the minds and hearts of the daughters of America.

Whenever orphans were to be cared for, deaf and dumb to be taught, the maimed, the blind, and the decrepit to be fed and clothed, the Sisters of St. Francis and Dominic, the Sisters of Mercy and of Charity, of Providence and of the Holy Cross, were found ready to devote themselves to the care of these afflicted yet loved ones of the Saviour. The Little Sisters of the Poor have thrown comfort, shelter, and happiness about the declining years of the aged and infirm.

Long before the nation had celebrated its centennial anniversary, the face of the country from the Atlantic to the Pacific, was studded with those jewels always so dear to the heart of the Catholic Church, monasteries, and convents of religious men and women, in all of which the members, while carrying out the counsel of Christ, "Be ye perfect, as also your heavenly Father is perfect," also labored for the well-being, temporal and spiritual, of their fellow-creatures. To-day the teaching Orders and the Orders for caring for the poor and destitute, are to be found in almost every town of any size within the United States and Canada, laboring zealously in the cause of religion and humanity.

Thus is plainly shown the plenitude of holiness that has flourished, since the dawn of Christianity, in all the religious Orders of the one true Church. We perceive that the life of Christ has been prolonged even to our own day in holiness of life among his children.

54. Concluding Remarks on the History of Monastic Life.

"And I beheld: and lo, a lamb," Jesus, "stood upon Mount Sion, and with him a hundred and forty-four thousand having his name, and the name of his Father written on their foreheads. And they sang, as it were, a new canticle; and no man could say the canticle, but those hundred and forty-four thousand, who were purchased from the earth,—the first-fruits to God and to the Lamb."—APOCALYPSE xiv. 1 *et seq.*

Unquestioned submission to God in voluntary poverty, unqualified obedience, virginal purity, and practical charity towards suffering humanity—such is the beau-ideal of monastic life.

Now, the impartial history of some few monasteries and of some few Orders informs us that the real state of those institutions did not always correspond to this ideal, that the practice was not always in keeping with the theory. For indolence, pride, and worldliness have in some instances not only influenced members of religious Orders, but in too many cases have proved disastrous and ruinous to whole communities. In this connection we must not lose sight of three all-important truths.

In the first place, Popes, bishops, Councils, and most holy and earnest saints,—as for example, St. Bernard, St. Teresa, and others,—have recognized these distressing abuses wherever they came to light. They were loud and determined in condemning them, and labored strenuously and unceasingly, yet prudently and judiciously, to root them out.

In the second place, it was often the very fault-finders themselves, sometimes the civil authorities, who placed the most formidable obstructions in the way of reform. They thwarted the efforts of bishops and other Church authorities, by encouraging the disedifying behavior of the wayward monks, and by forbidding the introduction of reformatory measures by the Church.

Finally, impartial history assures us that the greater part of these complaints, made against monasteries in most cases by the enemies of all religion, were founded on malice, falsehood, and ignorance. Among the worldly-minded there prevails, as St. Paul assures us, "concupiscence of the eyes, concupiscence of the flesh, and the pride of life, and desire of their own will." In the life of a true religious, the opposite virtues are scrupulously practised.

These virtues are voluntary poverty, virginal chastity, holy obedience; in other words, the perfection of Jesus Christ. Hence the worldlings, if true to their past history, must hate and persecute the religious Orders, for in them dwelleth the life of Christ. "The world will hate you, because it hath first hated me," was the significant promise of Christ to his followers. The world cannot believe in disinterested heroic virtue, because it has never known the supernatural power of those means by which virtue is acquired and securely maintained; has certainly never had any personal practical experience of the efficacy of those aids to virtue, the word of God, the Sacraments, humble prayer, sanctifying grace. Hence, basing their pretended judgment on their own experience, on their own interior life, worldlings affect to disbelieve the existence of virtue in the lives of the religious, and accuse them of deception and hypocrisy. The worldling feels acutely that the voluntary poverty of the monk, the self-sacrifice of the missionary, the heroic virtue of the Sister of Charity, is a reproach and a rebuke to his selfish indolence; and hence he would gladly rid himself of the presence of so persistent a monitor. Frivolous ridicule or malicious calumny, abuse of the rules of the Orders or reviling of the members, unfair legislation, and even open violence, have been made use of by the enemy, in the hope to destroy these institutions of the Catholic Church.

But we must not be deluded and led astray by the false opinions and malicious objections and fault-findings of the worldling. Though we may see the unfaithful member of a religious Order prove false to his vows, leave his community, and even lose his faith and preach heresy, we simply pity him, while we say to ourselves, "One traitor less in the camp, one coward less in the army of Christ." Let us rejoice, then, in our Saviour, and in the manner in which his life has been continued in the religious orders. Let us await patiently and confidently for his good time, when he will, in spite of the opposition of the enemy, renew and transplant these brightest, fairest flowers of his Church upon earth to the realms of everlasting glory.

CHAPTER VII.

THE HISTORY OF THE SAINTS.

CHRIST LIVES IN HIS CHURCH AS THE HOLY ONE.

55. The Martyr Saints.

ST. STEPHEN.

"We who live are always delivered unto death for Jesus' sake: that the life also of Jesus may be made manifest in our mortal flesh."—2 CORINTHIANS iv. 11.

NOT only in the religious Orders of the Church does Christ manifest his holiness, and repeat and continue his own holy life upon earth. He really and truly lives also in the holy and pure souls of men and women in all conditions of human society. Proud and self-sufficient worldlings choose to know nothing about these favorite servants of God, the Catholic Saints. To the worldly-wise, all pious legend, that is to say, the history of the lives, virtues, and miracles of the Saints of the Church, is something too despicable or trifling for their serious consideration. For they hold that only the names and memories of philosophers, statesmen, or warriors are fit themes of historical study, and they would ignore and forget all others.

This is unjust. Why, the fervent and persevering prayer of one sinless soul before the throne of the Almighty; the quiet, steady usefulness of a good man in his own sphere; the irresistible influence of his good example upon his fellow-men; the simple words of heavenly wisdom that fall from his lips, and like seed blessed by heaven, sink deep into the hearts of many, contribute more certainly and effectively to the advantage of humanity, and to the welfare of the Church, than the blood-stained victories of the conqueror, or the noisy words of the haughty orator or statesman.

Therefore, the Christian opens frequently the eyes of his soul and looks upward with joy upon that spiritual firmament, where, according to St. Paul's own testimony, the Saints of Christ's Church shine like brilliant stars, rivalling each other in beauty, power, and glory. Let us cast a glance also over this earth of ours, view the varied conditions and circumstances of human life, and then rejoice in the fulness of our hearts at the grand display of holiness and purity which Christ is pleased to make practically manifest in the lives of his Saints upon earth.

First of all, our gaze will alight upon that glorious army of martyrs, whose brows are decked with the laurel of victory, and whose garments are dyed crimson in their own blood. These Saints have received, and cherished, and reduced to painful practice the words of their Lord and Saviour: "Greater love than this no man hath, that a man lay down his life for his friends." As Christ had laid down his divinely precious life for them, they found it easy, and esteemed it but a poor return, to deliver themselves freely up to death, and to the martyr's death, and to seal with their life's blood not only the eternal truth of His doctrine, but also the intensity of their own disinterested love. What a glorious testimony in favor of Christian truth! If in the comparatively short period of the first three centuries in the Church, more than three millions of the purest and noblest of persons go cheerfully to death in defence of this truth; to death amid the most excruciating tortures; to a death unattended by world-honor or fame, and with bright and happy faces and joyous, tranquil hearts, and blessing their very executioners—who, in his sound mind, could longer question the truth of Christ? And if within the hearts of these three millions of victims to the truth and cause of Christ, the love for Christ burned so intensely as to be able to conquer all fear of the most painful and disgraceful of martyrs' deaths, who would or could refuse to pay his respect to this celestial ardor of self-sacrificing love? Hence the early Christians ven-

Martyrdom of St. Stephen.

erated with a tender love even the very bones of their martyred brethren. Hence, too, the true and fervent Catholic to-day loves to possess some of these precious relics, to venerate them as he remembers with pious awe and satisfaction that these relics were once animated by a great, God-loving, and heroic soul.

The Church honors as the first in the ranks of these champions, the holy martyr St. Stephen. He was chief among those seven deacons chosen to assist the holy Apostles; a man of strong faith and full of the Holy Ghost, working wonders and great signs among the people. The Jews, chafing under his severe and truthful rebukes, dragged him before the high council, and produced false witnesses, who stated: "This man ceaseth not to speak words against the holy place and the law." But all who were in the court-room looked with astonishment upon the youthful deacon, for his face shone in beauty like that of an angel. It was before this assembly that the inspired deacon delivered that eloquent and scathing discourse to the Jews, as given by St. Luke in his "Acts of the Apostles" [vii. 2–53]. His guilty audience fairly raved with anger, and gnashed their teeth at him in their fury. But Stephen, full of the Holy Ghost, directed his eyes towards heaven, where, being permitted to see the glory of God, and Jesus standing at the right hand of his Father, he exclaimed: "Behold, I see the heavens opened, and the Son of Man standing on the right hand of God." At these words his enemies fairly shrieked with rage, stopped their ears, and then rushed violently upon him, They dragged him out of the city, took off their outer garments, which they laid at the feet of a young man named Saul,* and then stoned their victim to death. But Stephen, offering no resistance, continued to look towards heaven and to repeat: "Lord Jesus, receive my spirit." On bended knees and with clasped hands, he at last cried out, as his soul was about to depart, "Lord, lay not this sin to their charge." Having said these words, he fell asleep in the Lord. Thus died the first of our Christian martyrs; a model of burning zeal for the truth of Christ, and of compassionate charity for evil-doers.

* This Saul, who was a willing witness to the death of St. Stephen, afterwards became St. Paul, the great Apostle of the Gentiles, and gave his life in defence of that same truth for which Stephen died.

56. History of the Bishops.

ST. CHARLES BORROMEO.

"God made to him a covenant of peace to be the prince of his people, that the dignity of priesthood should be to him and to his seed forever."—ECCLESIASTICUS xlv. 30.

Side by side with the holy martyrs, we see, standing in the temple of heaven, those glorious Saints who were once the worthy and faithful representatives, in the Christian temples on earth, of the great and veritable High Priest, Jesus Christ. These are our learned and holy bishops. Who can tell the names of all these anointed of the Lord, who, while on earth, wielded the sacred crosier with unswerving fidelity amid trials and afflictions; but who are now enjoying everlasting repose from their labors in the company of the Good Shepherd himself? Some distinguished themselves in their earthly careers by their sublime wisdom, others by their indomitable courage in the contest for truth and justice; some were remarkable for their child-like modesty in prosperity and success, others by their calm resignation in trial and persecution. All shone resplendent by the holiness of their lives, and the faithful discharge of their duties as shepherds of Christ's flock. Every land and every age has had its holy bishops, and in modern times the saintly Cardinal of Milan, St. Charles Borromeo, stands forth among the greatest of these successors of the Apostles.

In the government of his diocese, this holy bishop never lost sight of the bright and edifying example of his illustrious predecessor, the learned doctor and exemplary bishop, St. Ambrose. He endeavored constantly to find out the wants, necessities and abuses of his diocese, and immediately, and prudently, and effectively to remedy them. For this purpose he availed himself specially of conferences and synods; that is, the united counsels of his clergy and suffragan bishops. While listening in humble modesty and deference to the advice and suggestions of the aged and experienced, he knew how, by his magnanimity and ardent zeal for souls, to gain the unlimited confidence of his fellow-laborers, and to enkindle in their hearts the fire of apostolic charity and zeal. His own vast resources, as well as the revenues of the Church, he employed almost exclusively to the requirements of God's Church. Well-attended seminaries for the proper train-

St. Charles Borromeo.

ing and education of efficient carers of souls, several asylums for orphans, and hospitals for the sick and needy, were only a portion of his work. He himself lived so sparingly, that on one occasion, having returned home at evening sick and weary, after having attended during the entire day in a public hospital of Milan, consoling the victims of a contagious epidemic, he had neither bread nor money to buy it.

Even the limits of his own diocese were too contracted

for the generous zeal of this Apostle, and all Italy and even the wild mountain recesses of Switzerland became the scene of his labors. He made pilgrimages on foot to the most remote mountain districts, going from cottage to cottage, strengthening the inhabitants in the faith of their forefathers, warning them against the errors of that age, and consoling them in their trials and afflictions. By founding houses for the Jesuits and Capuchins, he provided religious consolation and instruction for the masses of the people; so that the interior districts of Switzerland escaped falling into Protestantism, and were thus indebted to him for the preservation of their ancient faith and Godworship. His vast and multiplied correspondence by letter with the bishops of various districts, with the heads of religious Orders, and with the reigning princes of his time, had no other object in view than to encourage and strengthen them by advice and exhortation to be true and loyal to the Church.

Above all was he obedient and loving towards Rome, which he knew to be the centre of Christian faith and unity. The chair of St. Peter was at that time worthily filled by his illustrious uncle, Pope Pius IV. This Pontiff, soon learning to appreciate the learning and sanctity of his nephew, allowed him considerable influence in the government of the universal Church. The most important work of that period was the successful finishing and closing of the General Council of Trent, in which the wise and prudent archbishop of Milan took an active and successful part. Thus did our blessed Lord and Saviour Jesus Christ raise up, in those dangerous years of the so-called Reformation, his faithful servant St. Charles, to be a pillar of strength in his persecuted Church, and a shining example of fidelity to all future bishops. He died in the odor of sanctity on the 3d of November, 1584, in the forty-sixth year of his age.

57. History of the Priesthood.

ST. JOHN NEPOMUCENE.

"The Priests shall enter into my sanctuary, and they shall come near to my table to minister unto me, and to keep my ceremonies."
—EZECHIEL xliv. 16.

Next to the glorious army of holy bishops in heaven, stand the countless rank and file of their fellow warriors, the holy priests of the Church. To these was intrusted upon earth the keeping of the sacred body of their Lord, though in a mysterious manner, and concealed beneath the sacramental veil. Faithfully and reverently they guarded the priceless treasure, offering it up as a perfect victim in the holy sacrifice of the mass, dispensing it faithfully and with priestly joy to the believing multitudes. But now the sacramental veil is removed from before their eyes, and they gaze with rapture on the glorified body of that Lord, whose merest glance on Tabor entranced the three favorite Apostles. To the priests, too, while upon earth, was intrusted the duty and power of pronouncing over the repentant sinner the consoling words of absolution. Zealously they corresponded; recalling wayward sinners to the ways of virtue, loosening them from their sins, and like true and faithful shepherds, leading them back to the fold of Christ. Now these faithful priests of the Church unite their voices with those of their converted souls in singing for all eternity the praises of their Redeemer. In those shining fields, no temptation can now assail them, no shadow of danger cast a moment's gloom upon their regenerated souls. All is peace and rest for all eternity.

In this grand army of priests we discover, among others, that heroic confessor and martyr, whom all Christendom has honored for the last five hundred years as the champion and martyr of the secrecy of the confessional, the glorious St. John Nepomucene of Bohemia. Having been chosen by Queen Sophia for her confessor, her husband, King Wenceslas IV., actuated by a wicked curiosity, had the presumption to approach the Saint with a view of extracting from him the subject of his wife's confession. St. John was shocked at the wicked presumption of the King, and replied boldly that he would die rather than violate the secrecy of the sacred tribunal by revealing a syllable of the Queen's confession. Furious at his discomfiture, the wicked King had the Saint stretched upon the rack, and as neither threats nor promises would induce him to yield to the tyrant's unreasonable demand, St. John Nepomucene was thrown from a bridge into the river Moldau, on the night of the 20th of March, 1393. Immediately the river became brightly illuminated, and the dead body of the Martyr of the Confessional was brought to shore, carried amid the tears and sobs of the people to the Cathedral, where it was buried with great solemnity. Three hundred years later, on the 15th of April, 1719, the Saint's grave was opened, and the tongue was found to be moist, fresh, and untainted. He has ever been and will continue to be the patron saint of our father-confessors, and the guardian of their eternal secrecy of the Confessional.

58. The Saintly Hermits.

ST. PAUL OF THEBES.

"Behold I will allure her, and lead her into the wilderness: and I will speak to her heart."—OSEE ii. 14.

Turn we now from those to whom was intrusted the offering of the Sacrifice of the new law, to the holy hermits of the Church. These men, buried in the solitary wilderness, offered sacrifice of prayer and mortification to their immortal Lord and master, Jesus Christ. Following the mysterious impulses of his heart, or rather obeying the call of divine grace, the solitary hermit, while abandoning the world with all its pleasures, also escapes its harrowing and exhausting distractions. Wherever a sweet fountain springs from the rock, or a sheltering cave supplies a roof, or a few herbs furnish a scanty means of subsistence, there we find the hermit settling himself down to lead a life of tranquil virtue and holiness. And whilst his hands are busy in useful industry, his heart is engaged in fervent contemplation of the goodness, mercies, and justice of his Creator. Although living apart from friends and kindred, still he remembers their difficulties, trials, and afflictions amid the busy throng of men, and offers his sacrifice of a lonely life, of prayer, and of self-denial, for their spiritual and temporal relief and advancement. These latter, also, sometimes make pilgrimages to the lonely retreat of the recluse, there to listen with comfort and edification to his wise teachings, salutary counsels, and consoling exhortations. Worldlings may mock and condemn the eccentricities of the man who has loved Christ more than the world, but they forget that many a pious recluse, ever since the days of John the Baptist, has rendered more real service to society by his prayers and mortification of the sensual appetites, than has been obtained by the eloquent words of the learned, or the restless sword of the conquering slaughterer of his fellowmen.

The most renowned among the holy hermits of the Church was St. Paul of Egypt, born in the year 227. During the persecution of the Emperor Decius, this devout and highly educated youth fled to the desert, where he passed ninety years without meeting a fellow-man. For the first twenty years, his subsistence consisted of the fruit of a palm-tree and the water of a brook which flowed in front of his hermitage. During the last seventy years of his life, the Lord sent to him daily, as to Elias of old in the desert, a raven bearing a half barley loaf. When Paul was 113 years old, another holy hermit, St. Antony, directed by God, and being himself then ninety years of age, came to visit this venerable recluse. These two holy men, enlightened by heaven, recognized each other at once, saluted each other by name at the first moment of their meeting, fell upon each other's neck in tender embrace, and thanked and praised the Lord. A sacred solid friendship was at once formed between them. While they were conversing, a raven flew down and dropped a whole loaf of bread before the two saints. Paul said, smiling: "Behold how good the Lord is! During sixty years he has sent me, in this way, a half loaf of bread every day. But now, when you have come to see me, Christ has doubled the pay of his servants." They ate together, drank from the spring, and gave thanks to God. On the following morning, after a night spent together in prayer and pious meditation, Paul informed St. Antony that his life was about to close, and requested him to go and bring for his shroud a certain cloak which the bishop Athanasius had some time previous given to him. Antony obeyed, and on his return with the mantle, found St. Paul in a kneeling posture, with head bowed down and clasped hands, apparently absorbed in silent prayer. But the soul of Paul had fled while he prayed, and he was now asleep in the Lord. Hardly had St. Antony enveloped the venerable remains of his friend in the mantle of the holy bishop, when two strong lions approached with gentle mien, and at once began to dig with their paws a last resting-place for the body of St. Paul. St. Antony, after placing the remains in the grave, and having smoothed the last sod, hastened back to his monastery to relate these miraculous events to his wondering disciples.

It is thus that the death of this great servant of God is described by one of the most credible authorities, namely, St. Jerome, Doctor in the Church.

59. The Royal Saints.

THE EMPEROR HENRY II.

And now, O ye kings, understand, receive instructions, serve ye the Lord with fear, and rejoice unto him with trembling."— PSALM ii. 11.

The infant Jesus, besides inviting to his crib at Bethlehem the plain and simple shepherds of Bethlehem, summoned also to his service and homage three rich and powerful kings from Eastern lands. And the Saviour's invitation has in all ages been directed, not alone to simple hermits and pious priests, but also to the great ones of the earth. Jesus Christ has been pleased to live, to act out his life, in the lives of many kings and princes. How edifying to society, how conducive to the spiritual and temporal well-being of mankind, for the head of the nation to take the lead in reducing to practice both in his public and private life the maxims of Christianity! How bright and honorable the crown of authority, when worn on a truly Christian brow! How serviceable and dignified the royal sceptre when wielded by hands unstained with blood, by hands ever busy in improving the condition of those committed to their care. How stately the regal ermine when covering the form of one submissive and docile to the teachings of Christ. Honor and praise are due to such wise, humble, and just rulers: to the saintly Ladislas, Stephen, and Emeuil of Hungary; to the pious Henry, emperor of Germany; to the devout Edward of England; to the religious Ferdinand of Spain; to the holy Guntram of Burgundy; to the just Canute of Denmark; to Saint Wenceslas of Bohemia, St. Leopold of Austria, and St. Louis of France. Honor and praise to these princely patrons of the Church; they were fathers to their people, and bright examples of every noble virtue.

In studying the life of the most glorious of all Christian.

rulers, of the saintly emperor, Henry the Second, we shall discover how princely wisdom is reconcilable with Christian simplicity, royal majesty with Christian humility, and dignified valor with Christian meekness. We shall observe what a torrent of heavenly blessings are poured out upon Church and State, when these virtues are found to exist in the soul of a civil ruler.

The foundation of Christian perfection was laid by pious parents, at an early age, in the heart of St. Henry,

The Emperor Henry II.

and the subsequent structure of piety and sanctity was reared by the skilled and careful hands of St. Wolfgang, bishop of Regensburg. St. Henry's espousals with St. Cunegunda, and his constant and familiar intercourse with great and good men, crowned his whole earthly career with a bright halo of holiness and wisdom. All through life his motto was, "Not unto me, but to God's name be praise and glory given: let everything be done for God and through God." The temple of the Lord was his happiest dwelling-place, and its embellishment was his chief and favorite care. Of this trait in his character, testimony is given by the many sumptuous churches that he built, or repaired and renovated. On the occasion of his coronation by the Pope, in the city of Rome, in 1014, the Sovereign Pontiff Benedict the Eighth, solemnly asked him: "Wilt thou be a firm and constant protector of the holy Roman Church?" St. Henry pledged himself to the Pope; and ever afterwards was so true to his promise that a pious historian observes: "That fraternal embrace between the Supreme Ruler of the Church and the highest potentate of the world, must necessarily have contributed immensely to the happiness of mankind." The bishoprics of Bamberg, Hildesheim, Magdeburg, Meissen, Merseburg, and Basel, which were either erected by him as new sees, or restored from poverty and decay, were by his special direction endowed with princely munificence. He restored to their ancient vigor and discipline, to their former temporal and spiritual prosperity, many neglected monasteries. For this purpose, he introduced fervent and learned monks from the renowned monastery of Cluny. He sent several zealous missionaries to Bohemia and Poland, in order to confirm and extend the influence of Christianity in those countries. How amply repaid for all these generous acts the saintly emperor must have considered himself, when in the year 1020, his illustrious friend and admirer, Pope Benedict the Eighth, in response to Henry's invitation, came in state to Bamberg to pass the Easter with him, and to consecrate the newly-erected church of St. Stephen!

In the midst of all these works, St. Henry never lost sight for a moment of the building up, in his own heart, of a glorious and lasting temple of inward sanctification. By prayer, meditation, mortification, and pious counsels he maintained that wonderful control over himself which enabled him to live, till the hour of his death, in a state of virginity with his saintly spouse and queen. Hence he could say when dying, as he commended his queen to her friends and relatives: "I received her a virgin; I give her back to you the same unsullied virgin."

It might be objected by some, that to such a pious man the garb of a monk would be more becoming than the sceptre of a monarch. We must not suppose, that on account of his devotion to religion, he neglected to maintain the dignity of his realm or to care for the worldly prosperity of his country. Even secular historians assure us that his piety never stood in the way of the discharge of his worldly duties. At the time when he ascended the throne, powerful enemies, some of them his own kindred, rose up to oppose him and his administration. St. Henry, fully conscious of the righteousness of his cause, met them with the courage of a soldier and succeeded in subduing them. Harduin of Ivrea sought to make himself king of Italy, but St. Henry's sword smote him to the earth. In the western portion of the kingdom, Prince Boleslas of Poland attempted to rebel against his emperor. The two opposing armies stood face to face. St. Henry with all his troops threw themselves upon their knees, and together received the Blessed Sacrament. Thus fortified, they soon won an easy victory over the forces of Boleslas. By means of his quiet, prudent, though efficient statesmanship, he succeeded in annexing to the German empire the important kingdom of Burgundy. Old prejudices estranged, from each other, the people of Germany and of France. St. Henry brought about the famous and interesting meeting between himself and King Robert of France, at Trois. Here these two princes held council how to render their people happy and contented, and vowed everlasting friendship to each other. A universal and continued peace was agreed upon, and law and justice were henceforth to replace disorder and rapine. An old chronicler of that day thus speaks of St. Henry: "All nations of the earth bow down before him. Rightfully he enjoys the highest reputation; for, by the assistance of God, he has triumphed over all other princes. The husbandman is contented on his broad acres, the ecclesiastic is happy in his sanctuary. Every man enjoys the blessings, both spiritual and temporal, vouchsafed to him by God; and under the benign sway of our emperor Henry, the poor feel themselves rich."

On the occasion of this holy emperor's death, which took place on the 13th of July, 1024, a writer of the time thus expresses himself: "The flower of mankind, the glory of kings, the pride of the empire, the protector of God's Church, the peaceful Champion of Christendom, our emperor Henry, is no more."

To this saintly prince may be applied the words of Solomon: "I have prayed, and the spirit of wisdom came upon me. I preferred wisdom to riches and to thrones, and kingdoms I have regarded as nothing in comparison to wisdom. More than health and beauty have I loved it. And with it were given to me all good and untold honors."

60. The Saintly Workingmen.

ST. CRISPIN.

"The foolish things of the world hath God chosen, that he may confound the wise: and the weak things of the world hath God chosen, that he may confound the strong."—1 CORINTHIANS i. 27.

Let us now leave the glare of the imperial palace, and enter into the tranquil precincts of the house of God. What a spectacle greets our eyes! The holy table of the Lord! And see kneeling around it the great and the powerful. They are not alone, for intermingled and side by side, you discover the poorest and most lowly of their subjects. They are all equal when in the house of God, and especially when kneeling to adore celestial, never-ending royalty—the King of kings. What a consoling and satisfactory solution of the difficulty concerning the equality of man, may be witnessed at the communion-table of a Catholic church! St. Paul, the Apostle of the Gentiles, exclaims: "The bread which we break, is it not the partaking of the body of the Lord? For we being many, all that partake of one bread are one body." (1 Cor. x.) That is to say: all receive equally the same bread of heaven, the same Lord and Master, Jesus Christ. Yes,

St. Crispin, and his brother Crispinian.

Christ lives equally in all men of good-will; manifesting his holiness, to precisely the same degree, in prince and potentate, as in the humblest beggar. For what is greatness, or what is lowliness in the eyes of him before whom the whole earth with all its vanity is but as a grain of sand in the desert? Did he not choose to be born in a stable and to pass many years in honorable toil and lowly poverty? Did he not mingle among the people, raising twelve simple fishermen to the twelve thrones of his kingdom, and likening himself to a farmer and a shepherd? Hence the truly Christian laborer is consoled, as, in the sweat of his brow and in the scorching heat of the day, he tills the field of his employer. Hence the contented brow and peaceful heart of the tradesman, as day after day, and year after year, he labors perseveringly for the support of his family. Perhaps in no other condition of life do we discover more easily the life of Christ continued and acted out in his Church, than in the life of the honest son or daughter of toil.

Among the many saints of lowly condition honored by the church is St. Crispin, who has ever been the patron of the Christian tradesman. Distributing all his goods to the poor, he went with his brother to Gaul, to preach the kingdom of Christ. The holy brothers took up their abode at Soissons, where they preached to the people during the day, and worked at manual labor the best part of the night. They made shoes, and divided the proceeds of their labors among the poor, whom they styled their brethren in Christ. An accident having revealed the nobility of their origin, many of the wealthy men, very much affected at the disinterestedness of these gentle strangers, supplied them with abundant material for their pious and useful undertaking. These two noble and pious brothers continued to reflect honor and credit upon an industrious avocation, till at last, in the year 287, they received the crown of martydom.

61. The Saintly Farmers and Shepherds.

ST. ISIDORE AND ST. WENDELIN.

"And he chose his servant David, and took him from the flocks of sheep."—PSALM lxxvii. 70.

In St. Isidore of Madrid the workingman possesses a model and a patron. In St. Wendelin from Scotland, the pious shepherd honors the patron of his lowly but honorable occupation. The Church recognizes both as illustrious Saints of God. Isidore, poor and unlettered, but eager to relieve his struggling parents of the burden of his support, entered, while yet a boy, the service of a wealthy man. At first he met with many a rebuke for coming late to work. "Have patience with me," he meekly replied to his exacting master, "and you will see that when harvest comes, my work will be blessed with abundant fruit." And so it was in fact; when harvest came, his fields surpassed all the others in quantity and quality. For Isidore had utilized the first hour of the day in repairing to church and hearing mass. During the weary hours of labor, he would look upon nature with all her beauty and rich and bountiful stores, and then raise his heart in contentment and joy to the Author of all this beauty and bounty. Dwelling upon God's wisdom, power, and providence, St. Isidore's heart and soul would brim over with humility and gratitude. He made use of the Sunday to fortify himself by the word of God and the Sacraments for the labors of the coming week. Out of his scanty earnings, he found means to help those poorer than himself. The very animals felt the influence of his gentleness and kindness. God's blessing, too, came down abundantly upon him, and upon all his undertakings. At the time of his death, the 15th of May, 1170, his countenance emitted a heavenly brightness, so that those standing about his death-bed said, in subdued whispers, "Truly this is the death of a Saint."

Far more romantic was the life of St. Wendelin. Descended from the royal family of Scotland, he was placed at an early age under the spiritual direction and tuition of a pious and learned bishop, who taught him all kinds of knowledge, but more the knowledge of heavenly things, and initiated him into the mysterious ways of Christian humility and self-denial. The Holy Ghost inspired the royal youth with the resolution to abandon all worldly honors and enticements, and to serve God in solitude and humble obscurity. Wendelin, therefore, leaving his father's home, went abroad clad in poor garments, and after making some pious pilgrimages, entered on the duties of a shepherd, in the employ of a nobleman, near Triers. Here, in order to give himself up to prayer, unseen and uninterrupted, he sought the most retired fields and meadows for pasturing his flocks. Whilst

St. Wendelin.

taking the most faithful care of the sheep entrusted to his keeping, he at the same time kept his thoughts on God and heavenly mysteries. Heaven's blessing descended on the pious shepherd, whose sheep escaped every harm, and grew and throve.

At the suggestion of his employer, who soon discovered Wendelin's high vocation, he entered the Benedictine Abbey at Tholey. Here, God granted to his servant the gift of miracles, so that the distressed and the sick flocked to his presence, and many, by virtue and efficacy of his prayers, obtained miraculous relief. At the death of the abbot, Wendelin's brethren chose him for their head, and under his guidance the community attained a high degree of monastic perfection.

When, in the year 1015, he felt his end approaching, he sent for the bishop of Triers, made known to him his royal extraction, and then, after receiving the last sacrament, he gave back his stainless soul to his Creator. The many miracles which took place at his tomb attracted crowds of pilgrims to the glorified spot. To shepherds, he has always been a true and powerful intercessor at the throne of God, for the protection of themselves and their flocks.

62. The Saintly Matrons.

ST. MONICA.

"Who shall find a valiant woman? The price of her is as of things brought from afar off and from the uttermost coasts. She hath opened her mouth to wisdom, and the law of clemency is on her tongue. Her children rose up and called her blessed: her husband praised her."—PROVERBS xxxi.

Although it was through woman that sin with all its accompanying miseries came into the world, yet, in accordance with the ancient promise of God, it was through woman, too, that the Saviour who was to remove all these calamities, was to come among men. Thus was woman, as well as man, chosen to be a channel of redeeming grace. And as Jesus Christ, even after his ascension, continued to live in men, so too was he pleased that his life should be prolonged for all time in the devout female sex: in pious mothers, chaste wives, and angelic virgins. The glorious queen amid all her sex, the model of all mothers, wives, and maidens, was David's humble daughter, Mary. In her the life of Christ was reflected, like the light of the sun in the gentle, faithful moon; for all her spiritual loveliness is naught else but the reflection of the glory and sanctity of Him whom she brought into the world. In a similar manner does Christ manifest his beauty of holiness, in all dutiful mothers. For when the Christian matron presses her cherished offspring to her heart, feeds it from her breast, and gazes with loving fondness upon its growth and progress; when she gives to it its first lessons in prayer and in love for God, and devotes herself to her child in health and sickness, she but presents to our admiring gaze a copy of the inexpressible love, wisdom, and fidelity with which Christ begets, sustains, guides, and preserves his regenerated child. Hence, the love and faithfulness of the Christian mother has ever been, in the Catholic Church, a subject of the tenderest respect and admiration; and holy mothers, such as Monica, Felicitas, Blanche, Bridget, and others have ever been regarded as graceful ornaments of God's kingdom.

St. Monica was the mother of a great Doctor in the Church, St. Augustine; his mother, too, in the fairest and most complete sense of the word. She bore him; and again, after he had become dead to God by sin and heresy, she brought him forth once more to God and the Church, in a regenerated life of penance and sanctity. Notwithstanding the careful training which Monica was ever solicitous to give her son, he permitted himself to be led astray by his inordinate passions, plunged headlong into licentiousness, and then, blinded by false worldly learning, he was ensnared into Manichæism, and thus lost his faith. Who can describe the anguish of the faithful Monica's heart? Yet, blessed are they who weep and mourn, for they shall be comforted. And comfort was granted to Monica; for her son was converted, and became a perfect model of the strictest virtue, was afterwards made bishop, and at last became a Doctor and a pillar of strength in the Church.

Now how was all this accomplished? By three powerful influences. In the first place, notwithstanding Augustine's errors, there lay buried, down deep in his heart, a smouldering love for virtue and truth, a love that had been implanted by a holy mother's care. And this love saved him from irredeemable destruction. Secondly, in the very depths of his sensuality, he experienced, besides remorse, a yearning for a higher and nobler, a more lasting and satisfactory happiness. The fallacies of heresy fascinated his imagination and captivated his intellect; yet, in the mysterious recesses of his heart, a secret voice ever admonished him, saying: "This is not truth." Moreover, there were not wanting warnings from without. In the third place, it was the gratuitous gift of heavenly grace which took so fast a hold upon his soul, pulling him out of the mire of iniquity, and supplying him with such strength, that he won a complete victory over himself, over vice, and over falsehood. And now, mark well, Christian reader, to whom Augustine owed this signal and final triumph—to his saintly and devoted mother, Monica. The pious counsels and steady example of her gentle love, her magnanimous forbearance, her purity and piety, had, from his earliest infancy, impressed themselves deeply and ineffaceably on the young man's heart, and imbedded in his soul a spark of charity, which would not be extinguished, but insisted on burning up brightly, as soon as the first breath of divine grace fell upon it. From his father, a rude and uncultivated pagan, whom St. Monica, in obedience to her parents, reluctantly married, the son could not have derived any spark of Christian sentiment. To his mother he was indebted, also, for an unceasing exhortation to penance. She even followed him through many long and weary journeys, never for a moment discontinuing her efforts to reclaim him, praying incessantly to the throne of grace for him. Even her dreams were so many prayers in his behalf. On one occasion, she called upon a holy and experienced bishop, for comfort and encouragement. And he said to her: "Persevere in your prayers; the child of so many tears cannot be lost." You know, Christian reader, how literally this prediction was fulfilled.

From these examples we may learn how much a holy mother's prayers can effect. St. Monica died at Ostia, near Rome, in the year 387, after having returned thanks to God for hearing her supplications, and after having piously requested her son to remember her when at the altar.

63. The Virgin Saints.

ST. CECILIA AND ST. CATHARINE.

"Incorruption bringeth nearer to God."—WISDOM vi. 20.

If the lives of Christian mothers and wives make manifest to us the beauty of Christ's holiness, how much more brilliantly, and beautifully, and closely must the life of Christ be exemplified in the lives of that lily-bearing army, of whom St. John writes, that they sing in the heavenly Jerusalem that mysterious canticle which they alone can sing; that choir whose state, according to the testimony of Christ and his Apostle, is sublimer than that of married people—the choir of the holy virgins. The virginal beauty of Jesus Christ, his complete victory over the lusts of the flesh, the pure glowing love of a life wrapped up in God—where are all these qualities more fully and truly reflected than in the pure life of a Christian maiden? Such virginal souls have been generated in countless numbers, during her entire existence, by our mother the Church. Two of the most sublime and remarkable, both within and without the cloister, are St.

Cecilia and St. Catharine; the former a Roman from the banks of the Tiber, the latter a Greek from the city of Alexandria. St. Cecilia has always been considered the patroness of Christian art; St. Catharine is honored as the patroness of Christian science. In the Catholic Church, these two stand side by side like the two graceful olive-trees or the two burnished candlesticks mentioned in the Apocalypse.

Cecilia, born about the year 205, distinguished alike by her virginal beauty and her brightness of intellect, dis-

St. Cecilia.

covered, in her tenderest years, that original well-spring of all beauty and of all understanding, the religion of Jesus Christ. Her chief delight lay in the holy gospels and in the beautiful chant of the Church. More than once, as tradition avers, while pouring out her soul to God in hymns, accompanied with instrumental music, the celestial choirs came down from heaven and united their voices to hers. At an early age she was betrothed, though much against her own will, to a young pagan named Valerian. But at their wedding-feast our Saint said decisively to her new husband: "Remember that I have already been espoused to Jesus Christ, and intend to preserve my virginity; and even now, an angel of the Lord stands by my side, as my protector and defender." Though astonished and disappointed at first, the youthful pagan entered into himself, became a convert, and was baptized. His brother Tiburtius, and their mutual friend Maximus, followed his example. Cecilia was very soon afterwards dragged to martyrdom, and died triumphant on the 22d of November, 230.

St. Catharine.

Like St. Cecilia in the department of music, St. Catharine of Alexandria has for centuries been honored in the Church as the patroness of Christian science; another evidence of the sincere, genuine sympathy of the Church for all true knowledge.

The following account will explain why this Saint and virgin was selected to be the patroness of science. One day, while the Emperor Maximinus was holding a grand and solemn festival at Alexandria in honor of the heathen deities, suddenly a fair young maiden emerged from the assembled multitude, and taking her stand before the throne spoke to them in words of such fervid eloquence and profound knowledge and wisdom against the absurdity of worshipping false gods, and in favor of the one true God, that neither the emperor nor any one of his assembled philosophers could reply. This intrepid virgin was St. Catharine. Without delay the emperor summoned the most distinguished philosophers in Alexandria, and others well versed in religious science, to refute the Saint. But they signally failed. Nay, more, at the convincing arguments of Catharine, the cloud of darkness was lifted from their understanding; her words penetrated their hearts; they professed themselves disciples of Christ crucified. Thus did Christian science, hand in hand with virginal innocence and childlike simplicity, win the victory over proud and self-sufficient worldly wisdom. St. Catharine was, however, condemned to die a martyr's death. The wheel on which she had been placed, having broken to pieces without injuring her fair person, she was dispatched with the sword on the 25th of November, 307.

Such are the nine choirs of Christ's chosen ones, in whom he manifests the beauty and glory of his holiness.

CHAPTER VIII.

THE HISTORY OF HERESY AND ITS AGGRESSIONS.

CHRIST LIVES IN HIS CHURCH AS THE DERIDED AND DESPISED ONE.

64. Nature and Origin of Heresy.

"There must also be heresies: that they also who are approved, may be made manifest among you."—1 CORINTHIANS xi. 19.

AS Jesus Christ is the light that came into the world to enlighten its darkness, should not all men turn towards that light with joy and gladness? As he came into the world for the purpose of overthrowing the idols of error and superstition, who would dare to stretch out his hand to restore these fallen gods? Since the truth preached by Jesus came from heaven, yea, from the very bosom of the eternal Father himself, should not all men cheerfully and unconditionally acknowledge and accept it? Alas! so it should be; so it could be. But we are too well aware that the Jews, even in the time of Christ, loved darkness better than light; that Jews and heathens alike used every effort at the outset, to replace upon their altars the false gods overthrown by Jesus Christ, and lost no opportunity to oppose and combat his teachings. When he spoke of his divinity, and consubstantiality with the Father, they charged him with blasphemy. When he asserted that he was older than Abraham, they sought to stone him. When he discoursed to them on the bread of eternal life, and proposed the institution of the blessed Sacrament of the altar, they treated his promise as an impossible one, and turned their backs upon him and his doctrine. They either denied his miracles, or, as they were stubborn facts well known to the people, endeavored to explain them away or attribute them to some evil power.

If, then, our beloved Lord and Saviour Jesus Christ was despised to such an extent, at the very time when he was perfecting visibly among men the great mystery of man's redemption, we must not wonder that his holy Church, the teacher of all nations, should have been despised, and her teachings denied and rejected in after times. Christ still lives in his Church; but he lives, and he will live, till the great day of judgment, "a sign that shall be contradicted."

As during his actual life upon earth, the human intellect will be ever unable to grasp the profound mysteries of his religion, and will therefore rise in proud and blind rebellion against his doctrines. It will always be as easy to find a pretext for doubting and denying, as it was in his own time. As in those days, the human heart will always be inclined to evil, and will therefore be ever ready to controvert the truth of those doctrines which inculcate humility, obedience, and self-control. In all ages, as well as in the days of Christ, will the human conscience endeavor to quiet itself, and justify its unbelief. As then, so will proud men ever entertain feelings of envy and hatred towards those who demand belief in the doctrines of an invisible master; and the more so, when these representatives of the spiritual are blameless in their own lives. Such is the origin of all heresy.

The history of heresy presents a sad picture to our view. Alas! how senseless must that man be, who sits in judgment on the truth brought down from heaven by the Son of God; the truth which he confirmed by miracles and sealed with his blood; the truth in whose defence millions of the holiest men sacrificed their lives; on the truth in whose possession the noblest and most intelligent persons have found peace in life and consolation in death! How lamentable the fate of the millions, who through the stubborn pride of heresiarchs, have been kept away from the well-springs of truth, from the source of grace and life, from Christ and his Church! And yet it may be salutary and useful for us, Christians, to cast a glance at this sad history of heresy and heretics. In the midst of the unholy conflicts stirred up by these unbelieving men, we shall see Jesus Christ, the great leader, in his sublime majesty and dignity, defending his Church against the powers of hell; rallying his faithful forces to her defence, enlightening them, strengthening them, inspiring them; thus covering his Church with the grand shield composed of his fathers of the Church and his holy councils; and bringing forth from the fires of persecution kindled by heretics, the gold of divine truth more bright and beautiful than ever.

65. Heresies Concerning Creation.

GNOSTICISM.

"Professing themselves to be wise, they became fools."—ROMANS i. 22.

Among the several species of heresy that afflicted the Church, there were four of very grave importance, for they were directed against the four principal articles of faith; namely, the creation of the world, the blessed Trinity, the divine-human person of Christ, and divine grace.

In opposition to the teachings of the Church on creation, the Gnostics rose and lived during the first three centuries. These heretics, although priding themselves on their superior wisdom, and despising the simple faith of the Christians, fell into the most ridiculous absurdities.

Thus, it seemed to them impossible that God, a sublime and infinite Spirit, should have created rough and chaotic matter. They maintained that the material composing the earth had, like God himself, existed from all eternity; that out of God had emanated a second and somewhat inferior spirit; and out of this one, a third spirit; still less perfect; and so on for a long generation, each spirit being less and less good, less and less wise, till at last one came who rebelled against God and sought to set up a separate and independent kingdom of his own. With this view he took possession of chaotic matter, and formed the world, with its three natural kingdoms of earth, fire, and water. The material world therefore, deriving its origin from a finite and evil spirit, all matter, or temporal creation, must be of itself evil and sinful. They taught that the man who is desirous of reaching and of being united to God, must abstain as much as possible from all bodily or material things, especially from the gratification of the senses, from wine and marriage; and that for this reason Jesus Christ, himself one of the lower spirits or emanations from the supreme God, had no real body, but only an imaginary one.

These heretics mixed up these and similar absurdities with maxims from the holy Scriptures, and from the books of pagan philosophy; and flattered themselves that they were in secure possession of perfect truth. Their system of morality was very austere; but the lives of most of them were dishonest and vicious.

The most remarkable upholders of Gnosticism were Cerinthus, Basilides, Valentine, Marcion, and Manes the Persian. The last was the author of Manichæism. Their errors were combated and refuted by the Apostles John and Paul,* by the first disciples of the Apostles, and by the

---

* Thus St. Paul had these heretics in his mind, when, in the 4th chapter of his first Epistle to Timothy, he warns him against apostates, who forbid marriage and the use of certain meats. If the

earliest Fathers of the Church, all of whom kept special watch lest the true teachings of the Church should be in the least degree changed or tainted by these absurd opinions.

66. Heresies against the Blessed Trinity.

ARIANISM.

"The god of this world hath blinded the minds of unbelievers, that the light of the gospel of the glory of Christ, who is the image of God, should not shine unto them."—2 CORINTHIANS iv. 4.

The doctrine of the holy Trinity was assailed as early as the third century. Among its opponents were Paul of Samosata, Beryllus of Bostra, the African priest Sabellius, and others more or less known. These heretics maintained that there is but one person in God, although this person reveals himself in a threefold manner as Father, Son, and Holy Ghost. Arius, a priest of Alexandria, undertook to combat and controvert this error, but fell himself into the opposite error. In his attempt to prove the Trinity, he destroyed the Unity of divine Being, and taught that the Son of God is distinct from the Father, not only in person, but also in nature; that he is not generated from the substance of the Father, but created out of nothing, and therefore is not co-eternal nor equal to the Father, but is merely the first and most excellent of his creatures. Thus we see that Arius is the father of the so-called reason-believing people of our own day, the rationalists, who deny the divinity of Jesus Christ. God

Church has forbidden the priests to marry, and prohibited all the faithful to eat flesh meat on forbidden days, it is not because she considers marriage wrong or flesh meat injurious, but because she knows that such abstinence from marriage, or from the use of flesh meat, when practised out of love for God, is good and salutary to the soul.

HERESIES AGAINST THE BLESSED TRINITY. 219

raised up in the person of St. Athanasius, that holy Doctor of the Church, a formidable adversary, a glorious confessor and defender of the truth against Arius, whose errors were formally and solemnly condemned in the General Council of Nice, in 325. However, God permitted Arianism to spread over a large part of Christendom, and for 300 years to disaffect many peoples, partly by the craftiness and hypocrisy of its teachers, but chiefly by the

St. Athanasius.

influence of the imperial court, which had banished St. Athanasius.

Allied with this heresy was that of Macedonius, which taught that the Holy Ghost was not of the same nature or essence as the Father, but less than either Father or Son. This sin of blasphemy against the Holy Ghost was condemned in the Council of Constantinople, held in 381.

67. Heresies against the Divine Person of Jesus Christ.

NESTORIANISM.

"Is Christ divided?"—1 CORINTHIANS i. 13.

One hundred years after Arius, Nestorius, patriarch of Constantinople, rose up against the Catholic doctrine concerning the unity of the person of Christ. He treated the mystery of the intimate and inseparable union of the two natures in Christ, of the divine nature and human, as absurd and untrue; and taught that in Christ there are two persons, a divine and a human person, and that as Mary had given birth to the human person only, she therefore must not be styled the Mother of God. In the year 428 he first preached this heresy publicly in Constantinople. The consternation and sorrow of the laity were indescribable, on being told from the pulpit that they were no longer to address the Blessed Virgin as Mother of God. "And how," they inquired, "if the human and divine natures are not inseparably united in Christ, if only the human nature of Christ suffered and died on the cross, how can we be saved? What value can the sacrifice so offered on Calvary have for our redemption?" This heresy was opposed and refuted by several bishops and priests, but especially by the holy Cyril, patriarch of Alexandria; and in the third General Council, held at Ephesus, it was formally condemned.

The Abbot Eutyches fell into the opposite error. In his imprudent zeal to refute Nestorius, he advanced the erroneous theory that the human nature in Christ is so closely united with the divine nature, that it is absorbed in the latter, so that we can predicate but one nature in Christ, which is the divine. He did not reflect, that if the human nature of Christ is eliminated, he cannot be our brother, and hence cannot be our Redeemer. Against this error, and those who maintained and defended it, called Monophysts, St. Leo the Great fought with the zeal and ability of an apostle. It was condemned in the year 451 by the fourth General Council of Chalcedon.

68. Heresies Concerning Grace.

PELAGIANISM.

"I can do all things in him who strengtheneth me.—For it is God who worketh in you both to will and to accomplish, according to his good will."—PHILIPPIANS ii. 13, and iv. 13.

About the same time, the British monk Pelagius, in Rome, and afterwards in Carthage, assailed the Christian doctrines on grace, and on free-will in man: elevating the latter too high and destroying the former. Like the rationalists of our times, this misguided monk taught, fifteen hundred years ago, that Adam's sin inflicted no injury upon his descendants, that consequently there is no original sin, that baptism is not necessary to salvation, and that man has within himself so much moral force that he can lead a virtuous life—pleasing to God and meritorious of heaven—without the aid of grace. The chief adversary of this heresy was St. Augustine. This pious and learned Doctor of the Church defended, against the Pelagians, the necessity of supernatural grace; and against the Manichæans the free exercise of the will in man. All our virtue and holiness can proceed only from the union of the divine and human; that is, from heaven's grace combined with free co-operation in man. It is divine grace that gives freedom, vitality, and strength to the human will, wounded and weakened as it is by Adam's sin, and renders it capable of genuine supernatural virtue. These ancient doctrines of St. Augustine were ratified in several Councils, and the errors of the Pelagians were again solemnly and formally condemned in the third General Council at Ephesus.

69. Iconoclasm.

"You shall not make to yourselves any graven thing to adore it."
—LEVITICUS xxvi. 1.

Towards the close of Christian antiquity, a difficulty arose in the Eastern Church regarding pictures and images. Away back in "the days of the martyrs," when the Christians were as yet compelled to celebrate the sacred mysteries, secretly, in the Catacombs, they used to set up pious images for their edification and consolation. This practice was founded in the very spirit of Christianity. Therefore, when Serenus, bishop of Marseilles, cast out all the images from his Cathedral, under the pretence of preventing divine honors being paid to them, the Pope, St. Gregory the Great, wrote to him as follows: " Thou shouldst not have destroyed what was intended, not indeed for worship, but for the instruction of the unlettered in your church. To adore a picture is quite another thing from learning, by that picture, the mystery which we are to adore. For, what writing is to the educated, a picture is for those who cannot read, for in it they can see and know the course they have to follow." In the Oriental Church some injudicious persons in that part of the world had been guilty of showing too much reverence towards images, and this fact furnished a pretext to the Greek emperor, Leo the Isaurian, in the year 727, to forbid all veneration to images as being idolatrous. The conflict, then begun, lasted nearly one hundred and twenty years; during which time many of the emperors forgot all care for the worldly welfare of their subjects, in order to meddle in Church affairs, and by repeated imperial orders, fines, and penalties endeavored to root out the lawful and ancient veneration of images. The pious empresses Irene and Theodora interested themselves in upholding this unduly disparaged ancient Christian custom, and the seventh and eighth

General Councils, at Nice and Constantinople, defended the veneration, but not the adoration, of images, as something lawful, and extremely useful to the Christian people.

70. The Greek Schism.

"The veil of the temple was rent in two, from the top even to the bottom."—MATTHEW xxvii. 51.

During the middle ages, three violent storms swept over the Church, threatening its unity and tearing many of her children from her motherly bosom. These were the Greek schism, the Manichæan fanaticism of the thirteenth century, and the aggressions of the restless, mischievous Hussites.

The author of the Greek schism which separated the Eastern or Greek Church from the mother Church at Rome, was Photius. This designing man, supported by the intrigues and power of the imperial court, assumed the patriarchal chair of Constantinople in 858. At first he sought, by flattery and bribes, to obtain the recognition of the Pope. Failing in this, he threw off the mask, and had the audacity to condemn the Roman Church as having departed from the faith and discipline of the Fathers. This hypocritical pretender, after being deposed by Leo VI., died in the year 891. The fires of this dispute continued to slumber till 1043, when the ambitious Michael Cerularius having been raised to the patriarchate of Constantinople, the flames again burst forth with fresh fury. This proud prelate repeated the charges of Photius against Rome, and so far succeeded in deceiving and stirring up the people that the revolt soon ended in the complete separation of the Eastern Church from the Roman or Western Church. Ever since that unhappy occurrence, the Popes and the bishops assembled in all the General Councils, have been untiring in their efforts to bring back the schismatics to the unity of the Church. But although these efforts sometimes promised happy results, and although some individual bishops have returned (United Greeks), yet the gulf between the mother Church and her schismatical children yawns as wide and as gloomy as ever. The Greek Church, once so fruitful in learned Doctors and holy saints, lies dead now like a dry branch broken from the vine. The same curse of religious Cæsarism, or imperial supremacy and tyranny over the Church, the same desolating blight brought about by the early emperors of Constantinople—which unlucky city fell into the hands of the Mohammedan Turks in 1453—still sits brooding over the unhappy Greek Church; and the supreme power, religious as well as civil, is vested in the hands of the irresponsible Russian Czar.

71. The Albigenses and Catherers.

"When they had stood up against Moses and Aaron, they said: Let it be enough for you that all the multitude consisteth of holy ones, and the Lord is among them; why lift you up yourselves above the people of the Lord? And immediately the earth broke asunder under their feet, and devoured them, with their tents and all their substances!"—NUMBERS xvi.

Hardly five hundred years after this unhappy event in the East, the Western Church was overrun and sorely afflicted by the fanatical Catherers and Albigenses. These were not two distinct sects of heretics, but rather a mixture of the Manichæans and Gnostics, who sprang into existence in Southern France and Spain, at the beginning of the thirteenth century. On account of their pompous pretensions to virtue, they were styled Purists, or Puritans, and sometimes Albigenses, from their chief stronghold, Albi in the south of France.

They rejected all the Christian fundamental truths concerning the creation of the world, the incarnation of

Christ, and his resurrection; all exterior worship, and especially marriage. They taught that it was not the God of light who created the world, but the god of darkness—Jehova. The men, therefore, descended from this god are, of their nature, enemies of light. But the God of light sent his chief angel, Jesus, into the world, with an imaginary body, in order to free men from the slavery of Jehova and his ten commandments. These freedmen formed a superior class of beings, and to them only is obedience due; for they alone live in the strictest detachment from corporeal life. Every one who promises to join this sect before his death, may meanwhile enjoy all pleasures; observing no commandments, especially those emanating from Jehova, who is styled by these heretics the god of darkness.

Such abominable theories, if reduced to practice, would have destroyed the foundations, not only of the Church, but also of the State. As the kindness and instruction vouchsafed to them by Pope Innocent III. were in vain, as the spiritual crusade of preaching and of the Rosary carried on by St. Dominic and his monks did not completely eradicate this heresy, as these rebels dared to lay violent hands upon the person of the papal legate, Peter of Casselnau, killing him while he was preaching on the 15th of January, 1209, it became necessary to resort to forcible means of subjugation. A body of soldiers, led by Count Simon of Montford, marched against them, and a number of cruel and sanguinary battles were fought. About the year 1229 the Inquisition came into existence, and handed these heretics over to the chastising hands of the civil power, as disturbers and mischief-makers dangerous to society.

72. The Hussites.

"As Sodom and Gomorrha, in like manner, these men also were made an example, who defile the flesh, and despise domination, and blaspheme majesty."—JUDE i.

Many other discontented and disappointed individuals allied themselves in these ages with the Albigenses, finding fault and creating disturbance in the Church and in society generally. The outward splendor of the Church, the princely magnificence and wealth of some few prelates, together with the disedifying lives of some few individuals among the clergy, scandalized many a well-minded person, who in his short-sightedness and prejudiced vision was unable to discern the exception from the general rule, the accidental from the essential and real. Persons thus affected easily fell a prey to the temptation of doubt, insubordination, and positive disobedience to the authority of the Church. In their blindness, they could not see beyond the surface of things, and fancied to themselves that the spirit of Christ had deserted the inner life of Christianity. They conceived a hatred and contempt for the Church, its ordinances, and even its mode of worship; and wished, or affected, to be altogether internal and purely spiritual, in order to become more intimately united with Jesus Christ and with the life beyond the grave; hence they gradually became immersed in the perilous quagmire of a false mysticism.*

Such was the fate of the Waldenses of the twelth cen-

---

* Mysticism is the doctrine whereby man learns to become closely united with Christ, and elevated to a higher plane of truth and grace, by the practice of prayer, contemplation, fasting, and the like. If this theory were strictly carried out, to the exclusion of other means of sanctification, such as learning, study, hearing of sermons, obedience to Church precepts, etc., it would lead to false mysticism, And this, after raising man aloft to the highest pinnacle of spiritual pride, invariably plunges him into the depths of sensuality.

tury; of the Brethren and Sisters of Liberty or of the free spirit, and of the Apostolic Brethren in the thirteenth century. John Wickliffe of England belonged to these restless mischief-makers. He railed vociferously against the temporal possessions of the Church, against the Pope; and, like the Protestants of the Reformation, he taught that every reader of the holy Scripture was an infallible interpreter of its meaning, and supreme judge in matters of faith. He died in the year 1384, but his writings were multiplied and widely circulated by John Huss, the Bohemian heretic. This man taught that some men are destined by God from all eternity for happiness, and these cannot help but be saved; that others are predestined to eternal perdition, and cannot escape it. Only the elect, or predestined, can be members of the Church; they only can be heads of Church or State: whilst to the others, obedience is not to be given. Huss was therefore dangerous to Church and government. With a letter of safe conduct from the emperor Sigismund, this heretic appeared before the General Council at Constance. Here the princes and the bishops, in the most friendly manner, tried to persuade him, by entreaty and explanation, to renounce his absurd yet dangerous notions, and thus save God's Church from a dreadful scandal. But this proud and obstinate man withstood both entreaty and threat, and was burnt to death, at Constance, on the 6th of July, in the year 1415, as a heretic and disturber of the public peace.*

* It is untrue to allege that the Church, in the Council of Constance, put Huss to death. The Council did nothing but its duty ; namely, to adjudge him guilty of heresy, to deprive him of his office, and to excommunicate him from the fold of the Church. He now became amenable to the civil courts, as a disturber of the public peace. These pronounced his sentence, and executed it, though the bishops of the Council, according to the testimony of Ulrich Reichenthal, who was an eye-witness, petitioned King Sigismund and the judges to spare Huss's life.

Some of the Bohemian nobility, under pretext of avenging Huss, and of demanding the reception of communion under both kinds, inaugurated against King Sigismund the dreadful Hussite war, which was ended only after twenty years of carnage, by the complete defeat of the Hussite heretics.

73. The Reformation, so-called.—Its Causes.

"I wonder that you are so soon removed from him that called you unto the grace of Christ, unto another gospel: which is not another; only there are some that trouble you, and would pervert the gospel of Christ."—GALATIANS i. 6, 7.

As we leave the middle ages and enter into modern times, we encounter, in the early part of the sixteenth century, three men who undertook to reform the Church of Christ. These men, while claiming to remodel and improve the work of our Lord, have in truth broken it into fragments, and severed from the centre of unity several nations of Christendom. These so-called reformers were Luther, Zwinglius, and Calvin.

How did this dismal and unhappy division take place? How was it possible that so large a part of the Catholic people in Germany, Switzerland, France, England, and other countries tore themselves away from the bosom of the Mother Church, to whose kindly and motherly care and labors these nations were indebted for their Christianity, and therefore for their civilization and prosperity?

Some superficial and insincere person might answer: "The scandalous traffic in indulgences introduced into Germany by the Dominican monk, John Tetzel, was the cause of the dismemberment of the Church. For it was this circumstance that opened the eyes of the hitherto deluded people, and made them discover the avarice and hypocrisy of the Papacy." But the announcement of grants of indulgences, for useful purposes, or for some common good, was nothing new in the ears of the Catholic public. Moreover, history has made it certain, that this Tetzel was not at all guilty of the scandalous absurdities which in later times have been attributed to him. Nor was he a rude fanatic, but rather an intelligent and educated man.

Then again it is insolently alleged that down to the time of Luther the Catholic people were buried in the grossest ignorance, that they had grown up for the most part without school instruction, that the clergy had neglected preaching and religious instruction, and that the Bible was a thing altogether unknown to the people. But when Luther, by the establishment of schools for the people, diffused education far and wide; but more especially when, by the translation of the Bible, he made the people acquainted, for the first time, with this holy rule of faith, and announced the *original gospel truth;* then did the people at last discover the great contradiction between the pure doctrine of the gospel, and the teachings of the Catholic Church. Hence they turned away with enthusiasm to follow the new religon.

But all this is as untrue as it is ridiculous. Before Luther was born, schools for the people flourished in his native country. And it was the Church, too, that, like an anxious mother, had provided these schools for her children. When we read in the old prayer-book which was in use among the laity at that time and previous, the following instruction for the head of a family, "Hear, on Sunday, the word of God diligently; attend the sermons in the morning and in the afternoon, lay the word of God seriously to heart," we learn from all this that preaching and religious instruction were not by any means so wofully neglected as some would pretend. In the cities and larger villages many endowments had been established for the special maintenance of preachers of the word of God. In the city of Nuremburg thirteen sermons were preached every Sunday in the various churches. Moreover, long before the sham Reformation, there were in the hands of the German people a large number of catechisms and other books of religious instruction.

Finally, as regards the Bible, long before the time of Luther, at least twenty different editions of the entire Scriptures in the vulgar tongue had been published, some with and some without explanatory notes and comment.

We must therefore go look somewhere else for the causes of the great falling away from the Church at the time of the Reformation. We shall find them in the civil disorders and disturbances and corruptions of those ages.

For some time previous, many of the German princes, great and small, had declared their independence of the German emperor. Of these many had become greedy and exacting, and very despotic and cruel to their subjects.

Instead of the ancient and well-tried German code of laws, another system had been introduced, namely, the old pagan Roman code. By this change the common people were subjected to injustice, losses, disadvantages, and made very discontented. The great wealth which the Church, by the generosity of her children and by her own care and industry, had gathered together, excited the covetousness of the princes and the governments. Princely and noble families often seized violently upon high Church dignities and officers for their unworthy, indolent, shiftless sons, who, having no fitness for the positions and no vocation from heaven, often gave the most shocking scandals. The unbelieving free spirits of that time, the so-called Humanists of the younger school, availed themselves of these scandals to arouse the hitherto contented people, by ridicule and hatred against the Church. Meanwhile the politicians broached again the old Roman doctrine Cæsareopapism; that is to say, they taught that temporal princes have a right to govern and control the Church as well as the State.

Thus, manifold doubt, disquiet, and discontentment had taken possession of the minds of the people. Hence, for the unfortunate priests who rebelled against their mother Church, it became an easy task to lead the people astray. And wherever the mass of the people wished to remain true to the old Church, their despotic and avaricious rulers, who meanwhile had appropriated to themselves the rights and the property of the Church, carried them away violently into the vortex of secession, then into schism, and finally heresy.

74. The Difference between Catholic and Protestant Teachings.

"But though an angel from heaven preach a gospel to you besides that which we have preached to you, let him be anathema." —GALATIANS i. 8.

The opposition to the Church was directed, in the beginning, by the self-styled reformers to outward things and to veritable abuses. But the obtuseness of their intellects, the pride of their hearts, and the dangerous flattery bestowed upon them by the great ones of this world, led them further and further in their mad career, till they enunciated false principles which threatened to undermine the doctrines of the Catholic Church. They were not themselves agreed, even in their errors; for they disputed with each other in most violent and passionate language. These conflicts are still going on among their respective followers. In our day, when unbelief is spreading far and wide; when believing Protestants and unbelieving Protestants are diverging farther and farther from each other, the teachings of the former, at least as far as they fall short of the truth, may be expressed in the following propositions:

1. "The Bible is the ground and source of all Christian faith; and every man who reads this book with good will, and lives accordingly, will participate in all truth and grace in Christ."

Catholic faith, on the contrary, teaches us that Christ did not leave his children depending upon the leaden types of a book, but referred them to his Apostles and their lawful successors; that he did not appoint a written or printed book to be the infallible guide of mankind, but founded for that purpose a living and a speaking infallible Church; and that she alone enjoys the authority and power to explain and impart to men the true meaning of the Bible, and the sense of oral and written tradition. The Bible has always been recognized and used by Catholics, in so far as it goes, as a duplicate on parchment of the doctrines which our Saviour had inscribed with a pencil of divine fire, in characters of living faith, on the heart of the Church.

2. "Faith alone is sufficient for salvation." The Catholic Church, on the contrary, teaches us that Christ requires from his followers, not only faith, but exacts also as a necessary condition to salvation works of Christian charity produced by faith.

3. "Christ alone is a priest forever, and therefore his Church needs no priesthood, but merely learned men to preach the word of God, and to maintain Church discipline among believers." The Catholic Church, on the other hand, teaches that Christ in his quality of highpriest communicated his priestly plenitude and power to the Apostles and their successors, and gave them a commission and authority, not only to preach his doctrine, but also to renew, in an unbloody manner, his ever-blessed sacrifice, and also to administer the sacraments and to dispense blessings in his name.

4. "The Church of Christ needs no head but Jesus Christ, and has no other." On the other hand, the Catho-

lic Church teaches that Christ has appointed St. Peter, and his lawful successor the Pope, to be his visible representative and the chief head of the Church, the centre of Christian unity, and the infallible teacher of the truths of faith.

5. "There are but two Sacraments: baptism and the Lord's Supper." The Catholic Church maintains that Christ ordained seven Sacraments, which have been dispensed to men from the beginning of Christianity.

6. "Christians have no other sacrifice than the bleeding sacrifice of our Lord on the cross." The Catholic Church holds that this bleeding sacrifice of the cross must, in obedience to Christ's command at the last supper, be renewed in an unbloody manner in the mass till the end of time, as the predicted clean oblation of bread and wine, according to the order of Melchisedech.

7. "As God wishes to be worshipped in spirit and truth, no images and but few ceremonies are to be allowed when we worship him." The Catholic Church teaches that pious symbols, and significant and sacred ceremonies, awaken and assist interior devotion and worship to God, and therefore may be employed in the practice of our religion.

8. "For the pardon of his sins, the sinner needs nothing more than faith in the atonement by Christ, and a firm resolution to amend his own life." On the contrary, the Catholic Church teaches that Christ commissioned the Apostles and their successors to absolve penitent sinners from their sins, when with the necessary conditions and dispositions they have revealed them in confession.

9. "The Lord's Supper is only a symbol and sacred memorial of the atoning death of Jesus Christ." On the contrary, the Catholic Church teaches that in the blessed Sacrament of the altar, the real promised Bread of Life, Jesus Christ himself, is really and truly present.

10. "To God alone are adoration, prayer, and praise

to be offered; therefore it is an unchristian practice to pray to Mary and the other saints." The Catholic Church holds that it is a useful, reasonable, and salutary practice to *venerate* Mary and the other saints, and to beg their intercession for us before the throne of God.

11. "Beyond the grave there are but two places: heaven and hell." The Catholic Church teaches that there is a third place, called *Purgatory*, and therefore that prayer and sacrifice should be offered for the souls of the faithful departed.

Thus we see how far away from the old faith modern heresy has gone, and how much those persons are to be pitied who have turned away to the " new gospel."

---

75. Martin Luther.

"Such false apostles are deceitful workmen, transforming themselves into the Apostles of Christ."—2 CORINTHIANS xi. 13.

Let us glance hastily at the history of the three unfortunate men who brought so much division, strife, contention, and hatred into the once united and happy Christian family.

Martin Luther, the most learned, active and efficient among the reformers, was born on the 10th of November, 1483, at Eisleben in Saxony, became an Augustinian monk, and was, later, a priest and professor at Wittenberg. During his lifetime, some monks, while preaching the doctrine of indulgences in Germany, solicited from their hearers some small offerings to aid in the erection of the most glorious temple in Christendom, St. Peter's Church at Rome. Luther found fault with the conduct of Tetzel, one of the preachers, and posted upon the door of All Saints' Church in Wittenberg a written exposition of his own individual views on indulgences, containing ninety-five propositions. This happened on October 31st, 1517.

The propositions created much excitement over all Europe, and many well-meaning persons sympathized with the daring friar, whom they looked upon as a zealous opponent of unchristian practices. Luther himself had no intention, in the beginning, of separating from the Church; for in March, 1519, he wrote to Rome, that "next to Christ, the authority of the Pope was to him above everything in heaven or earth." And a year later, he assured the emperor Charles V. that he wished to live and die a faithful and obedient son of the Catholic Church. But the evil spirit of contradiction had blinded him. Denying one Christian truth after another, and falling under the ban of the Church, he joined her enemies, and ridiculed, by speech and writing, in the most opprobious terms, the teachings of Catholic faith, its moral precepts and ancient practices; till finally, in 1525, he trampled under foot his solemn vows of religion, and married Catharine Bora, herself an ex-nun. With consummate cunning, Luther had recourse to the aid of princes, governments, and the nobility, whose attention he called to the wealth locked up in monasteries, to the episcopal revenues, etc. At the same time he preached the doctrine: the one hundredth part of the present wealth of the Church is sufficient for its support. This artful policy of the man who once, at the altar, had vowed undying fidelity to his Church, accomplished its purpose. Many princes and governments joined him, took possession of the Church property, and forced their subjects into the new religion. Luther died in February, 1546, complaining that, to his own personal knowledge and observation, the German people had become, since the beginning of the new religion, more immoral, wicked, and unprincipled than they had formerly been.

76. Ulrich Zwingli.

"Jesus I know, and Paul I know; but who are you?"—ACTS OF THE APOSTLES xix. 15.

Ulrich Zwingli was born January 1st, 1484, at Wildhausen in Switzerland; was ordained priest and appointed pastor, first in Clarus and afterwards in Einsiedeln. Although very learned, he was an unworthy pastor of souls, for, according to his own avowal, he gave great scandal by his unchaste manner of life. Yet, in 1518, he was chosen pastor at Zurich, where very soon, under the protection of the government, he preached against the Pope, against his worthy and pious bishop, Hugh of Constance, and against the ancient doctrines of the Church. He ceased to celebrate mass, destroyed religious pictures, dispersed the religious communities, and married. In his religious controversy at Zurich, on the 29th of January, 1523, Zwingli, among other absurdities, uttered the following proposition: "The so-called spiritual authority of the Church is not founded on the teachings of Christ, but the civil authority is. To the latter belong all the prerogatives to which the clergy lay claim; to the same civil authority do men owe exclusive submission." This was precisely the same dishonorable policy which Luther adopted, in order to completely win over to himself the civil authorities, in order with their help to force the success of his new departure.

Zwingli denied more strenuously and more absolutely than Luther himself the doctrine of the real presence in the Eucharist. He pretended to recognize in the Blessed Sacrament only a figure or symbol of Christ, and a pious commemoration of Him. His controversy on this doctrine with Luther, who wanted to retain that dogma, was so coarse and bitter, that when Luther afterwards heard of his death in the battle of Kappel, in 1531, he cried out with delight: "There is the end of the notoriety which he endeavored to acquire by blaspheming against the Eucharist. Now they will make Zwingli a martyr of Christ, in order to fill their measure of blasphemy till it overflows." Equally hostile to Luther were the adherents of Zwingli, and they styled Luther's short confession of faith so unclean, blasphemous, and diabolical a work, that it stood unequalled in its infamy, and was a disgrace to Christianity.

77. John Calvin.

"It must needs be that scandals come; but nevertheless, woe to that man by whom the scandal cometh."—MATTHEW xviii. 7.

John Calvin, born on the 10th of July, 1509, at Noyon, in France, was destined by his poor parents for the Church. However, he did not take priests' orders, but gave himself up to the pursuit of the positive sciences and to the study of jurisprudence. Becoming acquainted, in the University at Paris, with the principles of Lutheranism, he began the study of the Holy Scriptures under the direction of professors who were deeply infected with that modern poison. At once he entered upon the defence and advocacy of Lutheranism with such unmeasured violence, that he soon saw himself compelled to leave France. He went to Basel, in Switzerland, where he remained a whole year, and completed his work on "Instruction in the Christian Religion"—a book which his adherents declared to be "the most precious, next to the gospels." In this book the sour and gloomy Calvin introduced, together with Luther's innovations, his own dismal doctrine of predestination, or foreordained fate. "One portion of men," says he, "God has foreordained to everlasting happiness, in order to manifest his mercy in them. These are perfectly sure of their happiness, and cannot be damned. All other men God has from all eternity foreordained to damnation, in order to manifest his justice in them. These, notwithstanding all their efforts, cannot attain to salvation. In the reception of the sacraments, they receive neither grace nor justification."

From Basel, Calvin went, in the year 1536, to Geneva, where he remained some time. Here this restless but energetic man, by means of his great learning and iron will, succeeded in pushing his way into the highest and most exclusive society, both ecclesiastical and worldly, where he forced his errors upon very many. This apostolic advocate and defender of "Gospel liberty" composed a creed, which all the inhabitants and subjects of Geneva were forced to swear that they would follow. He persecuted with the most persistent and inveterate hatred all who did not agree with his views in every particular. He threw Bolsec the physician, Ameaux the senator, Gentilis, and several others into prison, or had them exiled. James Gruet he had several times put to the torture, and finally beheaded. The unfortunate doctor, Servetus, he burned to death at the stake. And all this wicked cruelty because these persons held views different from his own. He died on the 27th of May, 1564.

His heresies and Church ordinances forced their way principally into France, Holland, England, and Scotland. Lutheranism was confined mainly to Germany; while the doctrines of Zwingli prevailed most in Switzerland.

78. The Effects of the Reformation.

"By their fruits you shall know them. Do men gather grapes of thorns, or figs of thistles?"—MATTHEW vii. 16.

Concerning the significance and the consequences of the Reformation, we have the opinion of a very respectable man of that time, who at first greeted Luther's movements with joy, because, like thousands of others, as believed that his object was to remove certain abuses in the Church, and to improve the morals of the people, and not, as it soon proved to be, to change the very faith itself. Well and truly might this learned and admired Erasmus of Rotterdam say to the Reformers: "What do you want to do? You ask the world to despise and reject the traditions cherished by our fathers for centuries! Your new gospel lacks everything: prophecies, miracles, virtue, learning, the sanction of scholars, the testimony of martyrs; and yet you ask us to rush in and embrace this new gospel of yours? You want to make us believe that the Church was deprived of Christ for fourteen hundred years, and that while the bridegroom slept, the bride worshipped strange and false gods! There is no greater misfortune than to fall away from the Church. If you gather together all the sins of luxury, pride, avarice, and every other vice which is charged to the priest, the many-headed monster of all these vices would be nothing in ugliness to the monstrous crime of secession from the Church. The Apostles abstained from marriage; or, if married before their calling, lived with their wives as brother with sister, in order the more fully to devote themselves to the cause of Christ. Now a new gospel has come into full bloom, according to which priests and monks may violate their solemn vows and enter into matrimony. Of old, the gospel used to transform wild, wicked, and unruly men into peaceful lambs. But the followers of our new gospel become savages, rob, curse their benefactors, and preach rebellion to lawful authority. I see new hypocrites, new despots; but not a footprint of the Holy Spirit. Show me one man who has been made better by this new gospel. I, for my part, have not seen one who has not become, on embracing the new opinions, a worse man than he was before, if possible. Wherever this new gospel prevails, learning falls to the ground, and the writings of the ancient fathers are despised. The philosophy of Aristotle has been styled by Luther the work of the devil, and he condemns indeed all knowledge. Melanchthon is quarrelling with the Universities. Farel condemns all education as an invention of the devil. Perhaps, too, some other reformer might as well attribute to the fault of the priests the great falling off in the number of students. The fault-finders are wild enough in their charges to make this last one. For they forget how many colleges of England, Holland, France, and other places have been founded and richly endowed by bishops and priests, who also made ample provision for the decent support of the students. It would appear that lately some Protestant governments have advertised for professors. They will also find it necessary to advertise for students; so universal and incorrigible is the intellectual laziness and languor brought about by the so-called new gospel."

To these disorders and demoralization may be added the bloody persecutions which soon followed in many countries, especially in England, Ireland, and Scotland; the brutal violence with which many of the princes and governments compelled their subjects to abandon the religion of their fathers, and to embrace the new theories; the three religious wars of 1531, 1656, and 1712, in Switzerland; the nine Huguenot wars in France which lasted from 1562 to 1588*, and more especially the dreadful

* The unfortunate event which occurred in Paris during the night between the 24th and 25th of August, 1572, commonly known in history as the Massacre of St. Bartholomew, was instigated by the Duke of Guise, who sought to avenge himself for the death of his father on Caspar Coligny, the leader of the Huguenots, or French Protestants. By an unhappy chain of circumstances, and through the wilful blindness of King Charles IX., a man of little or no force of character, what was intended to be a mere act of private personal vindictiveness, was made to assume vast proportions never contemplated. It is stated that no less than four thousand persons, among them many Catholics, lost their lives at that

Thirty Years' War, which devastated Germany from 1618 to 1648, when it was at last brought to a close in the peace meeting at Westphalia. The unity of the German empire was rent asunder, the imperial power paralyzed, and Europe was drawn up into two vast hostile camps.

Such were the results of this sham reformation. The individual Catholic is far from wishing to hate and condemn his so-called Protestant fellow creatures. But the Reformation itself he must always look upon as one of the lamentable misfortunes which the Lord has ever permitted to overtake the Church.

79. The False Liberalism of our Day.

"You have been called unto liberty: only make not liberty an occasion to the flesh. Now the works of the flesh are manifest, which are contentions, emulations, wraths, quarrels, dissensions, sects, envies."—GALATIANS V.

If we cast a glance at the disturbances and conflicts that have arisen in the Church since the time of the Reformation, we find that they are owing chiefly to a spirit of false liberalism.* Let us endeavor to understand the meaning of this important word, liberalism. The Catho-

time in Paris and the provinces of France. The deceitful king, in relating the history of this event to Pope Gregory XIII., made it appear in the light of a discovery and frustration of a treacherous plot to assassinate the royal family.

* This pernicious system comprises Gallicanism in France, Josephism and Febronianism in Germany, the attempts of Bishop Ricci of Pistoja in Italy, Hermesianism in Bonn, and other absurdities. One of the most dangerous of these modern heresies was Jansenism, which in course of years joined hands with Gallicanism in France (1640 to 1718). This heresy took its rise in a misunderstanding of the teachings of St. Augustine on divine grace. It pretended that the Church was too mild and easy, denied the freedom of the human will, and maintained that man cannot resist the impulses of grace.

lic Church is opposed chiefly by three enemies: the civil power, which seeks to rule the Church and become omnipotent in all departments of society; Bible-reading Protestantism; and infidelity. Now there have always been, and there are to-day, individual Catholics, certain learned professors, even well-to-do and comfortably situated clergymen, who, instead of trying to preserve the legacy of Christ against these three enemies, and to defend it manfully, dally more or less with these enemies, and yield up now one portion and now another portion of Catholic truth and ecclesiastical right, with the laudable intention of saving the rest and purchasing peace at any price.

Bishop W. E. Ketteler.

They forget that Catholic truth is not the creation of man; nor yet merchandise, which we can cheapen and sell for the sake of gain. They do not remember how emphatically and positively the Lord commands us to hold fast with unshaken firmness and fidelity to the smallest tittle of doctrine and precept. They seem to forget that the enemy will not remain satisfied with such concessions, and that their own pretended sagacity will in the end prove a folly and a snare. It is true that these persons have for a long time won the applause of the world. They are called generous, tolerant, liberal, and enlightened Catholics, whilst their brethren who have stood firm and unyielding by the side of the Church have been derided, cursed, and persecuted as Ultramontanes. But this very flattering adulation of the world should make them afraid. For Christ the Lord has said: "Remember my word that I said to you. The servant is not greater than his master. If they have persecuted me, they will also persecute you.

If you had been of the world, the world would love you as 'its own;' but because you are not of the world, but I have chosen you out of the world, therefore the world hateth you."

Even in these degenerate days of our own time, the Lord has raised up great, learned, and fearless champions

Pius IX.

to combat this new heresy of liberalism, In the front ranks of this glorious army stand Bishop Ketteler and the other brave bishops of Germany and Switzerland. These faithful successors of the Apostles, equipped with the shining armor of faith, reposing their trust in God, possessing experience and knowledge, proof against the flattery and fearless of the threats of the mighty ones of this earth, faithful to duty, in perfect harmony with each other, and ready and eager to follow in the footsteps of the martyr-bishops of the primitive Church, they stand ready to repel the inroads of liberalism in the Church of Christ; defending, by pen and tongue, the legacy of faith, the freedom of the Church, and the rights of the Christian people.

Foremost in this sacred contest stood the late Father of Christendom, the glorious Pope Pius IX. Gentle and kind towards all men, he fought from the beginning of his pontificate, with the perseverance and courage of a hero, against the rise and growth of false principles. Like the venerable and aged Mathathias, in the days of the faithless and haughty king Antiochus, Pius IX. proclaimed: "Every one that hath zeal for the law, and maintaineth the testament, let him follow me. Now hath pride and chastisement gotten strength, and the time of destruction and the wrath of indignation: now therefore, O my sons, be zealous for the law" (1 Mach. ii.). In his letters and sermons, Pius tore the mask from the brow of that Antiochus, Godless enlightenment, proclaiming in fearless accents to the nations that timidity, cowardice, or liberalism, cannot lead to peace; that real, true, and enduring peace is to be found only in Christ, and in rendering to him honest, sincere, and undivided homage. The angels' song must ever be ours: "Glory be to God on high."

CHAPTER IX.

THE HISTORY OF THE PERSECUTIONS.

CHRIST LIVES IN HIS CHURCH AS THE CRUCIFIED ONE.

80. Persecutions from the Jews.

"Pilate saith to the Jews: Behold your king! But they cried out: Away with him, away with him; crucify him."—JOHN xix. 14.

WELL and truly hath the Saviour said: "If the world hate you, know you that it hath hated me me before you. If they have persecuted me, they will also persecute you. Father, the hour of my death is come; glorify thy Son. Keep and protect those whom thou hast given me in thy name, that they be one, I in them, and thou in me, and I am glorified in them."

These words of our divine Saviour contain and explain the whole mystery of Christian persecution. It is not the Church, it is not its leaders, nor yet its members that the world has persecuted and will persecute to the end of time; it is Christ himself who is the object of its fury: "Christ in *them;*" that is, Christ in his Church. Although he is now reigning in heaven's glory, at the Father's right hand, he is really and truly living over again, in his Church, his three-and-thirty years' life of martyrdom. "O ye of little faith! Is it not necessary for Christ thus to suffer, and so to enter into his glory?" The Church must follow in his footsteps. Against her, as it was against Him, the hatred of a dissolute world will ever be made practically and painfully manifest. But after the sword comes the palm; first the cross, then the crown.

The first persecution against the Church was waged by the Jews. They who had delivered the divine Master to be crucified by the heathen, now directed their fury against his disciples. The Council ordered them to be

The Crucifixion.

imprisoned, forbade them to preach the gospel, had them scourged, and sent Jewish minions into every town and rural district to find out the faithful and to bring them in chains to Jerusalem. It was the Jews who stoned St. Stephen, who effected the death of St. James the elder, slew St. James the Less, incited the heathen mob at Lystra to stone St. Paul; and it was they who afterwards sent this Apostle in chains to Cæsarea to appear and answer before pagan judges. But the measure was soon filled, and the day of vengeance dawned at last over the deicide city of Jerusalem. The blood of the prophets, the blood of the world's Redeemer, and of his saints, must be avenged, and the dreadful prophecies of Christ must be fulfilled.

The instruments chosen to inflict this chastisement upon the Jews were the Romans; whose forces, under the command of Titus, in the year 70, besieged the doomed capital; whose inhabitants, deceived by false prophets, had risen in rebellion against the imperial government. The sufferings undergone by the people of the beleaguered town during the three months' siege, have hardly a parallel in history; being "such tribulations as were not from the beginning of the creation."

The sword and arrow of the enemy from the walls, the wild and murderous gangs in the city itself, the poisonous effluvia of contagious diseases, and awful famine, all combined to produce a dreadfully abundant death-harvest. Seven and thirty years before had the Son of Man shed tears over this city, and foretold the destruction which has now come upon it. "O Jerusalem, Jerusalem, if thou also hadst known, and that in this thy day, the things that are to thy peace; but now they are hidden from thy eyes. For the days shall come upon thee, and thine enemies shall cast a trench about thee, and compass thee round, and threaten thee on every side, and beat thee flat to the ground, and thy children who are in thee, and they shall not leave in thee a stone upon a stone, because thou hast not known the time of thy visitation. Woe to them that are with child and give suck in those days, for there shall be great distress in the land, and wrath upon this people. They shall fall by the edge of the sword, and shall be led away captives into all nations; and Jerusalem shall be trodden down by the Gentiles, till the times of the nations be fulfilled."

Alas! the Jews, with their usual wilful obstinacy,

closed their ears to these dread prophecies of Christ, and now the measure of their guilt is overflowing and their punishment overwhelming. Not a spark of human feeling seems to be left alive in their hearts, for mothers feed upon the flesh of their children. Hundreds of thousands of her citizens were slain, or carried into captivity. The city, with its magnificent temple, was burned to the ground, and even the few remaining foundations were thrown down by Titus. Such was the punishment sent

Christianity departs from Jerusalem.

by Heaven on the first persecutors of the Church. The chosen city of God, the heaven-favored Jerusalem, the cradle of Christianity, was reduced to ruins; while Christianity, shaking the dust from her feet, and taking with her all her blessings, her heavenly peace, and her hopes of salvation, went forth from the ruins, to traverse the earth, to enlighten and comfort, and bring salvation to the heathen peoples who sat in darkness and in the shadow of desponding spiritual death.

81. The Ten Roman Persecutions.

"Behold, I send you as sheep in the midst of wolves. You shall be brought before governors and before kings for my sake, for a testimony to them and to the gentiles."—MATTHEW x. 16, 18.

The persecutions which the Church suffered at the hands of the pagan emperors of Rome were far more cruel and protracted and widespread than those inflicted by the Jews. Indeed, during the first three centuries the conflict between the powers of Rome and the struggling Christians was almost continual. Hence that period is specially known as the "age of martyrdom." From time immemorial the Roman emperors had considered themselves both as high-priests of paganism and as supreme rulers both in religious and temporal matters. Hence they looked upon themselves as attacked and

Nero.

defied in their most cherished rights by the "kingdom of Christ," which cannot know or recognize any authority superior to itself. Moreover, the imperial greatness and power, in a great measure, owed its rise, and great splendor, to idolatry, with which it had grown up into gigantic power and majesty. Hence it often happened that emperors, who in other respects were mild and gentle, became like roaring lions when brought in contact with the Christians.

During the greater portion of this "age of martyrdom" in the Church, namely from the year 64 to the year 313, history presents to our view ten emperors, who were the chief persecutors of the followers of Christ. These were: Nero, from 54 to 68; Domitian, from 81 to 96; Trajan, from 98 to 117; Adrian, from 117 to 138; Marcus Aurelius, from 161 to 180; Septimius Severus, from 193 to 211; Maximinian of Thrace, from 235 to 238; Decius, from 249 to 251; Valerian, from 253 to 260; Diocletian and his agents, from 284 to 313.

Injustice, cruelty, malignant hatred, diabolical lust: all the evil passions that slumber in the human breast, seem to have formed a conspiracy, and into this conspiracy to have taken hell with all its malice, for the sole purpose of destroying Christianity. Children, old men, tender maidens and gentle matrons, peasants and high dignitaries, were dragged before the judgment-seat of the emperor or of his representative officer; and when flattery and promises had no effect upon their faith, they were stretched on the rack, lacerated with iron hooks, burnt at the stake, beheaded, crucified, drowned, or buried alive, scalded to death in caldrons of seething oil, or molten lead; showing that Christ still lived, in his Church, a martyr's life. Those Christians who as yet had evaded death and imprisonment, took great pains to purchase from the executioners the martyrs' remains, and with touching and loving solicitude deposited them in the Catacombs. Then might be seen many a group of prayerful Christians, gathered in silence in the darksome vault, and by the uncertain light of a single torch, paying their last respects to a martyred brother or sister, blessing the sacred remains, and going forth only to be themselves brought back the next day and placed side by side with the one whom they had just left. The martyr's blood in which Christianity was to be extinguished became the seed of new Christians. While thousands of heroes and heroines of faith and charity fell dead on the field, millions rushed in to fill up the ranks, and in their turn fall in defence of truth; thus proving that the life of Jesus Christ did not close on Calvary, nor even on Tabor, but that he still lives, although persecuted unto death, immortal and unconquerable in his Church for all time. The survivors of the martyrs were careful to record quite fully and accurately the lives, capture, imprisonment, trials, and executions of their slaughtered brethren. These records are still extant, and are known to scholars as the "Acts of the Martyrs." They form one of the most tender and edifying chapters in the history of the Church.

When the Roman empire, after having spent its forces against the Christians, became powerless for further opposition, it, too, met its chastisement. Countless tribes of savages from the remote and unknown north of Europe invaded its territories, overran the empire with fire and sword, and in 476 drove the last emperor of the West, Romulus Augustulus, from the throne.

82. Persecutions by the Emperors of the East.

"God hath placed bishops to rule the Church of God."—ACTS OF THE APOSTLES XX. 28.

Less bloody, but more dangerous and wicked, were the persecutions undergone by the Church at the hands of the emperors of the East, at Constantinople. Most of these men were unworthy successors of Constantine the Great; and being addicted to Arianism and other errors and vices, they were constantly interfering in ecclesiastical affairs. They even presumed to issue ecclesiastical decrees and formal declarations of faith; and woe to the bishops and priests who would dare to oppose them. They would be deposed from their office, banished, imprisoned, beheaded, or strangled. The patriarchs of Constantinople especially were required to render blind obedience to the emperors, and to become the tools of their imperial whims in religious affairs. While some few submitted tamely, the greater number withstood manfully this invasion of their rights of conscience, and became martyrs in the cause of apostolic freedom, as became faithful shepherds. Such a conflict existed during the time of the Iconoclasts, when the emperors Leo the Isaurian, Constantine Copronymous, Leo the Armenian, Michael the Stammerer, and Theophilus endeavored to do away with the veneration of images by torturing and murdering its defenders.

These persecutors of the Church did not escape the chastisement of heaven. For while they were disputing on Church affairs, the Persians on the one side, and the Barbarians on the other, wrested from their possession the so-called Greek popedom, till finally the Turks and Saracens completely overturned forever the rotten throne of the Eastern empire.

83. Persecutions in the Middle Ages.

"Then Jesus saith to them: Render therefore to Cæsar the things that are Cæsar's; and to God, the things that are God's."—MATTHEW xxii. 21.

During the middle ages, many kings and princes of western Europe assumed the right to interfere in the government of the Church, and became its bitterest enemies and persecutors. They often nominated unworthy men to vacant bishoprics, and by artifice and violence sought to have them appointed and consecrated. The controversy about investitures between the popes and bishops

PERSECUTIONS IN THE MIDDLE AGES. 253

on one side, and the kings of Germany, France, and England on the other, lasted from 1074 till 1122. The most crafty and powerful of these enemies was Henry IV.,*

Henry IV. at Canossa.

Emperor of Germany who, after making his submission at Canossa to Pope Gregory VII., soon after violated his promises in the most disgraceful manner, the haughty Henry II. of England, and Philip the Fair of France, persecuted the Church and her ministers, and trampled

---

* Canossa was a strongly fortified castle, belonging to the noble marchioness, Matilda of Tuscany. Henry IV. came to this place of his own free will, as a penitent, to receive from the Pope absolution from the sentence of excommunication. Frivolous and superficial writers pretend to see in this proceeding a proof of the Pope's thirst for power, and an instance of his hard-heartedness. But even many Protestant writers of intelligence and discernment have acknowledged that the proceeding redounds to the credit of Pope Gregory VII., who showed himself a strong defender of principle, in opposition to an ambitious, yet weak and vacillating king.

upon her rights. Many episcopal chairs were dishonored by interlopers whom these monarchs, of their own accord, created bishops, while many monasteries were spiritually and temporally ruined by their so-called lay abbots; that is, by men who, without ecclesiastical training, and sometimes even without holy orders, were promoted by their sovereigns to the dignity of abbots in reward for services rendered to the State. These men appointed substitutes to exercise the duties of abbot, while they themselves, living sometimes in the monastery, but oftener out of it, squandered its revenues in profligacy and dissipation.

Amid the struggles and persecutions of those times, the name of St. Thomas à Becket, Archbishop of Canterbury, is the only one we have room to mention from the long catalogue of the defenders of the Church. Henry II., King of England, had promoted this gentle and cultured man to the dignity of lord chancellor, in the hope of making him a tool for the furtherance of nefarious designs. But when the king attempted to invade the rights of the Church, the holy archbishop rebuked and thwarted him. The saint preferred to incur the king's displeasure, and to be banished by sentence of the high court, rather than to prove untrue to his episcopal dignity. The king seemed to regret his unjust proceeding, and permitted St. Thomas to return to his diocese. But not long afterward some courtiers and friends of Henry slew the bishop at the altar of his cathedral. "Cheerfully I suffer death for God's Church," he said to the executioners as they were about to strike off his head. He died on the 29th of December, 1170.

84. Modern Persecutions.

"Many have abused unto pride the goodness of princes, and the honor that hath been bestowed upon them, and not only endeavor to oppress the subjects, but to violate the laws of humanity."— ESTHER xvi.

The false principle advocated by the reformers of the sixteenth century, that the civil rulers are the proper authorities in religious matters, led to cruel persecution at the time of the Reformation, and for centuries later.

This interference in Church affairs on the part of the civil power was augmented to an alarming extent. The reformers, on the one hand, in order to forward their cause, sought the help of the princes, and in return for their protection, surrendered to them many of the most sacred rights and privileges of the Church. These renegade princes often employed fire and sword to force their subjects into the new religion. On the other hand, those princes who remained Catholics and protected their subjects against heretical innovations, claimed to be the indispensable guardians of the Church; and under pretext of protecting it, and improving gradually its condition, assumed every imaginable authority. They discontinued many episcopal sees, closed several convents for the mere purpose of appropriating their revenues to their own private use, and by means of new laws injured the freedom of the Church very materially. Thus, for example, the German emperor, Joseph II., oppressed the Church in some of her most sacred rights from 1780 to 1790. He suppressed monasteries, forbade pilgrimages and processions, and restricted the ceremonies even at mass.* In order to place the Church at the foot of the throne, he

---

* Hence the Protestant Frederick the Great styled him "Brother Sacristan."

assumed the direction of ecclesiastical seminaries, and the training of candidates for the priesthood.

In the year 1790 a fearful storm burst over the Church in France. The successful revolutionists confiscated all the property of the Church, and closed all the convents and monasteries. Priests who refused to subscribe to the

Pius VI.

violent measures of the new government were sent into exile or put to death. After the execution of King Louis XVI., in January, 1793, Christianity was declared abolished, the so-called goddess of reason was set up in the churches, and the blood of the faithful ran like rivers over the soil of France. The father of Christendom, Pius VI., died in exile in August, 1799.

When, in 1801, a concordat was agreed upon between Pius VII. and Napoleon I., the oppression of the Church seemed to be at an end. But persecution soon raised its head again, and Pius VII., deeming it necessary and proper to refuse his consent to the extravagant and unlawful demands of Napoleon, and finding himself at last compelled to excommunicate the emperor, was brought a prisoner to France, where he remained four long, tedious years in ignominious confinement, till the defeat of Napoleon at Leipsic.

85. The Church and the Governments in Modern Times.

"If then your delight be in thrones and sceptres, O ye kings of the people, love wisdom that you may reign forever."— WISDOM vi. 22.

Napoleon I., having fallen from the pinnacle of power, was himself exiled to the island of St. Helena, where he died on the 5th of May, 1821; while the Pope, released from prison, returned in triumph to the Eternal City. The crime committed by this once powerful emperor against the Vicar of Christ was avenged in the snows of Russia.* His nephew, Napoleon III., also learned by hard experience that God does not permit his Church to be persecuted with impunity. After having for many years played a game of double dealing between the Vicar of Christ and the Revolutionists, he at last showed his true colors, and withdrew from Rome the French, soldiers

* When Pope Pius VII. uttered the sentence of excommunication against Napoleon, he laughingly inquired of his officers whether this sentence would paralyze the arms of his brave soldiers? It is remarkable that the history of his Russian campaign says: "The intense cold caused the arms to drop from the benumbed hands of the soldiers."

placed there by the French nation to protect Pius the Ninth. But on the very day, when the first detachment of his soldiers left Rome, the 4th of August, 1870, France lost the battle of Weissenburg. On the 2d of September, the tenth anniversary of his treacherous alliance with Victor Emmanuel against the Pope, he lost crown and freedom, to die in exile three years later.

Most trying persecutions overtook the Church in Italy, and, indeed, in most European countries, during the subsequent years.

Have princes and would-be statesmen profited by these examples? Alas! the history of the Church in modern days speaks the contrary; and even to-day, men in power seem to find no other enemy to meet in battle but the Church of Christ.

The religious houses are the next point of attack for the persecutionists. These sacred and peaceful retreats, and seats of piety and learning, seem to be objects of special dislike to the demon of unbelief. By means of falsehood, ridicule, and calumny, the unsuspecting people are first prejudiced against these religious institutions, and then, when the measures are all taken, and the people are demoralized, the mighty ones in the government, under pretence of its being the people's wish, and that the good of the State requires it, proceed to the ruthless invasion and suppression of these sacred abodes of faith, learning, and charity. The old consecrated halls, the products of our forefathers' generosity, are then perverted into penitentiaries, factories, or insane asylums. In many places, the freedom of bishops and pastors in the exercise of their duties is restrained by iniquitous laws; while the State, although publicly and fundamentally proclaiming its disbelief in all religions, still would arrogate to itself the selection and appointment of pastors of souls. The Church, that ancient and experienced schoolmistress of nations, is rudely and unjustly deprived of her right to direct the schools; and for no other purpose than to keep the tender children, whom the Saviour would have to come to him, in ignorance of the doctrines and precepts of that same divine friend of youth. In the colleges and universities, founded and supported as they have been from the revenues of the Churches, and by the generous bequests of our Catholic ancestors, we see the highest and most important positions intrusted to men of no belief, in order that our future lawyers, physicians, and statesmen may imbibe in the very bloom of their youth the poison of godlessness and of hatred for religion. By the enactment of unprincipled and unconstitutional laws, marriage, which is the very foundation of all society, is stripped of its sublime character of a Sacrament, and reduced to the level of a mere civil contract.

Moreover, whilst governments and law-makers thus circumscribe, oppress, and persecute the Church and religion, they concede to an evil press the most unrestricted license, and in many instances afford it governmental assistance and protection at the expense of the taxpayers. Countless copies of unprincipled newspapers, of tracts, pamphlets, almanacs, and magazines are circulated from house to house. The unsuspecting head of a family is persuaded that it is a proof of education, and very necessary to his success in life, to read the advanced newspaper of the day and to cause his children to do the same. And alas! what are the ordinary contents of these so-called progressive journals? They contain the poison of evil and soul-destroying principles, the filth of obscene anecdotes and indecent stories; ridicule for the Church, and even formal blasphemy. Many a Christian, blinded by the evil spirit of the times, pays for this literature with money earned by the sweat of his brow, and yet hopes and intends to be able to die a good Christian and a true Catholic.

The Popes of later years, especially the late Pius the

Ninth, and his illustrious successor, Leo XIII., have raised their voices in solemn protest against these persecutions of religion on the part of governments, of false science, and of an unprincipled press. And what return did the Vicars of Christ meet with? None other but the same that was made long ago to Jesus Christ, the King of Martyrs; and to St. Stephen, the firstling among the martyrs of the Church. As the Jews of old expelled the Redeemer of the world from the city of Jerusalem, and led him to Calvary for crucifixion; as they dragged St. Stephen out of the same city in order to stone him to death; in a very similar manner have the great powers of the earth, in collusion with the Revolutionary element of society, labored for many years to expel the Pope from the holy city of Rome, in order that he too might find his Calvary and death; "for," say they, "with the Papacy falls the Church; and with the Church the whole religion of Jesus Christ."

Such has been the history of the Church for eighteen hundred years. Fire and sword have been directed against her in vain; governments have opposed her; false science would tear her with its teeth; diplomacy has laid plans for her destruction; calumny would blacken her fair name, and even disloyal priests have given her the treacherous kiss of Judas. And now let us raise our eyes and scan the horizon of the world's history. Can we find in any age, or in part of the world, an institution which has been so persistently opposed as has been the Catholic Church? Nowhere, nowhere. Well then, in this unparalleled, unbroken persecution, we discover an incontestable and undeniable proof, that in the Catholic Church doth burn, really and truly and brightly, that divine Light which the darkness of the world has hated from the beginning; that Christ whom the world did nail to a cross, but who, in the very darkest hour of his trials, on the eve of his death, extended his arms over his faithful followers, saying to them, with courage and reliance upon God: "Amen, amen, I say to you that you shall lament and weep, but the world shall rejoice; and you shall be made sorrowful, but your sorrow shall be turned into joy. Have confidence: I have overcome the world."

CHAPTER X.

THE TRIUMPH AND GLORY OF THE CATHOLIC CHURCH.

JESUS CHRIST LIVES IN HIS CHURCH AS THE GLORIFIED CONQUEROR.

86. The Triumphant Existence of Nearly Nineteen Hundred Years.

"If this be the work of men, it will come to naught: but if it be of God, you cannot overthrow it."—ACTS OF THE APOSTLES v. 38.

THE congregation of all the Faithful on earth constitutes the Church militant or struggling. The glorified Elect in heaven form the Church triumphant. In each division of the Church Christ is the centre. As the Saviour, during his sojourn on earth, sometimes manifested his divine power in the midst of his humiliations, ignominy and persecution, so, too, in the Church militant, on earth, the triumph of Christ over his enemies is sometimes very positive and palpable.

Of all these triumphs, the most obvious and unquestionable is the prolonged and successful life of his Church for now nearly nineteen hundred years. Great teachers and philosophers in the world have meanwhile gathered disciples about them and founded celebrated systems and schools. All have disappeared. Ambitious men have distorted divine revelation, and founded for a time powerful and influential sects. These exist no longer, except as the dry branches of a withered tree. Mighty heroes have

CENTURIES OF TRIUMPHANT EXISTENCE. 263

fought their way to immovable thrones, and founded proud and haughty dynasties. They have perished, and are forgotten. Provinces and clans of people have confederated together, and formed mighty kingdoms and commonwealths. They have become dismembered, leaving only their name to history. Amid all these unceasing changes in human affairs, only one Power has remained unchanged and unchangeable during the long period of eighteen

Christ Triumphing over Death and Hell.

hundred years and more. One only kingdom has resisted dissolution, and defied destruction. That is the kingdom of Christ, the Catholic Church.

Though there has been growth, development, advancement, yet there has been no change. To those selfsame doctrines of faith in which the early Christians found such comfort, the Church, with her two hundred millions of followers in every quarter of the globe, still clings with invincible steadfastness. The self-same sacrifice which was offered up in the catacombs is still offered in all the Catholic Churches throughout the world. The same seven sacraments which sanctified our forefathers make us, to-day, partakers in the atonement of Christ. Around the present reigning Pontiff, Leo XIII., the multitude of believers gather, animated with the same sentiments of obedience that moved the Apostles and the other early Christians to gather about St. Peter. Another evidence that the power and influence of the Church are still undiminished, may be seen in the fact that not only Catholics, but more especially heretics and atheists, in their writings and in their public measures, always consider and recognize the existence of the Catholic Church.

"The Lion of Judah hath conquered," and he shall ever continue to conquer and triumph in his Church, till he attain the last and greatest crowning victory on the day of judgment. Can there be any more wonderful, glorious, decisive, and convincing victory on the part of the Church than the plain and obvious fact of her present existence among men, without a change in her doctrine or in her nature—as full of life and youthful vigor as in the days of the Apostles, directing and consoling the hearts and souls of millions of the noblest and best of men? Is not her very existence upon earth a crowning victory, after eighteen hundred years of the most deadly opposition from the world, from hell itself, from political powers, from error, unbelief, and false knowledge? Certainly, that ancient doctor of the law, Gamaliel, mentioned in the Acts of the Apostles, uttered prophetic words when, rising up in the high council, he exclaimed: "If this work be of men, it will come to naught: but if it be of God, you cannot overthrow it, lest perhaps you be found even to fight against God." [Acts v.] For nineteen centuries the powers of hell have waged war against this work, but they have not yet destroyed it. This fact constitutes the first glorious victory of our holy Church.

87. The Triumph of the Church in her Martyrs.

"Death is swallowed up in victory. But thanks be to God, who hath given us the victory, through our Lord Jesus Christ."— 1 CORINTHIANS xv. 54, 57.

Christ in the very moment of his deepest humiliation, by his death on the cross, won a victory over the great ones of this world. This victory won in blood he continues to repeat in the Martyrs, the bleeding witnesses to the truth of his Church.

The world employs all the ingenuity that hatred suggests, and all those means at which humanity shudders, in order to estrange the Faithful from Christ and his Church. Sword and gibbet, fire and wild beasts, everything that hell could invent to torture and kill, have all been employed against the confessors of Christianity, as well by individual tyrants as by fanatical nations. But behold! With a supernatural fortitude have these victims of cruelty mocked at all these torments, and thereby proved that a still higher mysterious power bore them up. Overcome at this spectacle, their opponents—aye, even their very executioners—have thrown themselves at the martyrs' feet, confessed Christ, and shared their sufferings and death. Hence, as Tertullian writes, the blood of the martyrs became the seed of Christians, and the enemies of Jesus were compelled over and over again to acknowledge, with the ancient Pharisees, the victory and triumph of the Saviour of the world. "The Pharisees therefore said among themselves: Do you see that we prevail nothing? Behold, the whole world is gone after him."—John xii. 19.

Each century, from the time of Nero down to the present day, furnishes us with examples of Christian martyrdom. Thus, for example, the soil of Japan was as profusely saturated as any other land with the blood of the martyrs who suffered during the persecutions which broke out in 1596, and lasted for fifty years.*

In China, too, from 1795 to 1820, during the reign of the emperor Hiaking, thousands of Catholics suffered martyrs' deaths. At their head stands the valiant and and pious Vicar Apostolic, Dufresse. In Corea, in the year 1839, the French bishop, Imbert, with two of his brethren

The Monks of St. Bernard.

and about one hundred native Christians, secured the crown of martyrdom.

Each and every such glorious death of a martyr is a new and separate victory for the Church. For what is this invisible mysterious power before which the rage and might of error and unbelief is so shamefully abused and

* The solemn canonization of these Japanese martyrs took place in 1862, in Rome, at a great gathering of bishops from all parts of the Christian world.

thwarted but the truth of Christ, the grace of Christ, the law of Christ, the supernatural treasure which he has deposited in his Church?

Hardly less brilliant than the Church's triumph in the martyrdom of faith is that testimony furnished during all ages by the martyrs in the cause of charity or love of neighbor. All those heroic confessors, male and female, of the faith, who at the risk of their lives penetrated to the cells of the Christian martyrs, in order to comfort them, are themselves so many martyrs of charity, and their lives form a victory of the faith taught in the true Church.

Those monks who, for more than nine hundred years, have, generation after generation, imperilled their lives amid the wild passes of Mount St. Bernard, in order to save the lives of perishing travellers, are also martyrs of charity, a shining triumph in the Church. Such, too, are the brothers and sisters who risk their lives on the field of battle, or in the hospitals and asylums. Their sacrifice of life, for the sake of Christ and his Church, is a continuous and repeated victory, a never-ceasing song of triumph, an indubitable proof of the power of Christ in his Church.

88. The Triumph of the Church over Heathen Powers.

"And this is the victory which overcometh the world, our faith."—1 JOHN v. 4.

The pagan empire of Rome had existed for more than a thousand years, and had extended its power to nearly all the countries of the earth. But at last the day was dawning when divine Providence would bring this power to the feet of Christ, and grant to His Church her proud victory over heathendom. The agent made use of by God for this purpose was Constantine the Great, the first among the Roman emperors to embrace the truth. This famous ruler, who possessed all the talents of a successful general and all the wisdom of a prudent legislator, was led into the bosom of the Church by an extraordinary manifestation of divine Providence. Although he had acquired a knowledge of Christianity in his early years, both from his devout mother, the empress Helen, and from his intercourse with the Christians who were found in large numbers in the imperial court of his pagan father, Constantius Chlorus, and was thus to a great extent pre-

Constantine the Great.

pared to receive the teachings of Christ, yet it was only on the occasion of his great victory at the Milvian bridge, on the 3d of October, 312, that he permitted himself to be finally conquered by the cross. With a very inferior force he had marched against the pretended emperor Maxentius, and gave him battle near the Milvian bridge, just before the gates of Rome. Constantine saw with extreme anxiety the very superior forces of his formidable opponent, and his heart was filled with sad forebodings of an unfavorable result; when, happening to raise his eyes to the clouds, he beheld in the sky a brilliant cross bearing the inscription, "*In Hoc Signo Vinces.*" "By this Sign thou shalt conquer." Admonished by this extraordinary vision, Constantine at once attached the sign of the cross to the imperial flag, and soon gained a brilliant and decisive victory over his opponent. Immediately all the cruel and bloody edicts against the Christians were repealed, the religion of Christ was recognized by the State, and glorious temples were erected for its worship.

The correctness of views held by Constantine, on the proper relations between Church and State may be inferred from his remarks at the first General Council at Nice. From his position amid the bishops, and which they had accorded to him, he said: "God has placed you as leaders of the Church; me He has appointed merely to protect and defend its temporal part.

Once more, in 323, paganism raised its head, under the pretender Licinus, in the hope of wresting Christendom from Christianity. On the morning of decisive battle, Licinus first offered sacrifice to the false gods, and then addressed his army, saying: "This day will make known whether we or the Christians are in error. It will decide between our gods and their crucified God." But he was defeated by Constantine, for the fortunes of war turned in favor of the Christians and their God. The efforts of Julian the Apostate, from 361 to 363, had a similar ending. This man, a nephew of Constantine, endeavored to restore paganism. But he was specially desirous to render false the prophecy of Christ concerning the Temple of Jerusalem. Hence he twice issued to rebuild it, but his designs were thwarted completely, and conquered by the Persians, he cried out, as he was dying: "Thou hast conquered, O Galilean!"

Thus the Roman power, after having waged war against Christ for centuries, finally bowed down before Christ's standard, the holy cross; and the spouse of Christ, his holy Church, had won another glorious victory.

89. Triumph of the Church over the Barbarians in the Days of the Northern Invasions.

"I will bring unto thee Sisera, the general of the army, and his chariots and all his multitude, and will deliver them into thy hand."
—JUDGES iv. 7.

Those invasions of the barbarians, which a century and a half after the death of Constantine were the cause of the downfall of the Roman empire, had already begun. Countless hordes of uncivilized tribes; namely the Suevi, Saxons, Goths, Huns, and Vandals, came from the inhospitable regions of western and northern Europe, and overran the southern countries in search of plunder and of fairer lands, spreading carnage and devastation on all sides. Torrents of blood, heaps of slain, and smoking ruins, marked the paths pursued by these ruthless invaders in their victorious marches through Gaul, Spain, and Italy. And who was the first to succeed in subduing and pacifying these powerful, but rude and uncultivated people, whose descendants are now the inhabitants of civilized Europe? Who taught them to understand and to love peace and civilized life, and trained them in knowledge and the arts of industry? Who defended and preserved for future generations—who rescued from amid the general wreck caused by these incursions—the remains of all that civilization, literature, arts, and sciences brought to such perfection by ancient Rome? The Catholic Church proved herself to be the saviour of civilized Europe in those trying times. She, and she alone, won the grand victory over the barbarous invaders. And when we see these wild and uncultivated people transformed into gentle and peaceful tillers of the soil, clearing the forests, laying out roads, building bridges, founding towns and cities, cultivating even the arts and sciences, we see but the result of the tact, wisdom, and influence of the Church. It is an indisputable fact of history that the Catholic Church, through the unceasing energy and piety of her bishops, missionaries and monks, established order, social and political; education, liberty, prosperity, and morality upon the ruins of the ancient Roman empire, and thus saved Europe from lapsing into barbarism, idolatry, and superstition.

90. The Triumph of the Church in the persons of her great Pontiffs.

"He hath deposed the mighty from their seat."—LUKE i. 52.

In return for these benefits conferred upon society, the Church received but little thanks; for we read in the history of the middle ages, that proud emperors and haughty kings raised their hands in threatening attitude against her, and sought to deprive her of her well-earned privileges and rights, to despoil her of her liberty, and to rob her of her possessions. Often during those centuries do we see the Church prostrate in affliction and oppression, but still always protesting against wrong and injustice. Yet the cloud of adversity soon passes away, and we again behold her rising from the dust, clad in the shining garments of victory of her divine-human spouse, and witnessing in her turn the downfall of her adversaries. For the divine conqueror of death and hell prepared glorious victories for his Church, by raising up in the time of need heroic men to hold the keys of Peter: men against whose wise efficiency the billows of evil dashed themselves in vain. Thus in early Church history, from 440 to 461, we meet the great popes, Leo I. and Gregory I. In the year 1077, we find the unrighteous emperor Henry IV. of

Germany, when deserted by his false friends, coming in the garb of a penitent to meet Gregory VII. at Canossa, in order to seek protection at the hands of that Pontiff whom he himself had abused and persecuted but a short time previous. In the twelfth century we see Alexander III., whose firmness and goodness made such an impression

PIUS VII.

on the wayward monarch Frederic Barbarossa that he was willing to kiss the Pontiff's feet.

Pope Innocent III. (1198 to 1216) made the Papacy more powerful than ever. On the 24th of May, 1814, we behold the illustrious sufferer, Pius VII., returning amid shouts of welcome to the eternal city of Christendom, while almost at the same hour his persecutor, the emperor

Napoleon I., was signing his papers of abdication in the Castle at Fontainebleau, which itself had been the prison of the now triumphant pope. From Gregory VII. to Pius VII. more than seven hundred years had intervened, and during that long and stormy period the Popes had won, by their wisdom, prudence, and indomitable courage,

His Holiness, Pope Leo XIII.

many signal victories over the enemies of Christ. Pius the Ninth of our own day won victories for the Church. History will call him Pius the Great, and his reign from 1846 to 1877 will be known as the age of Pius the Ninth. During his lifetime the enemies of the Church predicted; with Pius IX. the Papacy dies. On the 7th of February, 1877, the gray-haired Pontiff was called to his reward, and but thirteen days later the world resounded with the joyful cry, "Long live Leo XIII., Pope and King!" Catholics look with confidence on this "light from heaven."

"After a storm comes a calm, from night to day, from the cross to the crown," were the watchwords of the chosen pilots of Peter's bark.

91. The Triumphs of the Church over the Heresies.

"For I will give you a mouth and wisdom, which all your adversaries shall not be able to resist and gainsay."—LUKE xxi. 15.

The darkest of all the clouds that have ever passed over the bright disk of the Church were the clouds of heresy. But in this case, as in most others, the prophecy is verified: "From night to day, from cross to crown."

How often we have seen the holy successors of the Galilean fisherman presiding with wisdom, learning, and piety over the grand councils of the Church, and there winning glorious and decisive victories over heretics and their errors! The spectacle deserves our attention. A teacher of error arises. His new doctrines invariably flatter the senses and gratify the pride of men. Many persons, sometimes whole nations, and even priests and bishops, fall into the snare. The Church of God seems to totter towards complete ruin; her enemies are already rejoicing at her downfall. Anon a voice of authority is heard. The successor of St. Peter summons to his side, from every quarter of Christendom, the faithful and learned bishops of the Church, and together they discuss, often for months and even years, the disputed and denied dogmas of the Church. At last, in solemn session, the Fathers of the Church formulate for all time their inspired decisions, promulgate them to the world, and condemn the heretic and his errors. The world is astounded; and presumptuous and self-sufficient men of learning demur. Princes and statesmen pass enactments and issue protests against the decisions of the Fathers. The enemies of the Church are exasperated. But wait! one twelvemonth, or at most a few years elapse, and the storm has subsided; the opponents are silent; unity and peace once more prevail. What has become, for instance, of those men who in 1870 pronounced the Church as dying? Of the sect called "Old Catholics" hardly a dozen remain. The Church laments their disloyalty, but they have not weakened her. More than ever before she is the centre of all history, and even her enemies acknowledge her victory over the most recent assaults. The profane historian tries in vain to explain this result; while the believing Christian knows that it is Christ, the glorious Victor, who has secured this triumph to his Church. How many times has this grand scene been presented to the wondering eyes of men, from the days of the Council of Nice down to the glorious Council of the Vatican! It was not worldly wisdom that won the victory; "This is the victory which overcometh the world, *Our Faith.*" [1 John v. 4.]

Ever since the Catholic Church has become known to Americans, many of the best and purest as well as of the most learned among them have recognized her beauty and truth, and have sought, by entering her portals, to enkindle within their own individual souls the mysterious life of Christ, which they saw so strikingly reproduced in his one true Church. Among these only a few can be mentioned here, namely: Archbishops Bailey, Wood, and Eccleston; Bishops Gilmour, Young, Rosecrans, and Wadhams; Drs. Brownson and Ives; Rev. Fathers Hecker, Preston, Walworth, Deshon. Baker; Mother Seton, foundress of the Sisters of Charity, and many others.

92. The Triumph of the Church in her Conversions—The Converts.

"Saul, Saul, why persecutest thou me? It is hard for thee to kick against the goad."—ACTS OF THE APOSTLES xxvi. 14.

There are other victories too; choice and glorious and consoling, and won by Christ in his Church: namely, the return of many worthy men and women out of the slough of error to the bosom of their holy mother. It is not possible to enumerate these conversions, comprising the best men and women of all classes. Among them are eloquent orators, such as Joseph Emmanuel Veith, the preacher of the Cathedral in Vienna. Among the painters, Overbeck; the architect Häbsch; the theologian Stolberg; and many others.

Cardinal Newman.

England is especially the land of converts. In her metropolis mighty men, such as Cardinal Wiseman, proved to Englishmen that genuine love of liberty and civilizing knowledge are to be found chiefly in the bosom of the Catholic Church. Of the number of English converts we may form some idea from the fact that during the last fifty years, nearly four hundred Anglican ministers, among them Cardinals Manning and Newman, and more than five hundred of the students and professors, all learned men, have returned to the bosom of the Church of their forefathers. What influence has been at work to produce these countless illustrious conversions? Not indeed the lust of the flesh, nor greed, nor ambition, which have sometimes led weak and unfortunate Catholics away from their faith. No; it is the power of grace, the majesty, dignity, and beauty of the ancient Church that has brought them over. Many of these converts are men of education and refinement; while by far the greater number are men of unblemished lives and high intelligence, who have renounced friends, country, position, and ample means of livelihood; braved opposition, ridicule, and poverty, in order to obey the voice of truth and to heed the warnings of conscience. Many who had won fame and position among men, retired from the world in order to devote the remainder of their lives to prayer and penance in the cell of a monastery; interceding continually for the conversion of their still erring brethren. These are noiseless and bloodless, but precious victories for the Church, who whilst the enemies of light and truth are raging against her, in quiet and prayerful seclusion is multiplying her victorious laurels, all of which will deck her brow on the day of judgment.

Cardinal Manning.

93. The Triumph of the Church in the Arts and Sciences.

"Jesus spoke: I am the light of the world; he that followeth me, walketh not in darkness."—JOHN viii. 12.

Among the many countless and priceless treasures bestowed upon the human family by the goodness of its Creator, the arts and sciences take a prominent rank. But to the Catholic Church is due a debt of gratitude for the care with which she has encouraged the arts and

The Cathedral of Cologne.

sciences, and preserved them against the destructive tendencies of thoughtless, uncivilized, and malicious men. Art has at all times found a fostering mother in the ancient Church. The homes of her bishops, the halls of her cloisters, have always been thrown open to the artist. The Popes always endeavored to draw around them men of skill and cultivation, and to encourage and elevate them in the pursuit of their refined calling. In fact, where could the artist find himself more at home than in the beauteous precincts of the Church? The heavenly doctrines there proclaimed, the sacred story there related, the sublime and significant festival there celebrated, the solemn service, the very building itself in which the adoring worshippers kneel in silent prayer or raise their united voices in praise to the great Creator—these are themes well calculated to inspire the genius and awaken the enthusiasm of the poet, painter, musician, and architect. Hence, it was by true sons of the Church, devout Catholics, that those immortal works of art were produced, which even the heretical and unbelieving tourists are to-day compelled to pronounce beyond imitation.

In the department of music, the reader may recall the names of the founders of the majestic old Church chants; more especially the name of Gregory the Great, and later of Palestrina, Allegri, Cherubini, Mozart, Haydn, Lambillotte, and countless others of hardly less merit.

In ancient Catholic poetry, we possess such brilliant writers as Sts. Ambrose, Prudentius, Paulinus, and Sedilius. Later on, we have the devout poets of the middle ages, Conrad of Queenfort, John of Salzburg, Lopez, Calderon, Dante, Tasso, Chaucer, Spenser, Shakespeare, and many others.

Among the Catholic painters, we remember with pride Fiesole, Da Vinci, Raphael, Voneyck, Vandyke, Dürer; and in subsequent years, an endless array of painters, down to the devout and artistic Overbeck.

In the line of sculpture, the Church justly claims as her children, Pisano, Buonarotti, Schonhofer, Kraft, Styrlin, Canova, and many others.

To the skill and taste of Catholic architects, we are indebted for the stately and enduring monuments that rise in glorious proportions in almost every country in Europe.

A Church that has begotten, trained, and educated such a race of giant minds and intellects, should not certainly be taunted as the enemy of the arts and sciences.

The Catholic world in all ages has been prodigal in affording encouragement to genuine art.

The same is true with regard to Christian science. Ignorant and insolent writers and speakers call our beloved Church the enemy of science and enlightenment. But they forget intentionally all that the Church in her motherly love and solicitude has done for the education of her children, all that she is still doing. They fail to remember, or refuse to admit and to proclaim, that during long and troublesome centuries science had no protection or shelter save what it found in monasteries, churches, and cathedrals. They forget that those renowned seats of learning, the great universities of Europe, were to a great extent founded and maintained by popes and bishops, who by ecclesiastical regulations, liberal endowments, and many rights and privileges, have rendered these seats of learning the pride of all Christendom. These renowned Catholic men, so deeply versed in every department of science; the immortal achievements which they have bequeathed to posterity; the long-continued and successful, and eminently useful prosperity of the schools of learning which she called into existence, form but a portion, though a grand and proud one, of the triumph which Christ her founder and the "Light of the World," has achieved over darkness and ignorance. They forget that the most accomplished scholars and the deepest thinkers sprang from the bosom of the mother Church.

Conclusion.

THE TRIUMPH OF THE CHURCH ON THE LAST DAY.

"It triumpheth crowned forever, winning the reward."—Wisdom iv. 2.

Although no man can question all these triumphs of the Church, yet she must ever continue to be, here below, the Church militant, and be willing and ready to undergo all those humiliations and persecutions which her divine Founder was willing to accept during his life on earth. But on that great and glorious day, on which, at last, the weary conflict shall be brought to a final close, death be forever vanquished, and when the cross of Christ shall shine resplendent with celestial glory above the nations of the earth on the great Judgment Day, the Church militant will win her last permanent triumph, and become for all eternity the Church triumphant in heaven.

The history of early Christianity furnishes us with a feeble, though true and edifying picture of the great triumph which the cross—that is, the Church of the Crucified—will celebrate on the last day. In the year 326, the pious empress Helena, who from childhood had cherished in her soul the laudable design of recovering the holy cross upon which our blessed Lord and Redeemer had consummated man's redemption, set out, followed by the best wishes of her son Constantine the Great, and the prayers of all her Christian subjects, from her own country on her way to the holy city of Jerusalem. But alas! on arriving at her destination, she discovered that the places which had been once consecrated by the passion and death of Christ, had for more than two hundred years been desecrated by the heathens. The pagan emperor Adrian, in order to show his contempt for the teachings of the Cross, had permitted an idolatrous temple to be built on Mount Calvary. Relying confidently on divine assistance, the pious empress had the temple pulled down, the rubbish removed, and excavations made; till at last the grotto of the holy sepulchre was discovered, and lying near it were three crosses, with the nails and the inscription. This inscription having become detached from the cross, the question now arose which of the three was the cross of Christ. In this emergency, Macarius, the holy bishop of Jerusalem, conceived the idea of carrying the three crosses to a well-known pious lady of the city who was lying dan-

The Finding of the True Cross.

gerously ill. In presence of the empress and several court-attendants, two crosses were applied to the person of the invalid, but without any result. Hardly, however, had the third cross touched her, when she felt new life coursing vehemently through her hitherto withered and paralyzed limbs, and she arose immediately from her bed in the full enjoyment of health and strength. Who can conceive the joy that must have thrilled the heart of the pious empress and other witnesses of this miracle? The cross of Jesus, which was once a folly to the Gentiles and a stumbling-block to the Jews; the cross of Christ, once the sign of shame and disgrace; the cross of Christ, which for centuries had lain concealed in dishonor beneath the temple of Venus, now came forth from its obscurity to be lifted up in honor and triumph before the eyes of the nations. And while the grateful empress embraced the sacred wood with unspeakable reverence and consolation,

The Glories of the Final Triumph of Our Lord.

and the holy bishop Macarius proclaimed the wondrous works of God, a thrill of joyful gratitude ran through the hearts of the multitude, who with one accord raised their voices in joyful praise and shouts of triumph for Him who by his death on the cross had conquered sin and hell.

If then the Cross of Christ was thus victorious and triumphant in those days; if it is still so to an eminent degree even in our day of strife and oppression, how transcendently glorious will be its triumph on the day of judgment, when it shall appear in dazzling splendor above the heads of all mankind! The glories of this last great triumph of our crucified Lord, and of his persecuted Church, have been vividly portrayed by St. John the Evangelist in his book of Revelations:

"After these things, I heard as it were the voice of much people in heaven, saying: Alleluia! salvation and glory and power is to our God. And the four and twenty ancients and the four living creatures fell down and adored God that sitteth upon the throne, saying, Amen! alleluia! And I heard as it were the voice of a great multitude, and as the voice of many waters, and as the voice of great thunders; and the voice of harpers and them that play on the pipe and on the trumpet. And they sang a new canticle: Alleluia! the Lord our God, the Almighty, hath reigned. Babylon is fallen, the great is fallen. Let us be glad and rejoice, and give glory to him; for the marriage of the Lamb is come, and his wife hath prepared herself. And it is granted to her that she should clothe herself with fine linen, glittering and white. For the fine linen are the justifications of the saints. And I saw the heaven opened, and beheld a white horse, and he that sat upon him was called Faithful and True, and with justice doth he judge and fight. And his eyes were as a flame of fire, and on his head were many diadems, and he had a name written which no man knoweth but himself. And he was clothed with a garment sprinkled with blood; and his name is called *The Word of God.* And the armies that are in heaven followed him on white horses, clothed in fine linen white and clean. And he hath on his garment and on his thigh written: King of Kings and Lord of Lords."

Such will be the day of the Lord, the day of his last, greatest, most signal, and most enduring victory.

RETROSPECT

OF

CHURCH HISTORY, ACCORDING TO AGES AND CENTURIES.

1. The Three Epochs.

THE whole period of time embraced in Church history may be divided into three *ages;* namely, Christian Antiquity, the Middle Ages, and Modern Times.

I. Christian antiquity covers the period from the birth of Christ to the reign of Charlemagne, about the year of our Lord 800. During the greater portion of this age, we find Christianity most flourishing chiefly among the ancients; that is to say, among the Greeks and Romans. We see the Church maintaining her position, through bloody conflict, for three hundred years, against the imperial power of mighty Pagan Rome, making that time the "Age of Martyrdom." During that same period, as well as during the following three or four hundred years, she preached and developed, though amid mighty conflicts with heretics and heresies, the saving truths which had been entrusted to her keeping. This was the "Age of the Church Fathers."

As early as the second part of the age of Christian antiquity, several strange peoples, chief among them the Germans and Franks, invaded the Roman Empire, bowed down before the Cross of Christ, embraced Christianity, and gradually, under the reign of Charlemagne, took their places in the history of the Church, in lieu of the ancients.

II. During the Middle Ages, Christianity lived, acted, and flourished chiefly among these German and Romanesque* peoples. The apostolic chair of St. Peter's in Rome was the rallying-point, about which all these members of the various Christian families gathered together. Religious and civil life, Church and State, were, notwithstanding many a contest between Popes and Emperors, closely united together. The happy results of this union may be seen in the monastic life, and in the glorious monuments of religious architecture which even now awaken our admiration ; also in the Crusades and in the Orders of Knight-errantry, and in the renowned and crowded universities of learning.

III. Modern times in Church history usually take their date from the so-called Reformation. It has been a period of resistance to lawful authority on the one side, while on the other side it has been a time of most intimate and faithful adhesion of the true and stanch Catholics to their ancient Church. Social and civil life have been constantly losing their Christian character ; while the Church, on the contrary, in the midst of persecution, has been strengthening herself from day to day in her inner life, in preparation for the time when the nations of the earth, warned by the chastisements of Heaven, shall seek within her pale help, safety, and renewed vitality.

---

* The Romanesque people were those people in France, Spain, and Italy who sprang from the mingling of the Germans with the ancient Romans.

The First Century,

OR

THE CENTURY OF THE APOSTLES AND THEIR DISCIPLES.

A.D.

34 The Coming of the Holy Ghost on Whitsunday (page 17). The Rise and Growth of the First Christian Congregation (page 27). St. Peter converts 3000 persons on one day, and 5000 on another (page 29). Conversion of St. Paul (page 32).

36 St. Stephen the First Martyr is stoned to death (page 189).

39 St. Peter converts Cornelius the Centurion (page 29).

42 The Apostles go forth as Missionaries to all lands (page 41).

51 The Council of the Apostles at Jerusalem (page 124).

54–58 St. Paul preaches at Ephesus, Macedonia, Illyria, and Greece (page 35).

67 St. Peter and St. Paul are put to death by the Emperor Nero (pages 31 and 40).

70 Destruction of Jerusalem by the Romans under Titus (page 247).

95 St. John the Evangelist is cast into a caldron of boiling oil, from which he comes out uninjured (page 41). Beginning of the Gnostic heresy (page 216). After the Apostles appear Sts. Titus, Timothy, Clement, Ignatius, Polycarp, and the holy men who received the doctrines of salvation and their Apostolic Missions directly from the Apostles themselves. Persecutions of the Christians by the Jews, pagans, and the Emperors Nero and Domitian (pages 245 to 250).

The following are the four Popes who reigned during the first century:

	DIED		DIED
1. St. Peter	67	3. St. Cletus	90
2. St. Linus	78	4. St. Clement	100

The Second Century,

OR

THE CENTURY OF THE CHRISTIAN APOLOGISTS.

A.D.

107 St. Symeon, Bishop of Jerusalem, and St. Ignatius, Bishop of Antioch, are put to death (page 116).

125 to 180 Quadratus, Aristides, Justin, Athenagoras, Tatian, Theophilus, Tertullian, and other illustrious Apologists, by their writings and by word of mouth, ably and successfully deny and refute the unfounded calumnies uttered by the pagans against the Christians; such as being Atheists, or despisers of the Deity, traitors, murderers, and the like. The Founding and Growth of the Church in Asia (page 55), and in Africa at Alexandria and Carthage (page 60); also in Italy, Spain, France (page 45), England (page 47), and the Rhine Countries (page 50). The Gnostics arise. The chief abettors of this heresy are Basilides and Saturninus (about A.D. 125), Valentine, Marcion, and Bardesanes (page 217). The heretical moral reformer, Montanus (between 140–150), denies the co-operation of the Holy Ghost in the work of Christ. Praxeas (192–202) denies the doctrine of the Blessed Trinity. Violent persecutions against the Church under the Emperors Trajan, Adrian, Marcus Aurelius, and Septimus Severus (page 250).

The eleven Popes of the second century are:

	DIED		DIED
5. St. Anacle	112	11. St. Pius I	167
6. St. Evaristus	121	12. St. Anicetus	175
7. St. Alexander	132	13. St. Soter	182
8. St. Sixtus I	142	14. St. Eleutherius	193
9. St. Telesporus	154	15. St. Victor I	203
10. St. Hyginus	158		

The Third Century,

OR

THE CENTURY OF ORIGEN.

A.D.

202 Martyrdom of St. Irenæus (page 117).

203 Clement of Alexandria is succeeded by Origen. Among the men who, in the course of this century, amid the persecutions of the Christians by the Emperors Decius, Valerian, and Diocletian, keep the torch of Christian knowledge burning brightly, thereby exerting a decisive influence on their contemporaries and posterity, we find Origen, St. Cyprian, and Tertullian (pages 117 and 118); also countless anchorites and holy hermits, such as St. Paul of Thebes (page 196).

227 The Persian Manes (page 217) teaches Manichœism, the doctrine that there are two Eternal Beings, Light and Darkness, constantly warring with each other for supremacy.

230 Martyrdom of St. Cecilia (page 211).

240 Death of Tertullian, who in his later years is led astray from the Church by the doctrines of Montanus (page 118).

249 Death of Origen (page 118).

250 St. Antony, the first Hermit (page 158). The cities of Toledo, Leon, Tarragona, Cordova, and Elvira, in Spain, become bishoprics (page 45).

258 Martyrdom of St. Cyprian (page 118).

The fifteen Popes of this century are:

	DIED		DIED
16. St. Zephyrinus	220	24. St. Stephen I	260
17. St. Calixtus I	227	25. St. Sixtus II	261
18. St. Urban I	233	26. St. Dionysius	272
19. St. Pontian	238	27. St. Felix I	275
20. St. Anterus	239	28. St. Eutychian	283
21. St. Fabian	253	29. St. Caius	296
22. St. Cornelius	255	30. St. Marcellinus	304
23. St. Lucius I	257		

The Fourth Century,

OR

THE CENTURY OF THE GREAT CHURCH FATHERS.

A.D.

305 The celibacy of the clergy is made a fixed law by the bishops assembled at the synod of Elvira (page 141).

307 Martyrdom of St. Catharine (page 213).

312 Victory of Constantine the Great (page 268). With Constantine ends the "age of Martyrdom," and begins "the period of the Great Fathers of the Church." Within this century occurs the glorious period of Sts. Athanasius, Hilarius, Ephrem, Cyril of Jerusalem, Epiphanius, Basil, Gregory of Nyssa, Gregory Nazianzen, Chrysostom, Jerome, Ambrose, and partly of St. Augustine (pages 119–122).

313 Bishops assembled at Rome pronounce judgment against the Donatists, who held that baptism is invalid if conferred by a heretic.

325 First General Council at Nice (page 125), at which the Arian heresy is condemned (page 218).

328 St. Athanasius, at the age of thirty, is made Archbishop of Alexandria (page 118).

340 Death of Eusebius, Bishop of Cæsarea, the father of Church history.

356 Death of St. Antony, founder of monastic life (page 158).

361 Julian the Apostate becomes Emperor (page 269).

381 Second General Council at Constantinople, in which the Errors of Macedonius against the Divinity of the Holy Ghost are condemned (page 125).

386 Death of St. Cyril of Jerusalem (page 119).

387 Death of St. Monica, mother of St. Augustine (page 210).

390 Contest between St. Ambrose (page 119) and the

Emperor Theodosius, in which the latter submits and does penance for his crime.

During this century Ufila, bishop of the Western Goths, translates the Bible into Gothic.

The eleven Popes of the fourth century are:

	DIED		DIED
31. St. Marcellus I.	309	37. St. Liberius.	363
32. St. Eusebius.	311	38. St. Felix II.	365
33. St. Melchiades.	314	39. St. Damasus.	384
34. St. Sylvester I.	337	40. St. Siricius.	398
35. St. Marcus.	340	41. St. Anastasius I.	402
36. St. Julius I.	352		

The Fifth Century,

OR

THE CENTURY OF POPE LEO THE GREAT.

A.D.

407 Death of St. John Chrysostom (page 122).

410 Rome is taken and plundered by the Goths under Alaric.

430 St. Augustine dies as the Vandals are invading Africa (pages 61 and 120).

431 Third General Council, held at Ephesus (page 125), declares in opposition to Nestorius that there is but one person in Christ, and not two separate persons, and establishes and confirms the dignity of the Blessed Virgin Mary as Mother of God (page 220).

432 St. Patrick adds Ireland to the list of Christian nations (page 48).

440 Pope Leo I., who, during the pontificate of Popes Celestine I. and Sixtus III., though only in deacon's orders, wielded a great influence, is made Pope, and becomes in the hands of God an instrument to protect and honor the Church during the decay of the Roman Empire and the invasions of heathens and the assaults of the Arians (page 270).

A.D.

444 Death of the holy Father of the Church, St. Cyril of Alexandria (page 119).

449 Pope Leo the Great meets Attila, and saves Italy (page 149).

451 Fourth General Council, at Chalcedon, declares against the heretic Eutyches (page 220), and defines the revealed teaching of faith that in Christ there are two distinct natures, the divine and the human, hypostatically united in one divine person (page 125).

476 Fall of the Roman Empire in the West, under the Emperor Romulus Augustulus.

494 Feast of the Purification is introduced into the West by Pope Gelasius (page 109).

496 Conversion and baptism of the French King Clovis (page 46).

The eleven Popes of the fifth century are:

	DIED		DIED
42. St. Innocent I.	417	48. St. Hilary	468
43. St. Zozimus	418	49. St. Simplicius	483
44. St. Boniface I.	423	50. St. Felix III.	492
45. St. Celestine I.	432	51. St. Gelasius I.	496
46. St. Sixtus III.	440	52. St. Anastasius II.	498
47. St. Leo I. The Great	461		

The Sixth Century,

OR

THE CENTURY OF ST. BENEDICT.

529 St. Benedict, by his monastic rule, which is the foundation of monasticism in all ages of the Church, as well as by his founding of the Benedictine Order, works undying good for the civilization of Europe, for the development of the Church, and for the salvation of souls (page 161). With Pope St. Gregory I. he shares the glory of this century.

A.D.
553 Fifth General Council at Constantinople (page 126).
560 Council of Tours and that of Macon (586) enforce the offering of tithes (page 144).
565 St. Columkille carries the faith to Scotland (page 48).
570 Birth of Mohammed (page 57).
596 St. Augustine and forty missionaries found the Church in England (page 47).
597 Death of St. Columkille (page 48).

During this century the Western Goths in Spain, the Burgundians in Eastern France, and partially also the Lombards in Northern Italy, abandon Arianism and join the true Church.

The fourteen Popes of the sixth century are:

	DIED		DIED
53. St. Symmachus	514	60. St. Silverius	538
54. St. Hormisdas	523	61. Vigilius	555
55. St. John I	526	62. Pelagius I	560
56. St. Felix IV	530	63. John III	573
57. Boniface II	532	64. Benedict I	578
58. John II	535	65. Pelagius II	590
59. St. Agapitus	536	66. St. Gregory I, The Great	604

The Seventh Century,

or

The Century of Mohammedanism.

610 Mohammed pretends to have *visions*.
611 Mohammed first appears as a public teacher, declaring "there is but one God, and Mohammed is his prophet" (page 57).
622 Flight of Mohammed from Mecca to Medina (page 57).
630 Mohammed marches on Mecca, and takes possession of the city (page 57).
632 Death of Mohammed (page 57). During this century

A.D.

the Mohammadans overrun Western Asia, Africa, and Spain (page 57), while the Church in the East is convulsed with unceasing theological disputes. Whilst agitated by the violent interference of the Byzantine Emperors in ecclesiastical questions, and tending towards decay, new Church life is awakened in England, Scotland, and Ireland. The faith is carried from Ireland to Germany and Switzerland (page 49).

637 The Mohammedans take Jerusalem.

680 Birth of St. Boniface (page 51). The Sixth General Council, at Constantinople, condemns the Monothelites.

The twenty Popes of the seventh century are:

	DIED		DIED
67. Sabinianus	606	77. St. Eugenius I	656
68. Boniface III	607	78. St. Vitalian	672
69. St. Boniface IV	615	79. Adeodatus II	676
70. St. Adeodatus I	619	80. Domnus L.	678
71. Boniface V	625	81. St. Agatho	682
72. Honorius I	638	82. St. Leo II	683
73. Severinus	640	83. St. Benedict II	685
74. John IV	642	84. John V	686
75. Theodorus I	649	85. Conon	687
76. St. Martin I	655	86. St. Sergius I	701

The Eighth Century,

OR

THE CENTURY OF ST. BONIFACE.

718 Zeal and activity of St. Boniface. He is authorized by Pope Gregory II. to evangelize the Germans (page 51).

723 St. Boniface is made bishop, and changes the name Winifred, which he received in baptism, to that of Boniface (page 51).

727 The Greek Emperor, Leo the Isaurian, and the heresy of Iconoclasm (page 222).

A.D.

742 King Luitprand gives Pope Zachary the city and province of Sutri as *the lawful property of St. Peter*, thus forming the nucleus of the "Temporal Power" (page 150).

752 Pepin the Small, son of Charles Martell and father of Charlemagne, is anointed King of France (page 52).

753 St. Boniface receives the martyr's crown (page 52).

770 Death of St. John Damascene (page 119).

787 Seventh General Council, at Nice, sustains and confirms the time-honored and pious veneration of images (page 223).

The twelve Popes of the eighth century are:

	DIED		DIED
87. John VI	705	93. St. Zacharias	752
88. John VII	707	94. Stephen II	752
89. Sisinnius	708	95. Stephen III	757
90. Constantine	715	96. St. Paul I	767
91. St. Gregory II	731	97. Stephen V	771
92. St. Gregory III	741	98. Adrian I	795

The Ninth Century,

OR

THE CENTURY OF THE GREAT SCHISM IN THE EAST.

800 Pope St. Leo III. crowns Charlemagne Roman Emperor; that is to say, constitutes him protector of the Church, and chief among the Christian princes in the West.

831 Paschasius Radbertus originates the first controversy on the Real Presence, in which John Erigena appears, as forerunner of Zwingli (page 236).

848 to 849 The monk Gottschalk renews the controversy on Predestination, holding that some persons have been preordained by God to be lost.

869 Eighth General Council, at Constantinople, exposes

and condemns the wickedness of Photius, who was seeking to separate the Eastern from the Western Church, in which attempt he was successful (page 223). During this century the Saxons, Northmen, Swedes, Norwegians, and Bohemians are converted (page 52).

The twenty-one Popes of the ninth century are·

	DIED		DIED
99. St. Leo III	816	110. John VIII	882
100. Stephen V	817	111. Marinus I	884
101. St. Paschal I	824	112. Adrian III	885
102. Eugenius II	827	113. Stephen VI	891
103. Valentine	827	114. Formosus	896
104. Gregory IV	844	115. Boniface VI	896
105. Sergius II	847	116. Stephen VII	898
106. St. Leo IV	855	117. Romanus	898
107. Benedict III	858	118. Theodorus II	898
108. St. Nicholas I. The Great	867	119. John IX	900
109. Adrian II	872		

The Tenth Century,

OR

THE CENTURY OF THE ASSAULTS ON THE CHAIR OF PETER.

A. D.

911 Rollo, the most skilful and daring of all the Norman chiefs, is converted and baptized under the name of Robert, and shortly after marries the royal princess Gisela. Robert and his successors protect the frontiers of the West-Frankish Empire from invasion by the Normans, religion flourishes, and the great French Benedictine monastery, which afterward exerts such a powerful and salutary influence, is founded at Cluny.

942 Death of St. Odo, Abbot of Cluny.

950 Hierotheus, first bishop of the Hungarians (page 53).

955 The Russian princess Olga (Helena) is baptized at Constantinople. Her grandson, Wladimir the Great, labors to establish Christianity among the Russians,

A.D.
962 The Polish Duke Mieczyslaw, through the influence of his wife, Dombrowka, is baptized.

972– Geisa, Duke of Hungary, begins to introduce Chris-
997 tianity into his States.

998 Odilo, Abbot of Cluny, adds to the feast of All Saints a commemoration of the souls of the faithful departed. Feast of All Souls (page 111).

The twenty-six Popes of the tenth century are:

	DIED		DIED
120. Benedict IV	903	134. John XII	964
121. Leo V	903	135. Benedict V	965
122. Christophorus	904	136. John XIII	972
123. Sergius III	911	137. Benedict VI	973
124. Anastasius III	913	138. Domnus II	973
125. Landus	914	139. Benedict VII	984
126. John X	928	140. John XIV	985
127. Leo VI	929	141. Boniface VII	985
128. Stephen VIII	931	142. John XV	996
129. John XI	936	143. John XVI	996
130. Leo VII	939	144. Gregory V	999
131. Stephen IX	942	145. John XVII	999
132. Marinus II	946	146. Sylvester II	1003
133. Agapitus II	956		

The Eleventh Century,

OR

THE CENTURY OF POPE ST. GREGORY VII.

1014 The saintly Henry II. is crowned Emperor of Germany (page 200).

1054 Second controversy on the doctrine of the Real Presence. Michael Cerularius completes the severance of the Greek from the Roman Catholic Church (page 223).

1059 To the College of Cardinals is given the right of electing the Popes (page 137).

1073 Hildebrand, a monk of Cluny, who for thirty-three years had exercised a powerful influence in the government of the Church, becomes Pope, as Gregory VII. As supreme Pontiff, he works with equal energy

A.D.

for the advancement of learning and piety among the clergy and for the liberation of the Church from civil encroachments. Rise of universities under the special influence and protection of the Church. Rise of Scholasticism.

1076 to 1077 — Henry IV. of Germany is excommunicated, and goes to Canossa to implore pardon of the Pope (pages 253 and 272).

1084 Bruno of Cologne establishes the Carthusians.

1085 Death of Pope Gregory VII.

1088 Death of Berengarius, who denied the doctrine of the Real Presence.

1095 Enthusiasm for the first Crusade preached by Peter the Hermit (page 163).

1099 Jerusalem captured by the Christians under Godfrey de Bouillon (page 164).

The eighteen Popes of the eleventh century are:

	DIED		DIED
147. John XVIII	1003	156. St. Leo IX	1054
148. John XIX	1009	157. Victor II	1057
149. Sergius IV	1012	158. Stephen X	1058
150. Benedict VIII	1024	159. Benedict X	1059
151. John XX	1033	160. Nicholas II	1061
152. Benedict IX	1044	161. Alexander II	1073
153. Gregory VI. (abdicated in 1046)		162. St. Gregory VII	1085
		163. Victor III	1087
154. Clement II	1047	164. Urban II	1099
155. Damasus II	1048		

The Twelfth Century,

OR

THE CENTURY OF THE CRUSADES AND OF THE KNIGHTS ERRANT.

A.D.

1118– to 1120 — Establishment of the Orders of Knight-Templars and of Knights of St. John (page 167).

1122 Agreement made between Pope Calixtus II. and the Emperor Henry V. of Germany, by which the free

THE TWELFTH CENTURY.

A.D.

      election of bishops is guaranteed to the chapters of the respective cathedrals, subject to the approval of the Pope (page 143).

1123 Ninth General Council, at Rome, declares and maintains the independence and freedom of the Church from the civil power of the Emperor (page 126).

1139 Tenth General Council at Rome condemns the seditious demagogue, Arnold of Brescia (page 126).

1147–1149 The Second Crusade is preached by St. Bernard (page 164).

1152 to 1190 The haughty Emperor Frederic Barbarossa opens a controversy between the Empire and the Papacy which lasts more than a hundred years.

1153 Death of St. Bernard (page 163).

1170 St. Thomas A Becket, the holy Archbishop of Canterbury, is murdered at the foot of the altar (page 254). Death of St. Isidore (page 205).

1179 Eleventh General Council, at Rome, in which the errors of the Albigenses and Waldenses are condemned (pages 126 and 225).

1189 to 1192 The Third Crusade (page 163).

    The seventeen Popes of the twelfth century are:

	DIED		DIED
165. Paschal II	1118	174. Adrian IV	1159
166. Gelasius II	1119	175. Alexander III	1181
167. Calixtus II	1124	176. Lucius III	1185
168. Honorius II	1130	177. Urban III	1187
169. Innocent II	1143	178. Gregory VIII	1187
170. Celestine II	1144	179. Clement III	1191
171. Lucius II	1145	180. Celestine III	1198
172. B. Eugenius III	1153	181. Innocent III	1216
173. Anastasius IV	1154		

The Thirteenth Century,

OR

THE CENTURY OF ST. FRANCIS AND ST. DOMINIC.

A.D.

During this century the Papacy attains great power under the pontificate of Pope Innocent III., who died in 1216 (page 168).

1204 The Fourth Crusade (page 163).

1215 Pope Innocent III. sanctions the Mendicant Order of St. Francis of Assisi (page 168), and that of St. Dominic (page 171). Twelfth General Council, at Rome, rejects the errors of Berengarius, which had before been refuted, and more firmly establishes and elucidates the true Catholic doctrine by the adoption of the term *transubstantiation*. At the same Council the dogmas of the Blessed Trinity and of the Incarnation of the Son of God, both of which have ever been taught and believed in the Church, are reaffirmed and clearly and briefly formulated (page 126). The obligation of yearly Confession, and of receiving Holy Communion at Easter, is imposed upon all (page 91).

1219– Fifth, Sixth, and Seventh Crusades, in the second of
1270 which St. Louis is taken prisoner (page 165).

1245 Thirteenth General Council, at Lyons, in which all Christendom is exhorted to take up arms and defend itself against the incursions of the Saracens (page 126).

1245 The Western Carmellites are enrolled among the Mendicant Orders.

1246 Institution of the Feast of Corpus Christi (page 103).

1250 Frederick II. of Germany is reconciled to the Church, and dies December 13.

1273
to   The pious Rudolph of Hapsburg is Emperor.
1291

THE THIRTEENTH CENTURY. 301

A.D.

1274 Fourteenth General Council, at Lyons, in which the ancient doctrine of the Procession of the Holy Ghost from the Father and Son is renewed and confirmed, and the union of the Greek and Roman Churches is established, to be severed again after a short time (page 127). St. Thomas of Aquin dies while on his way to this Council, and St. Bonaventure during its sitting.

1294 Pope Benedict VIII. has a contest with the insolent Philip the Fair of France, who is seizing the property and revenue of the Church.

During this century are founded the Universities of Oxford (1249), Cambridge (1257), Vicenza (1204), Padua (1222), Naples (1224), Vercelli (1228), Piacenza (1246), Treviso (1260), Ferrara (1264) Perugia (1276), Toulouse (1228), Salamanca (1240), and Lisbon (1290). The three oldest of the Universities, namely, of Paris, Bologna, and Salerno, though begun in the twelfth century, are very flourishing in this.

The seventeen Popes of the thirteenth century are:

	DIED		DIED
182. Honorius III.	1227	191. Adrian V.	1277
183. Gregory IX.	1241	192. John XXI.	1277
184. Celestine IV.	1241	193. Nicholas III.	1280
185. Innocent IV.	1254	194. Martin IV.	1285
186. Alexander IV.	1261	195. Honorius IV.	1287
187. Urban IV.	1264	196. Nicholas IV	1292
188. Clement IV.	1269	197. St. Celestine V (resigned)	1296
189. B. Gregory X.	1276	198. Boniface VIII.	1303
190. Innocent V.	1276		

The Fourteenth Century,

OR

THE CENTURY OF THE EXILES AT AVIGNON.

A.D.

1305 to 1378 Yielding to the pressure of France, the seven Popes from Clement V. to Gregory XI. reside at Avignon, in France. After the death of Gregory XI., two Antipopes lay claim to the Chair of Peter. The Council of Pisa (1409), in order to put an end to the schism, declares both elections, that in Rome and the one in Avignon, null and void, and elect Alexander V. Christendom is thus distracted into three divisions. The great schism lasts from 1378 to 1417.

1311 The Fifteenth General Council, in Vienne, abolishes the Order of Knight Templars, at the instance of Philip the Fair (page 167). The Fratricelli, Apostolicals, Beghards, and Beguines, associations which, though originally formed with pious and charitable intentions, fell into excesses, and even into heresy, are condemned.

1315 Raymond Lullus is martyred at Tunis (page 61).

1347 Cola di Rienzi, the tribune of the people, re-establishes the Roman Republic.

1349 The Black Plague, a malignant contagious fever, ravages Europe and leads to a revival of penitential severity. A body of religious, calling themselves Flagellants, go about scourging themselves in order to avert God's anger. Starting with the best of motives, they finally become presumptuous and self-sufficient, and rejecting with contempt whatever comes from the Church, they are suppressed.

1360 The heretic Wickliffe disquiets England (page 227).

1361- 1381 Death of the Mystics (page 226), Tauler (1361), Suso (1365), and Ruysbroch (1381).

1393 Murder of St. John Nepomucene (page 195).

The fourteen Popes of this century are:

	DIED		DIED
199. B. Benedict XI.	1304	206. Gregory XI. (restored	
200. Clement V. (at Avignon)	1314	See to Rome)	1378
201. John XXII. " "	1334	207. Urban VI.	1389
202. Benedict XII. " "	1342	208. Boniface IX.	1404
203. Clement VI. " "	1352	209. Innocent VII.	1406
204. Innocent VI. " "	1362	210. Gregory XII. (resigned	1415)
205. B. Urban V. " "	1370	211. Alexander V.	1410
		212. John XXIII. (resigned 1415)	

The Fifteenth Century,

OR

THE CENTURY OF GENUINE REFORMATION.

A.D.
1409 The Council of Pisa.

1414 The Sixteenth General Council, at Constance, in which the dismal divisions caused by the Anti-popes are healed and the errors of Huss and Wickliffe (pages 127 and 227) are condemned.

1419 John Huss is burned at the stake (page 227). Death of the great Dominican St. Vincent Ferrer.

1431 to 1449 Seventeenth General Council, at Basel. It is continued by that of Ferrara, in 1438, and of Florence, in 1439 (page 127).

1440 Invention of printing.

1453 Capture of Constantinople by the Turks (page 224).

1457 St. Francis of Paula founds the Order of Minims.

1492 Discovery of America (page 62). Overthrow of Saracens in Spain by Ferdinand the Catholic.

1494 An altar erected on the island of Hayti (page 69).

This century is fruitful in eminent holy men, as St. Vincent Ferrer, St. Bernardin of Sienna, St. Francis of Paula, Thomas A Kempis, author of "The Imitation of Christ," the learned theologian Gerson, the noble Cardinal Nicholas of Cusa, the great preacher John Geiler.

The nine Popes of this century are:

	DIED		DIED
213. Martin V.	1431	218. Paul II.	1471
214. Eugenius IV.	1447	219. Sixtus IV.	1484
215. Nicholas V.	1455	220. Innocent VIII.	1492
216. Calixtus III.	1458	221. Alexander VI.	1503
217. Pius II.	1464		

The Sixteenth Century,

OR

THE CENTURY OF SHAM REFORMATION.

A.D.
1512 The Eighteenth General Council, at Rome (page 127).

1514 Cardinal Ximenes publishes a polyglot Bible, contain-
to ing Hebrew, Chaldaic, Greek, and other versions.
1517 He also publishes dictionaries and grammars to aid in the acquiring of the biblical languages. This eminent man, at once a statesman, warrior, scholar, and saint, dies in 1517.

1517 To the process of genuine reformation succeeds a false one, not improving morals, but attacking ancient belief and practices; not harmonizing, but dividing Christendom (page 228). The so-called reformers Luther (page 234) and his friend Melancthon (page 240).

1515 Francis I. of France strives for Church unity in his
to own country, and at the same time helps the
1547 "Reformation" in Germany.

1518– Zwingli preaches against the Pope (page 236). John
1564 Calvin (page 237).

1521 Charles V. of Spain, Emperor of Germany, opposes the "Reformation."

1524 Gustavus Vasa, of Sweden, introduces Protestantism into his country.

1525 The Peasants' war, in which it is computed a hundred thousand men fell in battle, spreads throughout Germany.

1526 The Capuchins, a branch of the Franciscans, is founded by Matthew Bassi (page 170).

1527 The Catholics of Antwerp publish a polyglot Bible.

1529 The Turks before the gates of Vienna.

1531– Religious wars in Switzerland (1531), in Germany
1588 (1546), and in France (1562–1588) (page 240).

THE SIXTEENTH CENTURY. 305

A.D.
- **1534** Henry VIII. of England, who at one time defends the Church against Luther, now embraces Protestantism in order to freely indulge his passions. Luther publishes his Bible. The Anabaptists take possession of Münster, but are finally subdued, and their leader, John of Leyden, is executed (1536).
- **1535** St. Ignatius of Loyola founds the Society of Jesus, which is confirmed in 1540 by Pope Paul III. (page 173).
- **1536** Death of Erasmus, "the scholar of Rotterdam."
- **1537** Apostolic brief of Pope Paul III. against enslaving the American Indians (page 65). St. Angela Merici founds the Order of Ursulines (page 180).
- **1542** St. Francis Xavier carries the faith to the East Indies (page 58).
- **1545 to 1563** Nineteenth General Council, at Trent, in which the errors of the so-called Reformers are rejected and condemned (page 127).
- **1546** Death of Martin Luther (page 235).
- **1548** St. Philip Neri founds the Order of the Blessed Trinity, which later on takes the name of the Oratory.
- **1551** Blessed Peter Canisius labors for the faith in Austria. He succeeds in stopping the advance of heresy, and brings back to the Church most of those who had gone over to Protestantism. He renders great service to both clergy and laity by the publication (1554) of a Larger and Smaller Catechism, and is called to his reward in heaven in 1597.
- **1552** Death of St. Francis Xavier (page 59).
- **1555 to 1598** Philip II. of Spain contends for the unity of the Church, though sometimes with questionable means.
- **1556** Death of St. Ignatius of Loyola (page 173).
- **1558** Elizabeth becomes Queen of England, persecutes the Catholics, and beheads her cousin, Mary Queen of Scots.

A.D.
1562 to 1588 Huguenot wars in France (page 240).
1566 Death of Las Casas (page 64).
1572 The Massacre of St. Bartholomew's Day (page 240).
1579 The Socinians, a heretical sect, arise in Poland.
1582 Death of St. Teresa.
1584 Death of St. Charles Borromeo (page 193.)

The seventeen Popes of the sixteenth century are:

	DIED		DIED
222. Pius III.	1503	231. Pius IV.	1565
223. Julius II.	1513	232. St. Pius V.	1572
224. Leo X.	1521	233. Gregory XIII.	1585
225. Adrian VI.	1523	234. Sixtus V.	1590
226. Clement VII.	1534	235. Urban VII.	1590
227. Paul III.	1549	236. Gregory XIV.	1591
228. Julius III.	1555	237. Innocent IX.	1592
229. Marcellus II.	1555	238. Clement VIII.	1605
230. Paul IV.	1559		

The Seventeenth Century,

OR

THE CENTURY OF THE THIRTY YEARS' WAR.

A.D.
1607 Death of the Church historian Cardinal Baronius.
1610 The Visitation Nuns founded by St. Francis of Chantal.
1618 to 1648 For thirty years a religious war rages in Germany, which is concluded by a treaty known as the Treaty of Westphalia, the execution of which is guaranteed by France and Sweden, the two countries that had done most to ruin Germany (page 241).
1620 Death of the theologian Bellarmin.
1622 Death of St. Francis of Sales. St. Vincent of Paul founds the Order of Priests of the Mission or Lazarists.
1629 St. Vincent of Paul establishes the Sisters of Charity (page 182).
1630 Rationalistic Deism in England.
1637 Death of the great theologian Cornelius à Lapide.

A D.
1643 Louis XIV. becomes King of France.
1649 Lord Baltimore promulgates religious freedom to all settlers in his colony (page 63). Charles I. of England is made prisoner and beheaded.
1650 George Fox, an Englishman, founds the sect of the Quakers.
1658 Death of Cromwell, "The Protector," of England.
1660 Death of St. Vincent de Paul.
1662 The Order of Trappists founded by Bouthillier de Rancé.
1678 Bishop Francis Stephen, of Pamiers, is condemned by Louis XIV. to lose the temporalities of his diocese because he rebukes the king for unjust and despotic actions in his dealings with the Church.
1681 Father J. B. De La Salle founds the Society of the Christian Brothers (page 180).
1683 The Siege of Vienna by the Turks is raised by the Catholic king John Sobieski.
1697 The Peace of Ryswick declares that the Catholic religion shall remain in the German countries occupied by France.

The eleven Popes of the seventeenth century are:

	DIED		DIED
239. Leo XI	1605	245. Clement IX	1669
240. Paul V	1621	246. Clement X	1676
241. Gregory XV	1623	247. Innocent XI	1689
242. Urban VIII	1644	248. Alexander VIII	1691
243. Innocent X	1655	249. Innocent XII	1700
244. Alexander VII	1667		

The Eighteenth Century,

OR

THE CENTURY OF REVOLUTION AND OF ANTI-CHRISTIAN PHILOSOPHY.

A.D
1725 Pope Benedict XIII. convokes the Council of the Lateran for the repression of abuses.

A.D.
- **1729** John Wesley founds the sect of the Methodists.
- **1738** Pope Clement XII. issues a bill condemning the Order of Freemasons.
- **1732** The Congregation of the Most Holy Redeemer (Redemptorists) is founded by St. Alphonsus Liguori (page 175).
- **1753** France, where, during the reign of Louis XIV., the higher classes became addicted to unbelief and loose morals, becomes the theatre on which the pretended philosophers Voltaire, Rousseau, D'Alembert, Diderot, and other atheists and enemies of the Jesuits, chiefly in their great Encyclopædia, make war on Christianity and prepare the way for the Revolution.
- **1764** The Jesuits are suppressed and persecuted in France in 1764, in Spain in 1767, and in Naples in 1768.
- **1773** The Jesuits are suppressed by a brief of Pope Clement XIV. (page 174).
- **1775** The battles of Lexington and Bunker Hill the beginning of the struggle for American Independence. John Barry, an Irish Catholic, leads the first naval battle of the American Revolution (page 66).
- **1776** The United States declares its independence.
- **1780 to 1796** Joseph II. of Germany becomes the leader of the enemies of the Church, and favors Illuminism and Freemasonry. The electors of Mentz, Treves, and Cologne, and the Archbishop of Salzburg, forming the notorious Congress of Ems, draw up a protest, known as the *Punctuation of Ems*, in which they insist on absolute and unrestricted episcopal authority. This protest, aimed at the Holy See, is sent to Joseph II., who gives it his hearty approval (page 255).
- **1785** First Catholic congregation organized in New York (page 72).

A.D.
1789 Outbreak of the French Revolution (page 256). The National Assembly confiscates all Church property, and establishes a civil constitution for the clergy.

1790 Rev. John Carroll is made first Bishop of the United States.

1792 First Synod of the Catholic Church in the United States (page 72).

1793 Louis XVI. is beheaded by the revolutionists (page 256). Every vestige of Christianity disappears and the worship of the Goddess of Reason takes its place (page 256).

1794 Robespierre decrees the existence of a Supreme Being and the immortality of the soul. Pius VI. protests against all these acts, is made prisoner, and Rome is proclaimed a republic (1798).

1799 Pius VI. dies in exile at Valence (page 256).

The eight Popes of this century are:

	DIED		DIED
250. Clement XI	1721	254. Benedict XIV	1758
251. Innocent XIII	1724	255. Clement XIII	1769
252. Benedict XIII	1730	256. Clement XIV	1774
253. Clement XII	1740	257. Pius VI	1799

The Nineteenth Century,

OR

THE CENTURY OF THE SEPARATION OF THE FAITHFUL FROM THE UNBELIEVERS.

From the time of the French Revolution, but more especially during the thirty-two years' reign of the late Pius IX., opposition to all authority, with unbelief, immorality, and rebellion, is rampant on one side, while on the other, faith and religious steadfastness grow stronger among Catholics. The various

A.D.

sects, detached from the true faith, fall into infidelity; whilst the bonds of belief among the faithful are drawn closer than ever before.

1800 Pius VII. elected Pope at Venice.

1803 The principalities and possessions of the Church in Germany are secularized to compensate the civil princes for their loss of territory on the left bank of the Rhine.

1804 The Jesuits are restored in Naples. Pius VII. crowns Bonaparte Emperor (page 257).

1806 The States of the Church are incorporated into the French Empire. The Pope is made prisoner and carried away to Savona (page 257).

1808 The See of Baltimore is raised to an archbishropric.

1809 Daniel O'Connell becomes the leader of the Irish Catholic party.

1814 After the abdication of Napoleon Bonaparte, Pius VII. returns to Rome and issues a bull re-establishing the Jesuits. Soon after Napoleon's return from Elba, the Papal States are invaded by the French troops, and the Pope is again obliged to leave Rome. Napoleon is defeated at Waterloo, and sentenced to exile for life at St. Helena (page 257).

1815 The States of the Church are restored in the Vienna Congress (page 272). Religious and ecclesiastical revival in France by Chateaubriand, De Maistre, Lacordaire, and others.

1817 The Irish Emancipation Bill is rejected for the second time by the English Parliament.

1825- Persecution of Catholics in Poland and Russia,
1855 especially under the Emperor Nicholas I

1826 The Episcopacy in England ask for a repeal of the penal laws against Catholics.

1829 O'Connell is elected to Parliament. Passage of the Irish Emancipation Bill by the efforts of O'Connell.

A.D.	
1836	Dr. (afterwards Cardinal) Wiseman and O'Connell start the *Dublin Review*.
1843	John Henry Newman (now Cardinal) embraces Catholicity, and is followed in 1845 by Father F. W. Faber and Dr. (now Cardinal) Manning (page 276).
1846	Piux IX. begins his pontificate (page 244). Oregon City becomes an archbishopric.
1847	O'Connell dies while on his way to Rome. St. Louis becomes an archbishopric.
1850	Catholic hierarchy is re-established in England.
1854	The dogma of the Immaculate Conception is promulgated on the 8th of December (page 108).
1860	Massacre of the pontifical army near Castelfidardo (page 153). The States of the Church are reduced to the "Patrimony" of St. Peter (page 147).
1865	Death of Cardinal Wiseman.
1869	Twentieth General Council, at the Vatican, defines the Infallibility of the Pope a dogma of faith (pages 125–131).
1870	Rome taken by the Piedmontese army and the temporal power wrested from the Pope (pages 152 and 258).
1872 to 1874	Persecution of the Church in Germany, Switzerland, and Italy. May laws against the free exercise of Catholic worship. Expulsion of the religious orders from Germany, and of the Catholic Bishops from Germany (page 243). General persecution of the Catholic press in Europe.
1875	Archbishop McCloskey is made the first American Cardinal.
1877	The Golden Jubilee of Pope Pius IX.
1878	Death of Victor Emanuel. Death of the great Pius IX. (page 273). Election of Pope Leo XIII. (page 274). The Catholic hierarchy is re-established in Scotland.

A.D
1880 The Jesuits and other religious orders are banished from France.
1881 Hierarchy in Poland and Russia.

The six Popes of the nineteenth century are:

258. Pius VII., from 1800 to 1823.
259. Leo XII.,   "   1823 " 1829.
260. Pius VIII., "   1829 " 1830.
261. Gregory XVI., from 1831 to 1846
262. Pius IX.,   "   1846 " 1878
263. Leo XIII.

A SKETCH

OF THE

CHURCH IN AMERICA,

BY

JOHN GILMARY SHEA, LL.D.

THE FIRST MASS IN THE NEW WORLD.

THE CHURCH IN AMERICA.

CHAPTER I.

Spanish America—Iceland and Greenland—The Voyage of Columbus—Missions—A See founded at St. Domingo—The Church in Mexico, Central and South America—A Bishop Martyr to his Zeal—The Dominicans oppose Indian Slavery—Indian Missions—Saints in the Episcopate and in the Clergy and Regulars—Negro Slavery and Blessed Peter Claver—Brazil—Martyrs on the Sea—The Suppression of the Jesuits—The French Revolution—Revolt of the Spanish Provinces—Decline of Religion—Efforts of the Holy See—Pius IX. in America—The famous Shrines.

THE discovery of the New World by the pious Christopher Columbus opened a new continent to the Church. A priest of the ancient Order of St. Benedict accompanied the discoverer, and Mass was offered up in the West Indies to consecrate the new-found lands.

Nowhere else in the western world was the Christian faith spreading its light, except in Iceland, where a church, with a bishop and clergy, had subsisted for some centuries. Greenland had indeed received the faith, and a series of bishops had governed the Church there, but all had been swept away, and in 1492 only ruins remained to mark the spot.

As settlers poured over from Spain to colonize the West Indies and plant colonies on the mainland of North and South America, clergy, both secular and regular, came to minister to the Spaniards and to instruct the natives in the pure doctrines of Christ. The Church remembered the Divine injunction to go and teach all nations. The riches of the New World called out all the covetous feelings of the settlers, and the clergy had a great struggle to check vice of all kinds, and especially cruel oppression of the Indian tribes who inhabited the country. Churches were established in the West India islands, and an episcopal see was erected at Saint Domingo in 1513, and a few years after there were bishops at Yucatan and Santiago de Cuba.

When Cortez conquered Mexico, Father Bartholomew de Olmedo, of the Order of Mercy, and the Rev. John Diaz began their labors among Indians and whites. The former of these pioneers of the faith in North America soon won the crown of martyrdom. In 1527 Mexico received her first bishop in the person of Julian Garces, Bishop of Tlascala. The city of Mexico became a see in 1530, the first bishop being the Right Rev. John de Zumarraga.

Soon after, Central America had bishops at Nicaragua, Guatemala, and Panama; and, as the Spanish power advanced, episcopal sees were erected at Carthagena; and at Cuzco, the seat of the Inca power; and before the close of the sixteenth century there were bishops at Paraguay, La Plata, Santiago de Chile, and Buenos Ayres. The nominations to these sees were all made by the Spanish kings, to whom the Holy See granted extensive powers in America. The early bishops were almost all remarkable men—full of zeal, laboring earnestly to bring to orderly lives both rulers and people, who were alike in those wild times disposed to excess. They preached the Gospel fearlessly, and not without danger. One of them, the holy Bishop Valdivieso, of Nicaragua, actually died by the hand of a governor whom he rebuked. The Spanish monarchs assigned part of their revenues from mines for the erection of churches; the religious Orders sent colonies to the various provinces, establishing seminaries, colleges, hospitals; and a new Order, that of Bethlehem, for the care of the sick, arose in Guatemala, founded by the Venerable Peter de Betancurt.

The Church has ever been the protector of the poor

and afflicted. In America she threw her shield over the Indians; as early as 1511 the eloquent Dominican friar, Antonio de Montesino, one of the pioneer missionaries in this part of the New World, raised his voice at St. Domingo against the system of enslaving the natives, and the great Las Casas, Bishop of Chiapa, a religious of the same Order, devoted his whole life to relieve the Indians from oppression. Meanwhile throughout Spanish America, Dominican, Franciscan, Jesuit, and Augustinian religious were study-

Columbus Planting the Cross in America.

ing the almost countless languages of the aborigines; drawing up grammars and dictionaries for future missionaries, and compiling works in the native dialects for the instruction of Indian catechumens and converts. By these missions millions of the aborigines, not only in the half-civilized states of Mexico, New Granada, Peru, and New Mexico, but in the wildest and fiercest tribes of the wilderness, were won to Christianity. The great Jesuit missions of Paraguay, and subsequently the Franciscan missions in

California, remain in history as monuments of the zeal and laborious efforts of the missionaries, many of whom died by the hands of those to whom they bore the Gospel of peace.

The bishops founded seminaries, held provincial councils and diocesan synods: one, St. Turribius Mogrobejo, Bishop of Lima (1578–1606), is already canonized; and the process of Bishop Mendiola of Guadalajara (1571–76), Bishop Aguiar of Mexico (1681–98), and Bishop Palafox of Puebla (1640—55), were introduced at Rome, with the sanction of the Popes.

Led by such examples, clergy and religious showed similar fervor. St. Louis Bertrand labored for years in Columbia; St. Francis Solano in La Plata and Peru; the Blessed John Masias, Martin Porras and Sebastian of the Apparition, lay brothers of the Orders of St. Dominic and St. Francis, edified all by their holy life ; St. Rose of Lima and Blessed Mariana of Quito became models for holy virgins.

The introduction of negro slaves into America gave the Church a new flock to save. The Blessed Peter Claver devoted his life to them, becoming the slave of the slave.

Brazil, settled by the Portuguese, followed the system of the Spanish colonies, and had an episcopal see at Bahia in 1550; and for a time religion flourished in the settlements and in the Indian mission, where the Ven. Father Anchieta led his wonderful life,

When Protestantism gained a foothold in some states of Europe, the missionaries on their way to America were exposed to fearful dangers before they reached the field where they were to labor. Piratical cruisers, veiling their cruel rapacity under a pretext of religion, murdered all Catholic missionaries found on vessels that fell into their hands. In this way the Blessed Peter Azevedo and thirty-nine companions were martyred on their voyage to Brazil.

Religion continued to be maintained and extended in Spanish America till the middle of the last century, when it received a severe blow in the expulsion of the Jesuits by order of Charles III. Missions were everywhere broken up and scattered, colleges and seminaries were closed, and

St. Rose of Lima.

churches left desolate. The state in vain endeavored to supply the void thus created. Some of the other religious Orders had grown wealthy, and had lost their early fervor;

the system of lay patronage had placed many unworthy persons in the benefices of the secular clergy, and a general decline of religion followed. When the French Revolution broke out, the infidel doctrines that produced it spread in books to Spanish America, and did more to wreck the faith of that once Catholic people.

Revolutions began in the provinces from Mexico to Patagonia, and gradually the Spanish authorities and forces were expelled, and new governments, nominally republican, were set up. Brazil followed a similar course, but became an Empire under a prince of the royal family of Portugal.

In these revolutions most of the bishops were driven out as adherents of Spain, and for years religion was at a low ebb. Gradually, Freemasonry, introduced into Mexico from the United States, spread over Spanish America and Brazil, and most of the leading men becoming its dupes and tools, no longer concealed their hostility to religion. In all these countries the Church has been for many years at the sport of impious men. Bishops are imprisoned or exiled for doing their duty, religious Orders and convents are suppressed, all attempts at reform are checked; even the pious sodalities and confraternities attached to the churches are made an instrument to oppress and insult the church.

The Holy See has been unceasing in its vigilance and efforts to revive religion, and has repeatedly sent pious and able men to operate the needed reform. With one of these, Monsignor Musi, sent by Pope Pius VII., came the Abbate Mastai Ferretti, afterwards the famous Pius IX., who spent two years in Buenos Ayres, Chili, and Peru.

Yet the faith is not dead. There are many learned and pious bishops and priests, and the pilgrimages to Our Lady of Guadalupe in Mexico, and to Our Lady of Capocabana in Bolivia, show that the faith is still alive, and that, under better auspices, religion may revive and regain its early and happier influence.

CHAPTER II.

The Catholic Church in the United States—Catholic Explorers—Spanish Attempts at Settlement—The English Colonies—Lord Baltimore—Catholicity coeval with the Settlement of Maryland—Its Progress—The Puritan Persecution—Oppression of the Catholics—Apostasy of Lord Baltimore—The Church in Pennsylvania—The Acadian Confessors of the North—The Revolution—Services of Catholics—Influence of the Alliance with France.

THE United States are remarkable for their rapid growth in wealth and products, the energy of the people, their great public works, and the general diffusion of education, and for being the most successful republic yet seen in the world. The spread of Catholicity is one of the most remarkable features in the history of the country.

In 1776, England was undisputed master of all North America east of the Mississippi River, but on the 4th of July in that year, thirteen of the colonies between Canada and Florida became an independent country, since known as the United States. At that time the Catholic religion had scarcely a foothold.

The early explorers of the coast, Cabot, Verazzano, Gomez, were Catholics. As early as 1521, Dominicans reared a Catholic chapel in Virginia; twenty years later, the Dominican Father Cancer perished in an attempt to found a mission in Florida. That colony was settled by Melendez in 1565, and a church established at St. Augustine, with attendant priests; settlements were also made on the St. John's, and at Port Royal, South Carolina. These were also attended by priests. Jesuit missionaries began to instruct the natives, and extended their labors as far north as the Rappahannock, where two

Jesuit Fathers and several companions died by the hands of the Indians. A few years later, Franciscans established a convent at St. Augustine, and converted the Timuquans, Apalaches, and other tribes of Florida. This Order too had its martyrs in Father Corpa and his companions, killed by apostate Indians in 1597, and in the beginning of the eighteenth century in the Fathers slain, amid the ruins of Ayavala, by Indians under English influence. Pensacola, founded in 1699, had its church and clergy, with missions among the neighboring tribes. These Spanish settlements, beside the parish churches, had hospitals, hermitages or rural chapels, confraternities, and were visited from time to time by the bishops of Santiago de Cuba, in whose diocese they were. At times, auxiliary bishops of that diocese resided for several years at St. Augustine.

When Florida was ceded to England in 1763, the Spanish population withdrew, but a large body of Minorcans emigrated to the colony, and finally settled with their clergy at St. Augustine, where their descendants still remain. Two bishops in the United States have sprung from this good Catholic stock.

The English colonies were all settled after the unity of the faith in Europe had been broken by the vagaries of Luther, Calvin, Henry VIII., and other innovators. Protestants, though professing to advocate private judgment, never permitted it; and many of the settlements in America were founded by Protestants, and others who sought to escape from Protestant persecution.

Virginia, settled in 1609, maintained the Church of England. English separatists, who had first emigrated to Holland, founded Plymouth Colony in 1621; and Puritans in 1630 began the Colony of Massachusetts Bay. Rhode Island was founded soon after by the zealot Roger Williams, who had been driven from Massachusetts; and Connecticut was an offshoot of Massachusetts, settled by men of the strictest Puritan ideas. All these colonies were intensely Protestant, and no Catholics entered them except when sent over as bondmen. Dutch Calvinists settled on the Hudson, Swedish Lutherans on the Delaware, each as much opposed to Catholics as their English neighbors. From all this part the true Church seemed to be excluded forever.

Lord Baltimore, a Catholic nobleman, after trying to colonize Newfoundland, sought a milder climate. The bigotry of Virginia refused him admission there, and he obtained a liberal charter for the new colony of Maryland on the Potomac. The first settlement was made at St. Mary's in 1634, by Leonard Calvert, who came over with two hundred families of emigrants, many of whom were Catholics. They were accompanied by Jesuit Fathers, whose ministry in Maryland has been perpetuated to our times. These Catholic priests were for many years the only clergy in the province, and most of the Protestant settlers, left without church or preacher, embraced the faith of their Catholic neighbors. Several of the native tribes were converted, with Chilamacon, the king or principal chief in that part.

The charter of Maryland was remarkable for its liberality, while the earliest legislation of the colony established religious freedom, and checked all that was calculated to disturb harmony; but a body of Puritans, to whom the colony afforded an asylum, availing themselves of the overthrow of the monarchy in England and the establishment of the commonwealth, rose against the authorities in Maryland, defeated the Governor, put many Catholics to death, transported the priests to England, and passed penal laws, prohibiting the services of the Church.

The restoration of Charles II. brought some relief, and the brief reign of his Catholic brother, James, who had become Proprietor of New York, opened that colony to Catholics. A few settled there, and English Jesuits, co-operating with those in Maryland, began missions in New

York and New Jersey. Pennsylvania, settled by the liberal William Penn, quietly admitted Catholics; and zealous Franciscan Fathers from England began a mission in Maryland, extending their labors to Pennsylvania.

The dethronement of James II. and the elevation of William of Orange to the English throne were followed by penal laws in many of the colonies; the missions in New York ceased; the Catholics in Maryland were subjected to double taxes and deprived of many rights; the Church of England was established by law, and Catholics were compelled to contribute to its support. To prevent all increase of the faithful by immigration, the introduction of Catholics was prohibited by law.

To the grief of the Catholics, Lord Baltimore, from worldly motives, abandoned the faith, and some Maryland families, led by his example and their own cowardice, basely followed his apostasy. About 1725 the Franciscans abandoned their American missions, and from that time till the Revolution the Jesuit Fathers in Maryland were left alone to maintain the faith and minister to the faithful. In constant peril, they not only attended to the Catholics in Maryland, but sought those in Virginia; they erected churches in Lancaster and Philadelphia, the first separate churches in the colonies, for in Maryland no chapel was allowed except as part of a dwelling house, and under the same roof. In times of pestilence the Jesuits visited the sick so devotedly that the Protestant clergy complained to the legislature; but the undaunted Catholic priests challenged them to a religious discussion.

Many of the Catholic settlers in Pennsylvania were Germans, and to attend them the Superior of the Mission obtained some Fathers from Germany. They were learned and zealous men, and in their apostolic journeys reached scattered Catholics in New Jersey and New York.

The frequent wars with France and Spain, whose colonies bordered on those of England, kept alive bigotry, and, from time to time, subjected the Catholics to fresh persecutions. In 1755 seven thousand French Catholics, who had been for more than forty years under British rule in Nova Scotia, were torn from their homes, and scattered in utter destitution along the coast from Massachusetts to Georgia. Most of them by degrees reached the West Indies, Louisiana, or Canada; those who were sent to Baltimore, however, remained, and were attended by the Jesuit Fathers, who thus for the first time began regular labors in that city.

The condition of Catholics in the country can thus be seen. There were no clergy out of Maryland and Pennsylvania, and the missionary excursions extended only to Virginia, at the South, and to New Jersey, and after a time to New York, at the North. Except in the neighborhood of the churches in Pennsylvania, and the chapels under the roofs of the houses of the missionaries in Maryland, Catholics had to travel many miles, sometimes more than a hundred, when the roads were wretched, in order to enjoy the consolation of hearing Mass, of receiving the Sacraments, even once a year, or of being married by a priest. There were no Catholic schools, except an academy maintained for a time by the Jesuit Fathers on the Eastern shore, and while the wealthy could send their children to the Catholic institutions on the continent of Europe, those less favored with worldly means trained their children in the faith at home. Catholic books were scarce and highly prized; priests wrote out the whole Missal for use; and among the people it was not unusual to copy a book which they could borrow; for it was not often that they could buy.

Laws and public opinion were against them, and their position generally was a hard one; but a change was at hand, prepared in the designs of Providence.

The fall of Canada and the occupation of Florida relieved the English colonies of all fears from Catholic neighbors, but trouble at once ensued between America and the mother country. The toleration granted the Catholics in Canada was one of the grievances of the English colonies, and excited bitter feelings against the king and Parliament. The Catholics in the colonies, however, enjoyed comparative quiet.

When the colonies finally took up arms in defence of the rights which they claimed, the Catholics of Maryland and Pennsylvania all joined heartily with their fellow-countrymen, and used their influence to bring the people of Canada and the western country to espouse the cause of the United States.

In the West the settlers of French origin and the Indian tribes under their influence, acting in concert with the Rev. P. Gibault, parish priest at Kaskaskia, secured the North-west to the United States.

Canada and the Indians, formerly under French influence in Maine, Canada, and the West, were favorably inclined to the United States; the great Catholic powers in Europe not only recognized the new Government, but sent envoys to represent them, and checked England in her work of hiring troops in Germany to fight against the Americans. Finally, France openly took part with the United States, and sent an army and fleets to co-operate with the American forces; and Spain, declaring war on England, attacked her in Florida and the West.

All this made the Catholic Church less unpopular, and when the war finally closed with the impetuous dash of French and American on the works at Yorktown, much of the bigotry entertained against the Church at the commencement of the war had faded away. Many of the States set aside by their constitutions all the unjust penal laws against Catholics; in others the most obnoxious parts were laid aside, and the rest became almost a dead letter.

CHAPTER III.

Spiritual Dependence of American Catholics—They ask a Prefect—Very Rev. John Carroll appointed—Condition of the Church—His Visitation—Necessity for a Bishop—Petition of the Clergy—The See of Baltimore established—Right Rev. John Carroll—Extent of his Diocese includes part of the Diocese of Quebec—Religion in Canada—Its Missions and Martyrs—English Conquest of the Colony—Present State.

Up to this time the Catholics in Maryland and the other old colonies had been subject to the Vicar Apostolic of London; and those in the French settlements on the Mississippi and the lakes were subject to the Bishop of Quebec. Both these bishops were in British territory, and for the Catholics in the United States to remain in dependence on them might awaken prejudice among Americans, who still viewed everything English with distrust.

The clergy in Maryland and Pennsylvania were nearly all priests who had belonged to the Society of Jesus before its extinction; in the West the few secular priests were from Canada, none of the old Jesuit missionaries surviving. Besides these there were a few priests without regular faculties who had settled in the country. Immigration was already beginning, and, as it included a number of Catholics, the clergy saw that they must be provided for, and that it was necessary to have a head and means for recruiting priests. Nearly all were opposed to the appointment of a bishop.

They accordingly petitioned the Holy See for the appointment of a superior. The Holy See had already taken into consideration the state of the Church in this country, and Pope Pius VI. on the 9th day of June, 1784, appointed Rev. John Carroll, Prefect Apostolic of the United States. In terms his authority extended to the whole republic, but the western part continued to be subject to the Bishop of Quebec.

The appointment of Dr. Carroll gave great pleasure to the Catholic clergy and people. Father John Carroll was well known, and from his services in the Revolution was favorably regarded by the government. He was empowered to administer the sacrament of Confirmation, which had never been conferred in what had been the English colonies.

As he proceeded to visit the various congregations, old and young flocked to receive that sacrament from his hands, feeling how much they needed the Holy Ghost, with all his gifts and graces, to confirm them in their faith.

The Holy See asked a report on the numbers, condition, and prospects of the Catholics in the United States, and asked that two young men who showed a vocation for the ecclesiastical state should be sent to Rome to study.

To carry out these wishes was the first care of the Prefect Apostolic. His own residence was at Rock Creek, where he attended the neighboring Catholics and a mission sixty miles distant in Virginia. Eighteen other priests were scattered in the various missions in Maryland, four too old and infirm for any further work. These various stations were Dr. Carroll's first care.

After visiting these the Prefect Apostolic set out for the missions in Pennsylvania, comprising St. Joseph's and St. Mary's in Philadelphia, St. John Nepomucene's at Lancaster, St. Paul's in Goshenhoppen, and St. Francis Regis in Conewago. These had all been under the Jesuit Fathers and been founded by them. But there were besides, Catholics scattered in various parts who had in some cases priests from Europe.

The Very Rev. Mr. Carroll left home, to visit Philadelphia, New York, and the upper counties of the Jerseys and Pennsylvania, there too to administer the sacrament of Confirmation.

The Pennsylvania missions long established gratified

him by their piety and zeal; but New York, where the congregation gathered before and since the war by the venerable Father Farmer had been confided to the Franciscan, F. Charles Whelan, showed a spirit less in harmony with the discipline and government of the Church.

Besides these missions, tidings came from various quarters of Catholics who now sought a priest and wished to erect chapels. At Boston, at Norfolk, at Charleston, on the Monongahela, in Kentucky and Illinois, Catholics no longer under penal laws avowed their faith, and found many others around them to be Catholics. Here and there a priest appeared, ex-chaplains in the French navy who were attracted by the country, or priests from abroad. Dr. Carroll had no power to receive new priests and grant them faculties. With the clergy in the country he at once urged the Holy See to erect an episcopal see and give the Catholics in the United States what the Episcopalians were about to have, a bishop. That no offence might be taken by the Federal or State authorities, it was asked that the selection of the candidate be left to the clergy.

Dr. Carroll encouraged the commencement of the publication of Catholic works, projected a college and seminary, and sent to Rome two young candidates for holy orders.

As time went on the number of Catholics increased by immigration and promised to grow steadily; but the experience showed in New York and Philadelphia, that the establishment of churches and the proper support of clergymen would be attended with peculiar difficulties, as many of the laity, witnessing the systems pursued in the Protestant denominations, began to claim for the congregation, wherever one was formed, the right to choose a priest to suit their fancy and make his salary subject to their caprice.

Except in Maryland, where from the settlement the clergy had possessed property, which made them, in a measure, independent of their flocks, the priests had to depend entirely on the voluntary contributions of the faithful, and a new system had to be organized.

Pius VI., after due deliberation, granted the prayer of the American Catholics, and on the 12th of July, 1788, the sacred congregation of the Propaganda authorized them to select the city where a see should be established, and to name the priest who, in their judgment, might be raised to the episcopal dignity with the greatest advantage to the Church. In May, 1789, the clergy then in the United States who could meet for the purpose, assembled to the number of twenty-six, and with heartfelt prayers to the Holy Ghost to guide their deliberation, offered the holy sacrifice of mass, and selected Baltimore as the city which seemed best fitted for a see, as being the chief place in the old Catholic colony of Maryland. Almost without exception these experienced priests united in recommending to the Holy Father the Rev. John Carroll as the fittest one to wear the new mitre, and assume the task of moulding into a Church the scattered elements in the broad republic. Dr. Carroll alone opposed their choice, for he felt how difficult the duties of the bishop would be.

At Rome the selection gave great satisfaction, and on the 6th of November, 1789, Pius VI. founded a hierarchy in the United States by his bull erecting the See of Baltimore, and appointed the Right Rev. John Carroll the first bishop, authorizing him to receive episcopal consecration from any bishop he might select.

The Diocese of Baltimore thus created comprised the whole United States, and any portion which had previously been subject to any other see was withdrawn from its jurisdiction. This added to what had been Dr. Carroll's district as Prefect Apostolic the French settlements in the West which had been up to this time in the Diocese of Quebec.

Canada was visited by the French almost immediately after the voyage of Columbus, by the pious and hardy fishermen of Brittany and the Basque provinces. In 1534 its great river was explored by James Cartier, of St. Malo, who named it in honor of the martyr St. Lawrence, and attempted a settlement on its banks. No permanent colony arose, however, till the commencement of the seventeenth century.

Nova Scotia and Canada, then settled by the French, had from the first received Catholic missionaries. The first settlement on Neutral Island in Maine had priests, and, as Nova Scotia was settled, Jesuits, Capuchins, and secular priests labored among the colonists and the Indians, exposed constantly to attacks from the English in the neighboring provinces. A Jesuit lay-brother was killed at Mount Desert in 1613; priests were on several occasions carried off to Virginia and Massachusetts; a pious Recollect Father perished in the snow; the Jesuit Father Rale was killed at his mission of Norridgewalk. Finally, the Nova Scotia Catholics were all swept from their homes and scattered along the coast, an army of confessors and martyrs for the faith.

Canada was happier. Champlain founded Quebec, and the colony was directed by Recollect or Franciscan Fathers, who were subsequently aided by the Jesuits till 1629, when the colony was captured by England. After its restoration in 1632, the Jesuits resumed their labors, revived the missions among the various Indian tribes from the St. Lawrence to Lake Huron, and founded a college at Quebec. The Sulpitians, another body of learned priests, founded the settlement of Montreal, and both towns soon had convent schools and hospitals for the sick. The Indian tribes along the St. Lawrence were instructed in the faith and many were converted. A great mission was established by the Jesuit Fathers among the Hurons; but the Iroquois, a confederation south of Lake Ontario, were bitter enemies of the Canada Indians. They obtained fire-arms from the Dutch and destroyed many tribes. The Hurons and their allies lost town after town, and were finally all killed, captured, or driven from their country. Many of the missionaries died by the hands of these cruel savages, who showed a bitter hate of Catholicity. The missionaries were not deterred by all the torments inflicted on them, but carried the Gospel to the nations in the far West.

With Christian audacity the missionaries at the earliest favorable moment undertook to civilize the fierce Iroquois themselves, and made many converts among that people. Led by Father Simon Le Moyne, they planted the mission cross near the salt springs of Onondaga, and were soon from their bark chapels instructing the various tribes from the Mohawk to the Niagara, winning many of the warriors, and especially of the women, to the faith. The pagan party, however, inspired with distrust by the Dutch and English of New York, showed great hostility to the converts. The missionaries were at times driven out, and finally established mission villages on the St. Lawrence, to which the converts removed from the Iroquois cantons. In this way several Christian villages grew up.

While the progress of the faith among the Iroquois gave peace to Canada the missionaries gained the Abenakis in Maine, and began new missions among the Algonquin tribes around Lakes Superior and Michigan, the Chippewas, Ottawas, Menominees, Sacs, Foxes, and Miamis. The Winnebagoes, a branch of the Dakotas, also received the faith.

The pioneer of these new western missions was the venerable Jesuit Father, René Menard, who had labored among the Hurons, Cayugas, and other tribes. Though broken by his severe labors and by age, he set out and reared the cross on the shores of Lake Superior. He suffered much from the medicine men, whose hideous superstitions he tried to suppress, but often could only pray when all argument failed. He died by the hand of violence while trying to reach some poor Huron Catholics.

In 1673 Father Marquette, accompanying Louis Jolliet, an explorer, descended the Mississippi to the Arkansas

FATHER RENE MENARD AMONG THE INDIANS.

and made known the course of that great river, announcing the faith to the Illinois, among whom he began a mission, which, checked by his death, was soon continued.

The Church in Canada for the first fifty years was considered as under the jurisdiction of the Archbishop of Rouen, and was governed by a Vicar-General. In 1658 Francis de Laval Montmorency was consecrated Bishop of Petræa and made Vicar Apostolic of New France. To protect the colony against the Iroquois, troops were sent

A Missionary Destroying Liquor.

over from France, and governors appointed to whom the religious influence in Canada was uncongenial. Piety declined, and the officials in many points opposed the action of the clergy. The Bishop, to prevent the ruin of the Indians by intoxication, took strong ground against the sale of liquor to the natives, which the governors encouraged.

In the missions liquor imperilled the lives of the missionaries and the Christians; and at times the only remedy was boldly to brave the wrath of the Indians and destroy the casks before them.

A see was at last established at Quebec in 1674, and Bishop Laval proceeded to organize parishes in his vast diocese, which soon embraced the whole valley of the St. Lawrence and of the Mississippi, and the great lakes. He founded a seminary at Quebec, encouraged the missions, and labored to strengthen the piety of his flock. The people of Canada are to this day one of the most fervent Catholic communities in the world.

England had long menaced Canada by fleets from Europe and by expeditions from her American colonies, stimulated especially by a hatred of Catholicity. The French repelled them for many years, and erected the Church of Our Lady of Victories at Quebec to thank God for the victory which on two occasions he granted to their arms. But at last, in 1763, England wrested the colony from France. This seemed a death-blow to Catholicity; but what seemed so to the eyes of men was, in the designs of Providence, the salvation of the Church in Canada. It was the moment when the war on religion in France gained its first triumph in obtaining the suppression of the Jesuits, and was preparing the overthrow of all religious institutions. By being removed from this infidel influence Canada preserved the faith. The English government had been hostile to the Church, but it now maintained Catholicity in Canada, and, beyond petty persecutions and a plan for the extinction of the Jesuits and Recollects, left religion free. The bishops, devoted to their flocks, labored to supply them with good priests. The Catholic population increased rapidly, and in the present century new sees have been established at Montreal, Halifax, Kingston, and Red River.

Canada now contains four archbishops, twenty-three bishops, the great Laval University, two great theological seminaries, several religious Orders of both sexes, and has schools where the young are trained in their religion.

CHAPTER IV.

Religious Condition of the French Congregations in the West—Bishop Carroll is consecrated at Lulworth Castle, England—Secures Sulpitians—Georgetown College—The Carmelite Nuns—The First Synod of Baltimore—Controversies—Bishop Carroll obtains a Coadjutor—Spread of the Church—Baltimore made an Archbishopric and new Sees erected at Boston, New York, Philadelphia, and Bardstown—Rise of Religious Orders—The Administration of the Diocese of Louisiana confided to Archbishop Carroll—State of Religion—Bishop Dubourg appointed to Louisiana.

THE parts of the old Diocese of Quebec that were incorporated in that of Baltimore under Bishop Carroll included the Catholic Penobscots in Maine, the Iroquois Indians at St. Regis in New York, the Catholic Wyandots at Sandusky, the town of Detroit and the Indian missions on Lake Michigan and Lake Superior, the settlements at Vincennes, Kaskaskia, Cahokia, and lower down the Mississippi the settlement at Natchez. The conquest of Canada had crippled the resources of the Bishop of Quebec, and the seminary at that city withdrew its priests from the Illinois country, while the suppression of the Society of Jesus was a deathblow to the Indian missions in the West and was disastrous to the white settlers; for the French officials in Louisiana seized the Jesuit property and ordered the destruction of their churches in

Right Rev. John Carroll, D.D.

Illinois; and they were actually levelled to the ground although the province had been ceded to England and the French had no jurisdiction whatever.

The American Revolution cut off the Catholics on the Mississippi and the lakes from the bishop at Quebec; most of the Jesuit Fathers had died, so that when the spiritual direction of that distant part of the republic devolved on the newly appointed Bishop of Baltimore it was almost destitute of clergy; many of the white settlers had crossed the Mississippi to live under Spanish rule in Missouri or Louisiana, while those who remained and the Indian tribes were fast losing all religious ideas.

Dr. Carroll, yielding to the will of his brethren, proceeded to England and received episcopal consecration at the hands of the Benedictine bishop, the Right Rev. Charles Walmesley, Vicar Apostolic of the London District. The ceremony took place on the 15th day of August, 1790, in the chapel of Lulworth Castle, the seat of his friend Thomas Weld.

Resisting the invitations of many warm friends to visit them, he embarked at Gravesend in October, and arriving at Baltimore, after a rough and unpleasant voyage, on the 7th of December, took possession of his see and commenced his arduous duties.

During his stay in England he saw the storm about to burst which had been gathering for years over Catholic Europe. Many of the clergy of France were already seeking refuge in England, and here the new bishop saw aid extended to him by the hand of Providence. The Rev. Mr. Nagot, one of the directors of the Seminary of St. Sulpice, entering into Bishop Carroll's views, agreed to found a theological seminary in Baltimore in order to train up young men for the priesthood. Other exiled priests learned of the wants of the vast American mission, and took heart at the prospect of being able to do God's work there.

The year of the consecration of the first bishop was

marked, too, by the publication of an edition of the Catholic translation of the Bible by Bishop Challoner, which was issued in a quarto volume by **Matthew Carey** at Philadelphia, where several Catholic prayer-books and other works had already appeared.

Bishop Carroll had the happiness of seeing Georgetown College enter on a career of prosperity, and give earnest of sending forth men to rise to eminence in all walks of life. Besides a seminary for the clergy, he also saw the troubles in Europe enrich his diocese with the first community of religious women; a colony of Carmelite nuns, English and American by birth, came from Antwerp in 1790, and founded a convent at Port Tobacco.

Another great step was to organize his diocese as the sovereign Pontiff desired, by convening a diocesan synod and adopting such regulations as the experience of the older missionaries and the great ecclesiastical learning of some of the more recent accessions should suggest. On the 27th of October, 1791, he issued his letters convoking the synod at his residence in Baltimore on the seventh of the ensuing month. This assembly numbered his vicar-generals, the Very Rev. James Pellentz, James Frambach, Robert Molyneux, Francis A. Fleming, O.S.D.; the Sulpitians Nagot and Tessier; Lavau, a Canon of Tours; the Rev. John Thayer, an American minister, converted at Rome at the time of the death of B. Benedict Labre, who had been ordained and returned to labor in his native land; Rev. Leonard Neale; Rev. Lawrence Graessel, who was to die a victim of his zeal when bishop-elect; and ten other priests: the little assembly including Americans, Frenchmen, Belgians, Hollanders, Germans, and English. After moving in procession to the cathedral of St. Peter with their bishop, the synod convened, and adopted regulations which in their wisdom excited the admiration of eminent clergymen in later days, and were formally adopted in the first provincial Council of Baltimore of 1829.

The Church in the Republic was now organized for its work. Already the old prejudice was beginning to rear its head. Dr. Carroll had been compelled to answer the insidious publication of Wharton, an apostate, and invidious articles in periodicals—as he always did with remarkable skill, clearness, and sound reason. In Boston the Rev. Mr. Thayer found it more than once necessary to enter the lists in defence of Catholic truth; and in Philadelphia, Father Fleming, in his "Calumnies of Verus," crushed an opponent who outraged truth in his attacks on Catholicity.

In a few years Bishop Carroll found the care of his vast diocese beyond his ability, and sought a coadjutor. The Rev. Mr. Graessel, first named, died of yellow-fever, and then the Rev. Leonard Neale created Bishop of Gortyna, was appointed. Meanwhile Kentucky, a growing State, had received several priests, others were sent to Vincennes and the West; Matignon and Cheverus were establishing the Church in New England; and from the Indians in Maine to the scattered Catholics in the Carolinas and Georgia, the faithful everywhere found opportunity, at least at intervals, to attend Divine worship and approach the Sacraments. In the South-west the newly appointed Bishop of Louisiana and the Floridas sent a priest to Natchez to minister till the Bishop of Baltimore could give a pastor.

The rapid increase of the Church in all parts of the Republic induced Bishop Carroll to solicit a division of his vast diocese and the establishment of new sees. Pius VII., on the 8th of April, 1808, made Baltimore an archiepiscopal see, and erected bishoprics at Boston, New York, Philadelphia, and Bardstown. To the last of these was appointed the holy French priest Benedict Joseph Flaget; the Rev. John Cheverus, another of the exiled clergy, became Bishop of Boston; the Rev. Michael Egan, a zealous Franciscan, who had been for many years on the mission in Pennsylvania, was appointed to the see of Philadelphia;

and for New York the sovereign Pontiff selected Father Richard Luke Concanen, O.S.D., who had shown great ability as agent of the Irish bishops at Rome. He was consecrated there and set out for America, but he never reached his diocese, dying suddenly at Naples, where he was detained by the French.

This division relieved greatly the venerable Carroll, who beheld religion progressing rapidly. Orders were springing up to meet the wants of Catholics. Miss Teresa Lalor founded a monastery of Visitation Nuns; Mrs. Elizabeth Seton, a convert of one of the best New York families, established a community of Sisters of Charity based on those of St. Vincent de Paul in France; Poor Clares and Ursulines came over from Europe; the Dominican Fathers revived their Order in Kentucky; monks of La Trappe established a monastery of their severe rule in the West; the Rev. John Du Bois, subsequently Bishop of New York, laid the foundation of Mount St. Mary's College at Emmitsburg, Maryland, which has continued to combine a theological seminary and a college, and has bestowed on America some of its most zealous priests and most educated and devoted laity.

It had been the desire of the venerable Archbishop to hold a Provincial Council; but as there were obstacles which prevented it, several regulations for some important points of discipline were adopted by him and his suffragans in 1810. One of these early rules formally excluded from the sacraments any Catholic who joined a lodge of Freemasons.

The purchase of Louisiana by the United States added new cares to the aged Archbishop. That province, settled by the French, had been subject to the Bishops of Quebec, but, having been ceded to Spain in 1763, was, a few years later, placed under the control of the Bishop of Santiago de Cuba; and an auxiliary bishop of that diocese, a pious Capuchin Father, who, already residing in Florida, superintended the affairs of that colony, proceeded to New Orleans and for several years labored to revive religion in Louisiana. He visited the parishes, administered Confirmation, and restored religious discipline. He also introduced some new clergymen to aid the few Capuchins on whom, for several years, the pastoral duties had devolved.

In 1793 the Holy See, at the desire of the Spanish king, established the Bishopric of Louisiana and the two Floridas, and appointed as first bishop the Right Rev. Luis de Peñalver y Cardenas, a native of Havana, a man of zeal and learning and unbounded charity. The Spanish government aided the new Bishop liberally; but religion had declined and he was unable to effect all his zeal desired. In 1802 he was transferred to the Archiepiscopal See of Guatemala. A second bishop was nominated but never consecrated; and Spain, amid the troubles in Europe, agreed to cede back the province of Louisiana to France in consideration of the elevation of the Duke of Parma to the new throne of Etruria. Before Louisiana actually changed its flag, the United States induced the Emperor Napoleon to cede it to the United States in 1803; and the revolutionary flag of France was raised only to be almost instantly lowered.

Most of the Spanish priests, and the Spanish nuns belonging to the Ursuline convent founded in 1726 by Mother Mary de Tranchepain, left the colony; the Vicar-General, on whom the administration devolved died, the next year; and everything fell into confusion. In 1805 the Holy See invested Bishop Carroll with the administration of the Diocese of Louisiana. He appointed the Rev. John B. Olivier his Vicar-General, but it was soon found that a resident bishop could alone remedy the disorders. In 1812, by virtue of a brief of Pope Pius VII., Archbishop Carroll appointed Rev. William Dubourg Administrator Apostolic, but even his authority was not recognized. At last, in September, 1815, Dr. Dubourg was consecrated at Rome as Bishop of Louisiana, and Archbishop Carroll was relieved of the heavy responsibility. Soon after, on the 3d of December, 1815, the venerable patriarch of the Church in the United States expired at the age of 80, having by his mildness, zeal, and firmness won the esteem of men of all opinions, and effected the great work of organizing this portion of Christ's fold. He had wisely guided its policy so as to insure the complete adoption of the canonical system elsewhere in use, without exciting prejudice without the fold, or alienating from the faith those who had unhappily caught too much of the uncatholic ideas amid which they lived.

CHAPTER V.

The Church in New England—Trial of Rev. Mr. Cheverus—Rev. John Thayer—The Progress of the Church—New York—Bishop Connolly and Trustee Troubles—Mrs. Seton and the Sisters of Charity—Bishop Egan of Philadelphia—Bishop Conwell and the Hogan Schism—Catholicity in Western Pennsylvania—New Jersey—Bishop Flaget and the Church in Kentucky—The Dominicans in Ohio—Devotion of Priests and Sisters during the Cholera.

THE Church in the other parts of the United States had grown even more rapidly. The wars which desolated Europe made many seek a home in America in spite of the difficulty of crossing the ocean; and after the fall of Napoleon this emigration went steadily on till, in later years, more than a quarter of a million of inhabitants were added to the country annually, a large proportion being Catholics. Only a small part of these immigrants reached the Southern States, where the existence of slave labor offered little opportunity for advantageous settlement. Hence the growth of Catholicity was the more remarkable in the North and West.

Right Rev. John Cheverus.

The New England States were all embraced in the Diocese of Boston, founded in 1808. The first bishop, John Cheverus, afterwards Archbishop of Bordeaux and Cardinal, was a man of learning, piety, and such winning sweetness that he seemed to draw all to him. His influence and that of his early associate, the Rev. Mr. Matignon, were all the more needed as the first priests at Boston had not been men to inspire confidence in Catholic or Protestant, or to advance the cause of religion; and the convert Rev. John Thayer, by indiscreet zeal, had excited lively opposition. Dr. Cheverus extended his labors over all the New England States, from Connecticut to the Indians and scattered Catholics in Maine, everywhere forming congregations, exciting zeal to erect churches and prepare to support a resident clergyman. He did not at first escape the old anti-Catholic opposition. In Maine he was arrested for marrying a couple without being the resident pastor, and he was actually placed in the dock to be tried with drunkards, thieves, and evil-doers. It was with no little difficulty that he escaped imprisonment, and the bigotry of the judges was satisfied with imposing a heavy fine.

The Rev. Mr. Thayer, though personally unsuccessful on the mission in his native land, closed a pious and devoted life in Catholic Ireland, possessed through life with one idea—that of establishing a convent of religious women in Boston. For this he collected means, which he left at his death; and he so imbued with his spirit three ladies of a pious family, that they came to America to carry out his plan. The Ursuline Convent was founded in 1818, and, having removed soon after to Charlestown, became in a few years a most successful academy.

Meanwhile churches were erected in South Boston, Salem, New Bedford; at Damariscotta and Whitefield in Maine; and in New Hampshire a little Catholic community grew up as by miracle at Claremont. There a Protestant clergyman, Rev. Virgil H. Barber, listening to the call of divine grace and not closing his eyes or heart to evidence, embraced the faith and devoted himself to extend it. His wife and daughters became members of religious communities. He himself became a priest in the Society of Jesus, and his son, growing up, followed his example; and his aged father, also a minister, became a humble lay brother. Other members of this remarkable family entered the fold, and a nephew in time became the first Bishop of Hartford.

In Connecticut the tyranny of the Congregational system had driven many to return to the Episcopal Church and established that form in the colony. These men were earnest, and had sacrificed too much to be influenced by temporal motives. They formed a school of religious thought which, in time, led many into the logical course of accepting Catholic truth.

In 1828 Rhode Island beheld its first church dedicated to the living God, and two years later, Hartford, where Catholicity had been struggling along, found enough of her children to open her first church.

When the American missionary, Rev. Benedict J. Fenwick, of the Society of Jesus, became Bishop of Boston in 1825, the prospects of the Church in that stronghold of Protestantism were highly favorable.

New York had been less happy. Its first bishop never lived to reach his diocese, and the zeal of Fathers Fenwick and Kohlmann had been unable to do what seems a gift of the episcopate. A Jesuit college, an Ursuline convent, a Trappist monastery, a nucleus of holy and vivifying influence, were established; but they all ceased before a bishop came to encourage them. When the Right Rev. John Connolly, who had displayed learning, ability, and wonderful energy in the management of affairs at Rome, came to the See in 1816, he found thirteen thousand Catholics in New York and New Jersey, with three churches—two in his episcopal city, and one in Albany; but the clergy consisted of a single secular priest, aided for a time by three Jesuit Fathers, who were soon withdrawn. Worst of all, there had arisen a spirit of contention. While the simple-minded Catholics of both sexes wished to practise their religion, some who had risen in the world and had become estranged from the faith and usages of the Church, wished to modify the whole government of ecclesiastical affairs in America. They elected men of their own stamp trustees in the churches, and these claimed the right of appointing and removing the clergy and even of the bishop.

Bishop Connolly struggled on as well as he could against these adverse circumstances. He obtained several priests, and introduced Sisters of Charity to direct an orphan

Mother Seton.

asylum; and made a visitation of his diocese, encouraged the erection of churches at Utica and Rochester, and sent a priest to Brooklyn to form a congregation there. With two of his small number of clergy he was carried off in 1825.

An event important to the whole Church in the country was the reception at St. Peter's, New York, of Mrs. Eliza A. Seton, widow of a prominent merchant of New York. Her husband, meeting reverses in business and failing in health, went with his family to Italy, hoping to regain his strength in a more favorable climate, but he died there; and Mrs. Seton, left alone in her distress, sought consolation in religion. The Catholic Church seemed to her so full of comfort and help, and its doctrines, as explained to her by a kind friend, seemed all that reason could ask; but she did not act hastily: she studied and prayed; and returning to New York, submitted all her doubts to the Protestant bishop Hobart, but could not be satisfied. God gave her light; and she, after full examination, made her profession of faith on the 14th of March, 1805. Her step brought many trials. She was abandoned by her friends, and opened a school to support herself. Unfortunately New York was not in a position to profit by this opportunity, and the Rev. Mr. Dubourg urged her to go to Baltimore. She acted on his advice, but her desire was to form a religious community and devote her life to the instruction of the ignorant and the care of the sick. Bishop Carroll deemed her vocation a real one and encouraged her project. Mr. Samuel Cooper, a Virginia gentleman, about this time embraced the faith, and wished to devote his fortune to good works and enter the priesthood. With this means and by the authority of the Bishop, land was purchased at Emmitsburg, Maryland, and some buildings erected. Meanwhile Mrs. Seton had been joined by four other ladies, and they took the habit of Sisters of Charity on the 1st of January, 1809, under the direction of Rev. Mr. Dubourg. Finding it impossible to obtain the rules of the Order in France, or Sisters from any community there, to form them to the life followed in Europe, rules were drawn up suited to the country, and a dress that, without being conspicuous, would mark them as women who had renounced all worldly ideas.

God blessed the work. Mother Seton lived to see her community number fifty Sisters, laboring at Emmitsburg, Philadelphia, New York, and other cities, caring for orphans, and saving Catholic girls from perversion, by instructing them in all branches without danger to their faith, which was solidly implanted. She died in 1821, having the consolation of seeing one of her daughters in her community and her son a fervent Catholic.

The community spread rapidly, and colonies were sent to all parts of the Atlantic States. After an existence of nearly half a century the Sisters adopted the French rule and habit, and placed themselves under the direction of the Priests of the Mission, or Lazarists, a community which, like the Sisters of Charity, had been founded by St. Vincent de Paul. This made some modification in their work. The Sisters were recalled from New York, but, by permission of the Holy See, were permitted there to retain their old dress and rule, as they do in New York, New Jersey, and the dependent missions. Both branches have extended wonderfully, and have flourishing academies for young ladies, parochial schools, orphan asylums, institutions for the insane, hospitals for the sick in general and for small-pox patients, refuges for the aged, reformatories for erring girls; in a word, institutions for all the works of mercy. Their record of Sisters who have died martyrs of charity in attending the sick during seasons of cholera, yellow-fever, and other epidemics, is one of the noblest in the annals of the country.

The Diocese of Philadelphia had churches organized for many years, but the more recently formed congregations, the German Church and St. Mary's, showed an insubordinate spirit. The first bishop, the Right Rev. Michael Egan, though pious and devoted, found his efforts thwarted; and Catholicity, instead of growing vigorously and acquiring its full development, was crippled and weakened by men of the loudest professions. The second bishop, the Right Rev. Henry D. Conwell, found as pastor at St. Mary's, then the pro-cathedral, a priest placed there during the vacancy of the See, who, on examination, proved to be utterly unfit. The attempt to remove him led to a schism, which continued for years and extinguished the faith in the hearts of many. The priest Hogan apostatized and became a violent calumniator of the Church; and there are at this day few Catholics descended from those who upheld him, so rapidly does the sin of schism lead to apostasy and to utter loss of faith.

Amid all these troubles the Sisters of Charity began their good work in the diocese; and the Augustinian Fathers were building up a church in which the true spirit of Catholicity prevailed, as it did in the missions served by the Jesuit Fathers. In the western part of the State Catholics began to settle soon after the peace. Those on the Monongahela appealed to Dr. Carroll for priests soon after his appointment as Prefect. Several priests endeavored to gather Catholic colonists. The Rev. Mr. Browers purchased land in Westmoreland County and, founding a church, bequeathed his property to it; and the great Benedictine Abbey of St. Vincent now fulfils his pious wishes. The Franciscan Father Lonergan also acquired land, and endeavored to draw Catholics to it, proposing, also, to found a convent of Sisters for their benefit. Soon after, Prince Demetrius Gallitzin, one of the first priests ordained by Bishop Carroll, founded the Catholic settlement of Loretto, and, renouncing his brilliant future in Europe, spent his life and means for the good of his flock in the Alleghanies.

Rt. Rev. Benedict Joseph Flaget, D.D.

In the neighboring State of New Jersey the faith was also spreading; the iron works at Macopin and Paterson being among the earliest centres of Catholicity.

In the West the appointment of Bishop Flaget to the See of Bardstown had been a great blessing. In this new field all was to be done. Though the first to enter the field had been discouraged, priests like Badin, David, Salmon, and Nerinckx adapted themselves to the country and their flock, imbuing them with the true faith and discipline of the Church. They shared the hardships and dangers of their parishioners; and in a few years, amid the log chapels, two religious communities of women, the

Father Fenwick visiting early Catholic Settlers.

Sisters of Loretto and Sisters of Charity, organized in the State, began their devoted labors. A college and schools soon gave the rising generation every opportunity for acquiring a sound education. The Dominican Fathers from Bornheim, in Europe, who had come to America, settled in Kentucky, and zealously entered into the mission work in that rising State. The Trappists also made an attempt to establish themselves in the diocese of Bishop Flaget, but they abandoned it for a time, though they ultimately returned.

Besides the State of Kentucky, Tennessee, Ohio, Indiana, and the then sparsely settled North-west were under the care of Bishop Flaget; and that saintly man, in his first visitation, travelled more than a thousand miles through what was then a wild country. In this vast field much was to be done. The Dominicans, led by Father Edward Fenwick, afterwards Bishop of Cincinnati, visited the scattered Catholics in Ohio, and were encouraged by their hearty welcome. They planted the first Catholic Church for whites in Perry County, Ohio; and a convent of their Order soon became a centre of religious instruction. The old churches at Vincennes, Detroit, Mackinac, Green Bay, and Kaskaskia began to echo again to the solemn services of the Church, and throughout that district Catholics began to organize congregations, inspired by the hope of at last obtaining pastors.

When it became evident that the territory north and west of the Ohio was increasing rapidly in population, with Catholics scattering far and wide, Bishop Flaget urged the establishment of a new see, and Father Fenwick was made Bishop of Cincinnati in 1821. How the Church has been built up may be seen in the very boldness of this step. To be appointed bishop of some venerable see, where there is a cathedral rich in memories, a residence where a long line of bishops had presided, churches, and schools, is one thing, but it was far different to be raised to the episcopate under conditions like those of the first bishop of Cincinnati. On reaching his see, Bishop Fenwick had to look out for a residence; and, having hired one, he sent out for the simple food that was to be his first meal in his unfurnished house. Cathedral, convent, college, school, were all dreams of the future. Yet all these came; and in 1831 the *Catholic Telegraph* was founded, to be a vehicle for diffusing Catholic intelligence among the faithful, as well as to repel the constant attacks made on the truth. The next year the first bishop of Cincinnati, while making a visitation on the upper lakes, was stricken down by cholera. He rallied from the first attack, and, on his way to Cincinnati, gave the last blessing to the veteran, Rev. Gabriel Richard, whom he found on his death-bed. He himself had the hand of death upon him, and soon passed away, dying without a Catholic near him, at Wooster, Ohio.

During the prevalence of the terrible cholera in 1832 and 1834 the Catholic clergy and Sisters devoted themselves everywhere to the care of the sick, giving several martyrs to the cause of charity. Where there were no Sisters, as at Detroit, Catholic ladies took on themselves the care of the sick.

Dr. Fenwick was succeeded by the Rt. Rev. John B. Purcell, who had been President of Mount St. Mary's College. He was consecrated Oct. 13, 1833, and occupied the see for nearly half a century, contributing by learning, zeal, and sacrifices to the wonderful extension of Catholicity in the West. He lived to see two other sees erected in Ohio, and Cincinnati become the metropolis of a province. He attended numerous Provincial and Plenary Councils at Baltimore, held Provincial Councils in his own city, and attended a General Council of the Church. He was early called to defend the true faith, his learning and ability being displayed in a famous controversy with Rev. Mr. Campbell, founder of a new Presbyterian sect. Under his impulse the Jesuits opened St. Xavier College, the Dominicans extended their churches, the Priests of the Precious Blood began to labor among the Germans. The education of the young was so dear to him that he had a series of school-books prepared, and introduced the Brothers of Mary to aid the Orders already laboring in Ohio.

CHAPTER VI.

Establishment of the Sees of Charleston and Richmond—Religion in Virginia—North Carolina—Bishop England and the Church in the Carolinas—Religion in Florida—Progress in Louisiana and Missouri—Miraculous Cure of Mrs. Mattingly—First Provincial Council.

THE southern part of the Republic next attracted the attention of the Holy See. Deeming the Diocese of Baltimore still too large, Pius VIII. founded the Sees of Charleston, S. C., and Richmond, Va., in 1820, naming to the latter the Right Rev. Patrick Kelly, and to the former a great prelate, the Right Rev. John England, a man of eminent learning, piety, and ability.

Catholicity was not in a prosperous state in Virginia; the old penal laws had excluded Catholics, and few now seemed inclined to settle there. The adherents of the ancient faith were so few and so poor that the newly appointed bishop opened a school in Norfolk to support himself. After struggling for a year, he was transferred to Waterford, Ireland, and for many years the diocese was governed by the Archbishop of Baltimore, the increase of the faithful not justifying the appointment of another bishop.

North Carolina had a priest soon after the Revolution; but it has remained to this day the State most impervious to the true doctrines of the Gospel. South Carolina and Georgia, also in the Diocese of Charleston, gave better hopes. So hostile had the people been that two men, discovered to be Irish Catholics, were tarred, feathered, and banished from South Carolina in 1775. Soon after the close of the war, Charleston and Augusta, in Georgia, had priests. Here, too, jealousies and scandals retarded the progress of religion, and repelled many from examining its doctrines.

Bishop England found only two priests in his large diocese, but he went cheerfully to work. He established the Sisters of Our Lady of Mercy at Charleston; introduced the Ursulines from Ireland, to provide for the great calls of education and charity. He soon had churches building wherever the number of Catholics justified it; and, to diffuse the truth and silence error, he established the *United States Catholic Miscellany*. In ability and power this long ranked as the foremost of the religious press in America. At his death he left twenty zealous priests ministering in nearly as many churches.

Right Rev. John England, D.D.

Florida was restored to Spain in 1783, and Catholics again returned to it. Not Spanish priests alone, but Irish also, were sent out from Spain; and they labored among the settlers who came from the neighboring States. St. Augustine, Pensacola, Mobile, and even Natchez, claimed then as in Florida, had thus their priests. This province was under the Bishop of Santiago de Cuba till the erection of the See of Havana in 1787, and formed part of the new diocese till a bishop was appointed for Louisiana and Florida in 1793. The Right Rev. Dr. Cyril resided for some years in St. Augustine, zealously superintending the scattered flock in the two large provinces. When Louisiana was ceded to the United States, Florida remained a Spanish province till 1821, connected with the See of Havana.

The consecration of Bishop Dubourg at Rome in 1815 revived religion in Louisiana. As Administrator his authority had been defied; and, finding it useless to make New Orleans his residence, the city of St. Louis enjoyed the advantage of his zeal, and Catholicity there received an impulse that has never been lost. He was a bishop of singular ability; and, by his appeals for aid in France, led to the establishment of the Association for the Propagation of the Faith, which has been such a wonderful succor to the Catholic Missions in all parts of the world. The first settlements in Missouri, St. Genevieve, St. Charles, and St. Louis, founded from 1750 to 1764, were attended by the Jesuits from Illinois, till Rev. Mr. Gibault built his log chapel in St. Louis in 1770. Bishop Cyril placed Capuchins here, and Bishop Peñalver did all in his power to keep religion alive in the hearts of that distant portion of his flock; but it was in no vigorous state when Dr. Dubourg arrived. He came accompanied by Father de Andreis, Father Rosati, and other priests of the Mission, who founded a seminary and college at the Barrens, which have been a hive for good priests and intelligent Catholic laymen. A band of young men, brought over from Belgium by Rev. Charles Nerinckx, and who had entered the Jesuit novitiate in Maryland, next came to Missouri under Father Charles F. Van Quickenborn, and founded houses at Florissant, St. Charles, and St. Louis; a noble university soon rising at the last-named city. The Ladies of the Sacred Heart opened, in this diocese, the first American house of their admirable Order for the education of young ladies, and the Sisters of Loretto from Kentucky, and Ursulines, soon joined them.

In 1824 New Orleans was virtually made a see, and St. Louis another, while the Right Rev. Michael Portier was stationed at Mobile, with jurisdiction over Alabama and Florida, the latter province having at last been acquired by the United States.

Miracles had been recorded from the early mission times in all parts of the country, but they were known only in limited districts or by a few, and exercised little general influence.

In the year 1824 a pious priest of the princely house of Hohenlohe, in Germany, labored earnestly to excite the faithful to fervor in prayer, promising to offer the holy sacrifice for the intention of all who wished to unite their prayers to his. A lady of Washington, Mrs. Mattingly, who had been for several years suffering from diseases which physicians failed to relieve, wrote to the Prince, and by his advice began a Novena in honor of the most holy name of Jesus. On the last day she received holy communion from the hands of the Rev. Father Dubuisson, S.J., and was instantly restored to complete health, all traces of the disease having disappeared.

The fame of this miracle spread, and the fact was, of course, denied; but a series of affidavits from physicians and other witnesses was published, leaving no reasonable ground for doubt. An anonymous writer, however, attempted to gainsay it and break down the testimony; but Bishop England, in a publication full of sound and able reasoning, completely silenced all opposition.

This miracle of prayer tended greatly to revive faith in all parts of the country, and the enemies of the Church had helped to this consoling result.

Catholicity was thus spreading over the country, swelled by emigration from abroad. Her ecclesiastical organization was derived from England, France, and Spain, while the flocks were mainly of English, Irish, French, or German origin. All felt the necessity of uniform discipline and action, to guide the clergy, and imbue the faithful with genuine piety and devotion. It was necessary, too, to adopt measures to meet the bigotry which was reviving against the Catholic Church, and to thwart the insidious attempts which were made to tamper with the faith of the poor.

About the end of the first quarter of the present century, the Catholic agitation in England and Ireland for a relaxation of the penal laws, and a general emancipation, evoked a bitter warfare against the Church, and the press teemed with attacks on the Church. The spirit spread to America, and a spirit of hostility began to show itself. Catholic newspapers established in various parts defended the doctrines, ritual, and devotions of the Church. Controversies, oral and written, became common, and the whole Catholic body felt that great sacrifices were necessary to preserve the faith dear to their hearts, and transmit it to their children.

The holding of a Provincial Council had been proposed as early as 1810, but obstacles intervened. Archbishop Leonard Neale and Archbishop Ambrose Maréchal had, while extending religion in the Diocese of Baltimore, labored to secure this end; but it was not till 1829 that the Most Rev. James Whitfield, the fourth Archbishop, was able, with the sanction of the Holy See, to convoke a Provincial Council, to which he invited Bishop Rosati of St. Louis, then Administrator of New Orleans, and Bishop Portier of Mobile. The imposing ceremonial of the opening of a Provincial Council was witnessed for the first time at the Cathedral of Baltimore on the 4th of October, 1829, when the Archbishop, with the Bishops of Bardstown, Charleston, Cincinnati, Boston, and St. Louis, and the Administrator of Philadelphia, with their theologians, and the heads of the religious Orders in the country, met before the altar of God to deliberate for the welfare of the Church.

The decrees approved by the Holy See were a great encouragement to priests and people. They revived discipline, struck a death-blow to the pretensions of trustees, showed the necessity of Catholic schools, periodicals, and books, upheld the sanctity of Christian marriage, and provided against scandals.

The Catholics at this time in the whole country were

estimated at about half a million: and this Council marked their coalescing into one organic body, imbued with the utmost loyalty to the Holy See, anxious to preserve unity in the bond of faith and discipline. It had no heresies to condemn originating among the faithful; there had been no general falling away from the ecclesiastical rules or precepts. On the contrary, the faithful—scattered over a vast continent, few of whom had ever witnessed many of the rites, ceremonies, and practices of the Church in lands which she had moulded for centuries—were now rapidly and eagerly reviving the old Catholic life of their ancestors, and showing the inherent vitality of their faith.

CHAPTER VII.

Religion in Michigan—The See of Detroit—Bishop Rézé—Bishops at Vincennes and Dubuque—Early History of the Church at Natchez—Religion in Tennessee—Anti-Catholic Movements—Vile Fictions and Libels—The Ursuline Convent destroyed—Increase of German Catholics—The Redemptorists—Councils at Baltimore—Missions from Quebec and St. Louis to Oregon—Beginning of the Church in Minnesota—Rate of Progress.

WITHIN the ten years following the first Council of Baltimore, several new sees were established in the West to meet the wants of the increase in the faithful. Detroit, a town where Catholicity had flourished since the year 1700, was made an episcopal see in 1832. It was nearly two centuries after the first missionaries entered the limits of the State of Michigan ; for as early as 1642 the Jesuit Fathers Jogues and Raymbault planted the cross at Sault Ste. Marie among the Chippewas. In 1665 the venerable missionary, Réné Menard, while on his way from Lake Superior to visit a distant band of Hurons, was murdered by prowling Indians.

The first church at Detroit was burned in 1704. Two years after the priest stationed there, F. Benedict Constantin de Chasle, was killed by the Miami Indians in a sudden attack on the Ottawas. A succession of priests was kept up till 1785. When the district devolved on Bishop Carroll he sent priests to attend Detroit and two other churches ; but religion received no impulse till the arrival of the energetic and able Sulpitian, Gabriel Richard, who, in 1798, took up his residence there. He was not only a learned and devoted priest, but a man of progress. He established the first printing-press in Michigan, and was the first to print any portion of the Bible in the West. He was not only a leader of the Catholics, but of the whole community, and was elected the Delegate of the Territory to Congress. In 1805 St. Anne's Church, Detroit, perished in a conflagration, but was once more rebuilt. Under Bishop Flaget, of Bardstown, and subsequently under Bishop Fenwick, of Cincinnati, the Indian missions were revived at Arbre Croche, where the Indians had long solicited a priest. Catholicity spread, too, beyond Lake Michigan; the veteran priest Badin, the first ordained in the United States, restored the old mission at Green Bay, which soon had its log chapel. In 1834 a priest tells us that he had visited a spot called Milwaukee, where he found about twenty Catholics.

Bishop Fenwick died after visiting this part of his diocese.

When the See of Detroit was erected, the Very Rev. Frederic Rézé, a zealous missionary in Michigan, was chosen bishop. He found nine churches in his diocese, and introduced the Redemptorists and Poor Clares. Before the close of the period we here include, he could count more than twenty churches.

In 1834 Vincennes, another old French settlement, received as bishop the learned and pious Right Rev. Simon Gabriel Bruté, who had contributed to found Mount St. Mary's and the Sisters of Charity. The post had been served from early in the last century to the year 1789 by Canadian priests. The Rev. Mr. Flaget revived the faith in 1792, and subsequently as bishop cared for the old flocks. Bishop Bruté appealed to the charity of the Old World and gained zealous priests. Alive to the importance of education, he also introduced the Sisters of Charity.

Three years later Dubuque, the capital of Iowa, a district rapidly settling, was made an episcopal see. The bishop had no priests, churches, or institutions, but these soon came under his zealous action. Within two years after the building of the first log hut in Iowa, there were two Catholic churches. Natchez, another ancient French settlement, was also made a see in this year. Early in the last century it had an Indian mission under the Rev. Mr. St. Cosme, a Canadian priest who was killed by prowling savages on the Mississippi; and Rev. Mr. Foucault, a missionary to the Yazoos, met the same fate. The Capuchins then became chaplains of this French post; but in 1727 the Natchez, roused to fury by the injustice of Chopart, the commandant, plotted a general massacre of the French. The Jesuit Father Poisson, stopping in charity to minister to the French, was slaughtered there, and Father Souel was killed by the Yazoos to whom he had been preaching, and a third missionary escaped almost miraculously from the hands of the infuriated Indians.

After a time the settlement was restored and was regularly attended to the fall of French power. In 1787 the Spanish government sent Irish priests to Natchez, and a church was erected there and another at Cole's Creek. When this part was fully recognized as American territory the Spaniards withdrew; but Bishop Peñalver, at the request of Bishop Carroll, sent priests to Natchez, and for years the Catholics in that part depended on New Orleans for spiritual aid. When Natchez was erected into a see in 1837, all trace of churches and of the French and Spanish labors of the last century had vanished: but, though Bishop Chanche found the field of so little promise, he zealously bent himself to the work; and at his death, even in that State of Mississippi where little of the tide of immigration reached, left eleven churches and ten priests where he had found none.

Nashville, established as an episcopal see in the same year, has seen Catholicity grow slowly. The Dominican Father, Richard Pius Miles, on his consecration repaired to Nashville, but he had scarcely secured a temporary home in a boarding-house when he was prostrated by a dangerous fever, and might have died unattended had not Providence guided a priest to his bedside. Yet he lived to see thirteen priests, fourteen churches, three convents, with academies and parish schools.

But the very increase of Catholics in the country envenomed the hatred against them. Brownlee, Beecher, Morse, and others, by wildest appeals to prejudice, aroused the worst passions of the low and ignorant against Catholics; others went further, and by the grossest and most indecent fictions, like "Six Months in a Convent" and "Maria Monk," excited the mob against the pious and helpless ladies in our Catholic institutions. On the 11th of August, 1834, a mob, under the very eyes of the authorities, attacked the Ursuline Convent at Charlestown, near Boston, Massachusetts; set fire to it; and, driving out the inmates, plundered and destroyed the building. One of the nuns, flying with the pupils from the sacrilegious mob, died soon after from the effects of that terrible night. A mock trial shielded the guilty, and all redress was denied. This fearful enormity led many misguided Protestants to reflect, and for a time the storm was lulled.

The immigration into the country had by this time become largely German, and many of the new-comers were Catholics. To minister to them was a difficulty, as there were few priests able to address them in their own language.

The Germans in Pennsylvania had early had priests of their own tongue, and their Church of the Holy Trinity in Philadelphia is one of the oldest in the country. For the later immigration, the pioneer priest in the East was the Very Rev. John Raffeiner, who erected German churches in New York, Boston, Williamsburg, and Macopin, and labored among his countrymen far and wide.

Bishop Rézé of Detroit, himself a native of Hanover, took an active interest in their welfare. His appeals to the clergy and faithful in the various German States brought great aid in various ways to the Church in the United States, and were to some extent instrumental in establishing the Leopold Society. This did, in Germany, the work accomplished in France by the Association for the Propagation of the Faith. At his appeal the Redemptorists, worthy followers of their founder, Saint Alphonsus Liguori, came over to devote themselves to the Indian missions in Michigan, though they soon found a wider and more extended field for their labors among their German countrymen. Bishops gladly committed to their zeal

Father Lemcke's First Meeting with Prince Gallitzin.

and piety the new congregations they found it so difficult to supply.

The devoted Frederic Baraga, an Illyrian priest of rank, also devoted himself to the Indian missions of Michigan, and labored among them till, as bishop, his zealous life was closed.

A soldier of the old European armies, the Rev. Peter Lemcke, becoming a priest, devoted himself to the American mission, and, seeking out the venerable Prince Gallitzin, became the assistant of that pioneer priest during his later years. After long service in the Alleghanies, Father Lemcke induced a Benedictine Father, Boniface Wimmer, to undertake an establishment of his ancient Order in the United States; and from this grew St. Vincent's Abbey in Pennsylvania, which has spread its houses and filiations through the country, giving excellent priests to the German-speaking part of the Catholic community; and at various points, Jesuits, Franciscans, Priests of the Precious Blood, soon had charge of German congregations, and among them all the cause of education has received steady and constant attention.

The wants and difficulties of the time led to several Councils at Baltimore, in 1833, 1837, 1840, and 1843. Under their impulse the Indian missions, which were confided to the Society of Jesus, were pushed beyond the Rocky Mountains; and the Fathers reached Oregon to labor beside the secular priests from Canada, who were ministering there to their countrymen.

Quebec was still the centre whence Catholicity radiated over the North. In the olden time it had sent missionaries from the St. Lawrence to Hudson Bay, the Lake of the Woods, Natchitoches, and Mobile. French Canadian trappers and voyageurs, crossing the continent, had settled in Oregon; and in 1834 they applied to Mgr. Provencher, on Red River, in what we now call Manitoba, for a priest, as he was the nearest bishop they knew. That zealous missionary had few for his immediate work. Quebec took the matter in hand, and in 1838 despatched the Rev. F. N. Blanchet and Rev. Modest Demers to Oregon, which thus owes its origin to the old missionary Church of Canada, the child of France, while the Jesuits came from Louisiana, whose bishopric was founded by Spain.

The Fathers in Missouri had from 1836, under Father Van Quickenborn, begun missions among the Kickapoos, Pottawotamies, and Kansas, gaining many to the practice of the Christian virtues, and, aided by the Ladies of the

LAYING OUT AN INDIAN MISSION.

Sacred Heart and the Sisters of Loretto, forming them, especially the female portion, to the life of civilized Christians. Out of these missions grew the Vicariate Apostolic of Indian Territory and the present Diocese of Leavenworth.

Through the French, and especially through a Catho-

Father De Smet instructing the Indians.

lic Iroquois from Canada who had settled among them, the tribe of Selish, or Flatheads, learned to esteem Christianity, and desired a missionary. They sent three delegations to the Bishop of St. Louis, failing however twice, the Indians perishing on the way by disease or by hostile bands. The third embassy was more successful, and Father Peter J. De Smet was sent to them in 1840, beginning a course of missions among the red men of the Rocky Mountains which has made his name familiar and endeared to all. A result of these missions is seen in the Catholic tribes of the Flatheads and Kalispels, and Catholic communities among the Nez Percés and Sioux.

In less remote parts of the country, too, the faith was spreading.

In 1839 Bishop Loras, with the Rev. Mr. Pelamourgues, pushed into Minnesota to begin the ministry among those who came to settle the land explored by Father Hennepin two hundred years before.

These were times of beginning. In 1834 there were only twenty-five thousand Catholics in the City of Philadelphia, and as many in the large Diocese of Portland. There were only two priests in what is now the Diocese of Buffalo. It was two years later before Chicago had a resident priest, and Cincinnati was then proud of having two churches; and it took another year before Columbus, which has since had two successive bishops, saw the first church erected. Even then it excited such bitter feeling that it was soon robbed of its vestments and altar furniture.

CHAPTER VIII.

Catholic Schools—State Schools hostile to the Faith—The Fourth Council of Baltimore—The School Question in New York—Spread of Catholic Educational Institutions—Death of Bishop England—New Dioceses and Orders—Texas added to the United States—History of Religion there—Bishop Odin—The Native American Party—Philadelphia Riots and Destruction of Catholic Churches—A Priest in Indiana unjustly sent to Prison—Conversions—Madame Gallitzin—Catholic Literature—Dr. O. A. Brownson.

In the rapid increase of the Catholic body, especially in the Northern States, the resources of the faithful were taxed to the utmost to provide churches where they could hear Mass and approach the sacraments. Many were poor and struggling, and found it hard to do this and maintain the priests, when they succeeded in having one stationed among them. But the necessity of educating their children in the faith was also felt. There were schools supported by general tax in many parts; but, so far as Catholics were concerned, these, instead of being a benefit which they could enjoy, were deadly weapons used against them—part of a set scheme to weaken the faith of their children. In most of these, Protestant doctrines were openly taught to the children, who were compelled to learn them, as well as to use Protestant Bibles and Protestant prayers under pain of expulsion.

From the first, Catholics had sought to remedy this by establishing parochial schools; and with this view the Sisters of Charity, so far as their numbers permitted, the Sisters of Loretto and Charity in Kentucky, Sisters of Our Lady of Mercy in South Carolina (all Orders originated in the country), as well as the Sisters of St. Joseph who came from Lyons to St. Louis in 1836, the Sisters of Providence who came to Indiana a few years later, the Sisters of Notre Dame, were laboring for the general diffusion of sound religious and general instruction; while the Sulpitians, Jesuits, Augustinians, Ursuline and Visitation Nuns and Ladies of the Sacred Heart were furthering the higher education.

There was a faint hope that their Protestant fellow-citizens, who as a majority could control the result, would allow the public schools to be such that Catholics could conscientiously use them; and the Fourth Council of Baltimore urged pastors to endeavor to secure this just concession wherever they saw any possibility of obtaining it. The only other alternative was to induce the government to recognize Catholic schools as part of the State system, while the State retained the power to make the public schools as sectarian as Protestants might desire. But the time was not a propitious one. It was one of sharp religious controversy, and Protestant leaders were in no mood for any temperate or honest course.

The Fourth Council of Baltimore met on the 17th of May, 1840, Most Rev. Samuel Eccleston, Archbishop of Baltimore, presiding, and among the Fathers the holy Bishop Benedict J. Flaget of Bardstown, the great Bishop England of Charleston, Bishop Kenrick of Philadelphia (of great theological fame), and nine others. The Coadjutor Bishop of New York, on whom the administration of that important diocese had devolved in the age and weakness of the Venerable Dr. Du Bois, was then in Europe seeking aid to carry out the works he deemed necessary for the interests of religion.

The Council had, as we have seen, not been silent in regard to the school question; but during the absence of Bishop Hughes, the issue was directly raised at New York; and on his return he had to take a leading part in it, less as he wished than as he found it. New York had, for many years, granted an allowance to the various schools maintained by the different denominations, and also to those supported by "The Public School Society," an organization expressly intended for those not connected with any particular church. This system was at last abandoned in consequence of frauds committed by a Baptist Church to obtain more than it was entitled to. The Catholics of New York, in 1840, asked the Common Council to revive the old system and give aid to the Church schools. As it would clearly benefit the Catholic schools, several denominations remonstrated; their ablest ministers and famous lawyers were selected to argue the matter before the Common Council and on the 29th of October, Bishop Hughes, alone against this array of talent, with wonderful skill, learning, and ability, maintained the justice of the Catholic claim. From that moment he was, in the eyes of the American people, the leader of the Catholic body—a man whose power they respected.

The Common Council, as had been expected, decided against the Catholics; conviction could not weigh against the strong anti-Catholic prejudice aroused throughout the country. The next appeal was to the Legislature, in the hope that a law might be passed that would prevent teachers in public schools from compelling pupils to learn doctrines, theories, prayers, or religious opinions at variance with those professed by their parents. Meetings were held, and in addresses and publications the Catholics endeavored to bring home to the sober-minded members of the community, the fact that they were combating for the great principles of human freedom, while their antagonists were reviving the odious systems of intolerance.

To the surprise of the Catholics the candidates put forward for the Legislature by both Whigs and Democrats pledged themselves in advance to vote against the Catholics. There was no alternative. Catholics could not, without degrading their manhood, vote for either ticket; their only course was to nominate a ticket of their own; and that course entailed the complete defeat of the Democrats. Then both parties sought to gain the Catholics, and the old Public School Society gave place to a new system of State Schools, in which many steps were made towards preventing evils of the past; but this was only in theory, little difference resulting practically. The public schools are to this day distinctively sectarian and anti-Catholic.

The evil passions aroused in the country by the mere petition of the Catholics for what they deemed their rights as citizens, taught them that they must do all themselves for the education of their youth, and that, though the State had been the protector and benefactor of all Protestant establishments, to Catholics it would be persistently hostile.

As a result of their efforts, St. Xavier College, Cincinnati, was opened by the Jesuits in 1840; the next year the Very Rev. E. Sorin, founder of the Priests of the Holy Cross in America, began the College of Notre Dame, Indiana; St. John's College, Fordham, New York, opened in 1841; followed in the succeeding years by Villanova College, under the Augustinians, in Pennsylvania; and the College of the Holy Cross at Worcester, directed by the Jesuit Fathers, though Massachusetts long denied this college an act of incorporation to enable it to bestow degrees. About the same time those accomplished educators, the Ladies of the Sacred Heart, opened academies for young ladies in the Dioceses of New York and Philadelphia. The diffusion of this Order was due, in no small degree, to the ability of a remarkable lady, Madame Gallitzin, a Russian Princess, who, after a long struggle, renounced the schism in which she had been brought up, and, entering the Ladies of the Sacred Heart, came to the United States as visitor. She founded several new houses, and died of yellow-fever, in December, 1843, while pursuing her career of usefulness.

In April, 1842, the Church in the United States lost

one of its pillars, Bishop England of Charleston, who had been for many years the ablest exponent of its doctrines and life. Singularly gifted, able, eloquent, he instinctively appreciated the spirit and mind of the American people, and, identifying himself thoroughly with the country, acquired a reputation in all parts of the Union. Eloquent in the pulpit and with the pen, his words carried conviction. Before his time slanders against Catholics had been feebly met: Bishop England took them up with the skill of an able dialectician, with the widest range of learning; and he presented the truth in such colors that, after one or two essays, few ventured to cope with the Bishop of Charleston. When he appeared in the field they retreated ingloriously.

Conscious of the extent to which the Protestant mind has been biased by the distorted pictures of Catholic doctrine and history which are alone presented, he happily used this to make his language tell when addressing Protestant bodies, whether the Congress of the United States, the Legislature of his State, or academic and civic gatherings. He not only presented Catholic doctrines fairly to non-Catholics, but wrote much to reveal to the faithful the richness and beauty of our liturgy and rites, to which he was deeply attached.

The organization of the Church was furthered by the sessions of the Fifth Council of Baltimore in 1843, and by synods at New York, Boston, and New Orleans. New sees were erected in 1843 at Pittsburgh, Milwaukee, Little Rock, Hartford, and Chicago, the last of these dioceses having only a single church in the city when the bishop took up his residence. Oregon gave promise of such progress for the faith that it was made into a Vicariate Apostolic.

The cause of religion gained also by the introduction of the Redemptorists into the Diocese of New York, and the foundation of a community of priests of the Congregation of the Most Precious Blood by the Very Rev. F. de Sales Brunner in Ohio, and by a filiation of the Sisters of Mercy, who opened the first house of their Order in Pittsburgh in 1843, to begin the various charitable works for which Mother Catharine McAuley designed them.

Meanwhile Americans who had settled in Texas, unable to endure the oppressions and spoliations of the fluctuating governments of Mexico, declared that State an independent republic and secured recognition in Europe and America. As settlers at once poured into that country, the Holy See in 1840 made the Very Rev. John Timon, who was at the time Visitor of the Lazarists in the United States, Prefect Apostolic of that republic. The religious condition of Texas may be seen in the fact that it was necessary at once to suspend the two priests who were the only clergy remaining there. The Very Rev. John M. Odin, as Vice-Prefect, revived religion, secured the old church property to the Catholics, and in 1842 was made Bishop of Claudiopolis and Vicar Apostolic of Texas.

In 1685 Robert de la Salle landed in Texas with a force designed to seize some of the rich mines in Northern Mexico; but his projects, through his incompetence, ended in his death and that of nearly all his party. Among them were three Recollect Fathers and two Sulpitians, with powers from the Propaganda and the Archbishop of Rouen. In 1689 the Spaniards occupied the country, Father Damian Macanet being the first priest. The next year missions were established among the Cenis Indians, which were revived a few years later; but the real founder of the Texas missions was the Ven. Father Antonio Margil, who founded churches among the Cenis, Bidaies, Nazones, Nacogdaches, Ays, Adayes, and Caddoes: while the Spaniards settling at San Antonio were soon attended by secular priests and a parish established. The Texas mission ere long had its martyrs: Father Pita was killed by the Lipans, a lay brother by the Apaches, but the missions were extended to other tribes and fine churches built, although several of the fathers were killed in their apostolic labors.

Meanwhile the Spanish settlements increased by emigration from the Canary Islands, whose spiritual wants were attended to by the Bishop of Guadalajara, till the province was made part of the Diocese of Linares. These bishops visited this remote portion of their flock, and one of them died from the hardships encountered on the visitation of Texas. An Irish colony was established in Texas in 1829 which had priests from their own country.

Bishop Odin repaired the ancient church of San Antonio, and erected new churches at Galveston, Houston, Lavaca, Fort Bent, St. Augustine, and Nacogdoches, opening schools wherever he could. In a few years the new republic was merged in the Union by annexation and became one of the United States.

Meanwhile the evil spirit of bigotry, evoked by the discussion of the school question, was imbittered by other elements—the jealousy of mechanics excited by the competition of immigrants, and by the active part taken in elections by naturalized citizens. A new political party, called Native Americans, was formed, and the country rang with incendiary appeals to the ignorant and prejudiced. The great cry was that Catholics wished to banish the Bible from the public schools. In fact, however, all that Catholics had asked was that Catholic children should not be forced to learn anti-Catholic doctrine and practices in schools for which they were taxed. But the cry took with people who never stop to think; and the vilest rabble of the great cities, ignorant alike of the letter and spirit of the Holy Scriptures, were shouting about the Bible. In Philadelphia the excitement was very great, and when a rain storm disturbed a public meeting of Native Americans in May, 1844, and they took refuge in Kensington Market, collisions occurred between some of the members and Irish Catholic spectators. The next day the newspapers, in inflammatory articles, hounded on the mob; public meetings were held; and the placards put up by Bishop Kenrick urging his flock to abstain from all violence were torn down. On the 8th of May a mob set fire to St. Michael's Church, the Fire Department refused to save it, and the edifice consecrated to divine worship was reduced to ashes. Then a house occupied by Sisters of Charity was fired; and in the evening St. Augustine's Church and rectory, with an extensive library belonging to Villanova College, were set on fire and destroyed. Houses of Irish Catholics in various parts were pillaged and burned, and many persons murdered; the rash attempt of a few to defend their homes only increasing the bloodthirsty instincts of the mob. During all this scene of incendiarism and murder, the city authorities remained inactive. The next day martial law was proclaimed, and for a time the violence ended. No one was punished for the destruction of the Catholic churches and other property, and no compensation was ever made to the Catholics.*

But the demon of violence evoked was not crushed. On the 5th of July the pastor of St. Philip Neri's was warned of an intended attack on his church. On his notifying General Cadwallader, the militia were called out. The rioters had seen the militia stand idle while they did their work in May, and at once attacked the church, but were driven off by Cadwallader, who convinced the mob that he was in earnest, on which the civil authorities came forward to save their dupes and suppressed the riots.

When all was over the Catholics had to begin anew; many fled from such a place; the others sought patiently to rebuild the homes and shrines that had been immolated to the demon of bigotry.

The well-known decided character of Bishop Hughes and the firm position taken by the Catholic press and people saved New York from similar scenes, although the

Native Americans had just elected one of the publishers of the "Maria Monk" fraud as Mayor of that great city. A meeting that had been called to create a riot and inaugurate scenes of incendiarism was countermanded and the disaster averted.

While minds were thus inflamed with hatred of Catholicity, a priest in Indiana became the object of a persecution before unparalleled. A wretched woman accused him of crime; the public eagerly took up the charge; the case was hurried through, the judge evincing the utmost prejudice and gloating over his opportunity. A jury as partial as the judge convicted the priest; but the prison doors had scarcely closed on the confessor of the faith than inquiries made as to the woman's character in New York, whence she came, proved her to be a most degraded and wicked creature. In a short time there was a general revulsion of feeling, and the Governor was but too glad to open the prison doors and release an innocent and injured man.

The violence and hatred of 1844 were beneficial to Catholics. Many of the weak, deluded by the soft whispers of heresy, had looked on it favorably; but they now beheld it in its true colors, and felt that in fidelity to their Church lay their true happiness. Many Protestants, in order to attack Catholics, began to read Catholic books, which had been previously utterly unknown. The result was often fatal to their Protestantism. A singular case of this occurred at Pompey in New York State. A pedler's wagon broke down near the house of a worthy miller and farmer named Dodge, who, going to the pedlar's aid, found the damage beyond immediate remedy and invited the man to pass the night at his house. There, by the clearer light, he saw that he had asked an Irishman and undoubtedly a Catholic within his walls. After a night spent in great anxiety, Mr. Dodge took his guest to a smith to make the necessary repairs. When all was completed the pedler wished to compensate his entertainer for his kindness, but neither Dodge nor his wife would accept anything. Out of curiosity, however, he took a little "Butler's Catechism," and when the man had gone his way began to read it. Every statement seemed to him clear and reasonable. Bible in hand, he examined, and conviction increased. He ordered from New York all the books found in a catalogue at the end of the Catechism, and, reading them to his family and neighbors, led many to regard the Catholic as a very sound and sensible system. Knowing no Catholic, and above all no priest, even by name, except Bishop Hughes, the gentleman wrote to him, asking to be received into the Catholic Church.

About this time died a remarkable man, who had taken a prominent part in Catholic affairs. Prince Demetrius Gallitzin was the son of the Russian ambassador to Holland and of the Princess Amelia, a lady who, breaking away from the fashionable free-thinking of her time, became a model of piety. Her son, intended by his father for the army, was sent at the outbreak of the French revolution to travel in America with a tutor. Here he resolved to devote himself to the sanctuary, and, renouncing the brilliant career before him in Europe, entered Bishop Carroll's seminary, and was the second on whom he laid his hands in the sacrament of Holy Orders. His first labors were in Conewago, Pennsylvania; but he soon conceived the idea of a Catholic colony, and, as has been incidentally stated, devoted all the resources he could command from Europe to gather Catholic settlers around his Church of Loretto in the Alleghanies. Though thus seeking obscurity and flying all honors, zeal led him to meet in controversy some who assailed religion in those parts. His "Defence of Catholic Principles" showed such clearness and precision that it has been frequently reprinted in Europe and America, in English, French, and German, and his other treatises were widely disseminated, doing great good. In the care of his congregations he was strict and exact, but won all by untiring zeal and devotedness to their welfare. Deprived of property to which he was entitled in Europe, he was harassed by cares in his later days, and a sufferer from painful diseases; but he bore all with unshaken courage and equanimity, and died a holy death at Loretto, May 6, 1840.

This period marks, too, the rise of Catholic literature. The early publications in the United States had been reprints of standard works published in Europe, and of controversies, like those of Carroll, Thayer, Gallitzin, and Edelen. The Rev. C. C. Pise initiated works of a pleasing and attractive style and Catholic periodicals for the faithful. Catholic publishers, Dunigan, Sadlier, Murphy, undertook new works, and increased greatly the libraries of our readers. But in 1844 the Church received, as an humble catechumen, one of the most profound and logical minds in the country, Orestes A. Brownson. His *Review* became Catholic, and was for years the bulwark of Catholic thought. Though he occasionally issued other works of a less severe cast, his reputation rests mainly on the Review which bore his name, and which for nearly a quarter of a century was the most learned and philosophical Catholic publication in the English language.

Orestes A. Brownson was born in 1803 in Vermont, a State noted for the vigor of her sons. His mind was too clear to rest long cramped by New England theology, and in the narrow circle of local dissent he sought a religious system that he could respect. But Universalism and Unitarianism, though he embraced them and advocated their doctrines as a minister, proved hollow and unsubstantial. They were not the Church, and during the year 1844 grace enlightened his mind so that he saw in Catholicity what his heart had yearned for. He at once sought instruction with all the docility of a child, and was received into the Church. To the day of his death, April

17, 1876, he was constant in all his Christian duties, having found true peace in the unity of Catholicity.

Besides the Catholics from abroad and those born of Catholic parentage in this country, the Church received constant accessions by conversion. She had to deplore serious losses; many Catholics who settled far from all opportunity of attending Mass and frequenting the sacraments, in time lost all trace of Catholic piety, allowing their children to grow up without any instruction in their faith. In such homes, prayer, catechism, and instruction were unknown, and the children learned in the sectarian public schools all manner of slander and insinuation against the religion of their parents. In other cases, Catholics rising in the world forgot their God, who bestowed prosperity; and, instead of giving their poorer and weaker brethren an example of fidelity to their religious duties, concealed their Catholicity to win favor with the empty and irreligious society in which they sought to mingle. Others sought to cover the criminal life which excluded them from Catholic fellowship by ostensibly adopting some form of Protestantism.

But while the Church thus lost some of the weak and wicked, she received constantly men and women of education, thought, and position, who, conscious of all that the step would cost them, bravely responded to the grace of God and humbly entered the Church. These conversions had been going on from the settlement of Maryland, through the colonial times. After the Revolution, Thomas Simms Lee, who had been Governor of Maryland, became a Catholic; Rev. Mr. Thayer at Boston; Mrs. Seton in New York; the Barbers in New Hampshire; the Rev. Mr. Richards, a Methodist clergyman of Western New York; but the great movement was in the Episcopal Church. That church was established in Connecticut as a protest against the tyranny of Calvinism; and while Episcopalianism in some parts sought to approach Calvinism, there it questioned every form of the old tyranny. The school of thought established in Connecticut led many to the Church: Rev. Messrs. Kewley, Ironsides, White, Bayley, besides laymen who examined and prayed.

When Oxford became the centre of a school in England, reviving the study of the Fathers and examining calmly what doctrines were professed, what worship followed, and what religious ideas were entertained by the Christians of the earlier centuries, they began to adopt one point of Catholicity after another, till there was no logical course but to become Catholics, though many faltered, occupying for years a false position.

The writings of this Oxford school found many readers among American Episcopalians, especially among the students of their theological seminaries, who became arrayed into two distinct parties. Alarm was given, and the question had to be met. Many of the Episcopal clergy and students who had embraced Tractarian views, lost all hope of being able to restore their denomination to fellowship with the Church, and came to seek admission to the true fold. A number were received by the Redemptorist Fathers, some entering that zealous Order, to do immense good in that congregation and the Paulist Society as missionary priests; others as secular priests, editors, or writers helped to defend the truth, refute error, and diffuse sound thought.

A strange persecution in Prussia, where the King tried to mould Lutheran and Calvinist into one body, sent many emigrants to this country; but the staunch Lutherans found their church in America so lax that many, with their clergy, sought peace in the Catholic Church.

Among the distinguished converts may be mentioned Archbishop Eccleston of Baltimore, Archbishop Bayley of the same see, Archbishop Wood of Philadelphia, Bishop Rosecrans of Columbus, Bishop Tyler of Hartford, Bishop Gilmour of Cleveland, Bishop Young of Erie, Bishop Wadhams of Ogdensburg, Rev. I. T. Hecker, editor of the *Catholic World;* Rev. C. A. Walworth, Rev. F. A. Baker, Rev. A. F. Hewit, Mrs. Connolly, foundress of the Society of the Holy Child Jesus; Dr. Levi Silliman Ives, who had been Protestant Episcopal Bishop of North Carolina; Mrs. Peters of Cincinnati; James A. McMaster, editor of the *Freeman's Journal;* Governor McLoughlin, Governor Burnett of Oregon.

CHAPTER IX.

The Mexican War—Military Chaplains—Catholic Territory annexed—Sketch of Religion in New Mexico—Bishop Lamy, Vicar Apostolic—California and its Early Missions—Father Juniper Serra—Bishop of both Californias—See of Monterey—Right Rev. Joseph S. Alemany—Emigration—Archbishopric of Oregon and Diocese of Nesqually—Sees at Albany, Buffalo, Cleveland—Bishop Cretin and Minnesota—Other New Sees.

THE annexation of Texas to the United States led to a war with Mexico, and among the troops sent to the frontier were many Catholics. The bigotry so recently excited in the country had reached the army, and Catholics were punished for refusing to take part in Protestant worship. This aroused a stern protest, and steps were taken to prevent such tyranny. Government even solicited Catholic chaplains for the army; and two Jesuit Fathers, McElroy and Rey, were sent to the post of danger, Father Rey soon to be murdered while in the discharge of his sacred calling.

The war was disastrous to Mexico, and the treaty of Guadalupe Hidalgo not only renounced all claim to Texas, but also ceded to the United States New Mexico and California. All this was Catholic territory, and had been from the earliest settlement. An Italian Franciscan Father, Mark, of Nice, had penetrated to the strange towns of the Pueblo Indians, built of sun-dried bricks and rising several stories in height, as early as 1539. Five missionaries, following in his steps, perished in attempting to plant Christianity on the upper waters of the Rio Grande. When the Spaniards at last, in 1595, under Don Juan de Oñate, occupied the country, Father Roderic Duran, of the Order of St. Francis, reared a convent and church in the town of San Gabriel del Yunque, the first white town, known since the commencement of the following century by the name of Santa Fé. Missions were established in all the pueblos, or towns; and though the priests of their old fire-worshipping creed made strong opposition, especially at Picuries and Taos, nevertheless in 1626 there were twenty-six churches in the country, and Catholic converts numbering many thousands, some of the tribes having all embraced the faith. Every mission had its school, where the children learned to read, write, and sing.

The Franciscans extended their labors to the Moquis, the Navajoes, and even to the fierce Apaches. But Paganism, though defeated, was not crushed. It had many secret votaries; and in 1680 these, led by a chief named Popé, made an outbreak at Jemes, butchering the missionary Father Morador with great cruelty. Then other towns rose, and in a few days twenty-one missionaries lay dead among the ruins of their churches and convents. The neophytes were paralyzed with terror, and forced to join the heathen bands in the attack on Santa Fé. Unable to hold it, Governor Otermin evacuated the territory, which was not recovered till 1692. The next year the missions were restored; and, though some of the Fathers lost their lives, the good work was maintained till early in this century. Regular parishes were founded at Santa Fé, Albuquerque, and Santa Cruz, with secular priests to attend them. The Bishops of Guadalajara and, on the division of that diocese, the Bishops of Durango watched over the missions of New Mexico; and several visitations made at great peril and amid constant hardships show how faithfully they discharged their duties.

Early in the seventeenth century the erection of a bishopric had been urged, but this was not carried out. In November, 1850, the Holy See made New Mexico a Vicariate Apostolic, and confided it to the Right Rev. John B. Lamy, consecrated Bishop of Agathonica. It contained sixty thousand Mexicans and eight thousand Catholic Indians, who had twenty-five churches and forty chapels.

Bishop Lamy labored earnestly to give his flock good priests, and to revive education, which had been greatly neglected under Mexican rule. He introduced the Sisters of Loretto, the Brothers of the Christian Doctrine, and the Fathers of the Society of Jesus, so that colleges, academies, schools and charitable institutions soon gave token of improvement. The Territory has never been admitted as a State, and the administrations appointed at Washington have been generally hostile to the faith of the people, and persistent effort has been made to deprive the Indians of their religious teachers.

A still more important acquisition by the treaty with Mexico was the province of Upper California, which, in its history, rivals Paraguay as one of the greatest triumphs of Catholic missionaries. Before there was an English settlement on our Atlantic coast, two Carmelite Fathers offered up the Holy Sacrifice beneath an oak tree on the shore of Monterey in 1601; and only thirty years later a Vicar Ecclesiastic of the Bishop of Guadalajara exercised jurisdiction in Lower California. There Jesuit missions grew up that gradually extended to the upper province, winning the natives to Christianity and civilization, and marking the soil with the death-blood of Fathers who laid down their lives in the zealous discharge of their apostolic duties.

When the Society of Jesus was driven from its missions and colleges by the Spanish Government, the field of Upper California was assigned to the Franciscans. Providentially they had as Superior a holy and able priest, Father Juniper Serra. On the 16th of July, 1769, he founded the Comaya mission of San Diego, and erected a chapel and mission-house, which was almost at once consecrated with blood, Father Vizcaino being wounded and an altar-boy killed by hostile Indians.

San Carlos de Monterey, San Antonio, Carmel, San Gabriel, San Luis Obispo, San Juan Capistrano, were the next missions established before the end of 1772, each with zealous Fathers, who began to learn the language of the Indians and train them to useful trades, while imparting the doctrines of Christianity and disabusing them of the old fables. While all seemed to promise the complete conversion of the province, the mission of San Diego was again attacked at night, and the buildings set on fire. Father Louis Jayme, awakened by the noise, went forth and greeted the Indians with his usual pious words: but his body, exposed in the glare of the burning buildings, was soon bristling with arrows, and as he fell the savages rushed upon him and despatched him with their swords of hardened wood.

Yet the Franciscans continued their work, founding San Francisco in 1776, and Santa Clara in the following year. At all these missions there were fine churches and buildings. The Indians, trained to agriculture and trades, supplied large quantities of produce and manufactured goods, which were shipped yearly by the missionaries, and necessary supplies for the Indians purchased and money obtained for new improvements. The Indians were not only no expense to government, but were self-supporting and rapidly increasing in means. Near each mission was a presidio, or military station, with a few soldiers for defence against hostile Indians; and around some of these white settlements gathered, chiefly of discharged soldiers and their families. The most important villages were Los Angeles, San José, and Branciforte, near Monterey.

In 1774 Father Serra was made Prefect Apostolic and died the same year, having lived to see ten thousand Indian converts. His successors extended the missions till the revolution began which made Mexico a republic. Then trouble came; the new government showed little regard for religion. In 1832 an act of Congress dissolved the missions; the lands were seized, the Indians driven off, and the missionaries left so destitute that one, Father Sarria, fell dead at the altar of pure starvation. Subsequent legislation endeavored, though too late, to remedy the mischief; but the income of the Pious Fund of California, established by charitable benefactors in the last century, was withheld. In 1840 the Holy See established the Diocese of Both Californias; and the Prefect of the Mission, Father Francisco Garcia Diego, became Bishop.

He took up his residence at Santa Barbara, and attempted to found a convent and seminary; but the Fund income was not paid, and, though a large grant of land was made, he died in 1846 without accomplishing any of his projects. He did what he could to revive a spirit of religion among his flock, and especially to save the remnant of the Mission Indians, which had dwindled from thirty to four thousand.

When California became part of the United States some emigration from the older States began, the climate and soil offering attractions; but within two years gold was discovered, and the whole country proved to be rich in that precious metal. At once thousands poured in from all parts, making their way by land and water. A city sprang up at San Francisco, and many of these new-comers were Catholics. The administrator of the diocese, Very Rev. J. M. Gonzales, a man of zeal, had no priests for this new flock till some came from Oregon, when a wooden shanty at San Francisco was bought and blessed in 1849. The next year the Holy See divided the California diocese and established a new see at Monterey, the Very Rev. Joseph S. Alemany, Provincial of the Dominicans in Ohio, being appointed bishop. Fathers of his Order soon came, with nuns of the same rule. From Oregon, nearly depopulated by the rush of gold-seekers to California, came Sisters of Notre Dame. A few years later Sisters of Charity and Jesuit Fathers began to labor in the same field.

The remnant of the Mission Indians became subject to the control of the Indian Department at Washington, which has almost always been managed in a spirit hostile to Catholics. These Indians were assigned to Protestant hands and cut off from the ministry of Catholic priests. The Mexicans, who had first wronged these Indians, were already punished, and were pushed aside by the energetic new-comers.

While religion was thus consolidating her institutions in the newly acquired territory, she had lost nothing in the older portions. Emigration from Germany, bringing many who were practically infidels, few zealous Protestants, but many Catholics, steadily increased; and in 1847 the famine in Ireland caused thousands to fly from that unhappy island to seek homes in the New World. Fever broke out in the crowded ships and many died soon after landing, but priests and sisters were at hand to give them tender care and all the consolations of religion, not a few of them winning the crown of martyrs of charity.

The organization and legislation of the Church went on. In 1846 Oregon was raised to an archiepiscopal see, with Wallawalla, (now Nesqually) and Vancouver's Island, as suffragans. The next year St. Louis became an archbishopric, and sees were erected at Albany, Buffalo, and Cleveland. How Catholicity had increased in New York State may be seen in the fact that, in his first year, the new Bishop of Albany found in his diocese twenty churches and thirty-four priests; and in Ohio the Bishop of Cleveland began with sixteen churches and thirty-three priests.

The great tendency of immigration was to still more westerly parts, where land was almost free and of the greatest fertility. In 1849 Bishop Cretin was consecrated for a new see, established at St. Paul, Minnesota. He had been a missionary among whites and Indians in Wisconsin and Iowa, and knew the country and people well. He devoted himself to encourage Catholic immigrants to come and settle in his diocese, and was gratified with beholding a fine, industrious, intelligent flock gather around him. In 1850 sees were established at Wheeling and at Savannah, although the Catholic body had not increased very rapidly in Western Virginia and Georgia. At the same time New Orleans became a metropolitan see, and the old province of Baltimore was divided by the promotion of the Bishops of New York and Cincinnati to the dignity of archbishops. In New York State the Catholic body had so increased that it became necessary to make Long Island a diocese; and at the same time the State of New Jersey, hitherto divided between the Dioceses of New York and Philadelphia, was placed under the jurisdiction of a bishop at Newark. The Indian Territory east of the Rocky Mountains and New Mexico were made Vicariates in 1850, and for the latter territory a see was erected at Santa Fé three years later, and in the East another at Erie, in Pennsylvania.

The province of Cincinnati embraced also the dioceses of Cleveland, Detroit, Louisville, and Vincennes. The venerable Archbishop Purcell had already founded the Theological Seminary of Mt. St. Mary's of the West, which became for thirty years a nursery of pious and learned priests. In 1855 he held his first Provincial Council, which devoted itself mainly to Catholic education and the cause of temperance. A second Council followed in 1858, and in October of that year he celebrated the Silver Jubilee of his episcopal consecration. Although Cleveland had been made a separate bishopric, the diocese in 1860 contained 160,000 Catholics, with 148 churches and 123 priests. Rt. Rev. S. H. Rosecrans was appointed bishop auxiliar in 1862, and some years after Bishop of Columbus, the diocese being again divided. In 1870 the Catholics tested in the tribunals the right of the Public School authorities to inculcate Protestantism on Catholic pupils, but failed to obtain justice. In 1880 the churches, priests, and people in the diocese of Cincinnati exceeded those in its larger extent in 1860; while religious of more than fifteen Orders are laboring in education or works of mercy.

CHAPTER X.

The Blessed Virgin Conceived without Sin chosen Patroness of the Church in the United States—Progress of the Benedictines in the United States—The Passionists—Brothers of the Christian Schools—Brothers of Mary—Sisters of the Good Shepherd—The First Plenary Council of Baltimore—New Sees—The American College at Rome—Archbishop Bedini sent by the Pope as Nuncio to the United States—Anti-Catholic Agitations—The Know-Nothings—Acts of Violence—Father Bapst—Churches destroyed in New Hampshire and Maine—At Williamsburg and Newark—Anti-Catholic Laws—The Louisville Riots—Archbishop Hughes—Bishop Spalding.

THE Sixth Provincial Council of Baltimore, besides adopting salutary rules of discipline, sought supernatural aid in the extension of religion and morality by placing the country under the protection of the Blessed Virgin Mary Conceived without Sin, who was formally chosen as the Patroness of the Church in the United States. Oregon held its first Provincial Council in February, 1848, and Baltimore her seventh in 1849. Synods were held, too, in various dioceses.

During this period the ancient Order of Benedictines began labors in the United States, which have been signally blessed by God. In 1846 the Rev. Boniface Wimmer, of the Abbey of Metten, in Bavaria, came to Pennsylvania with some candidates for choir and lay brothers, and was placed by Bishop O'Connor, of Pittsburgh, on property in Westmoreland County purchased in the last century by the Rev. Mr. Browers, the first priest in that part. Here Dom Wimmer founded a monastery, to which he annexed a seminary and college, and received so many postulants that the institutions attained great prosperity, and the monastery was erected into an abbey. Missions were established in other parts of the State, in New Jersey, Kentucky, Illinois, Kansas, Minnesota, North Carolina, and Georgia. These prospered so that other abbeys were established at Atchison, Kansas, and St. Cloud, Minnesota. The Fathers of the Order labored almost exclusively among the Germans, and have rendered great service to religion. One monastery, that of Creston, Iowa, is, however, altogether English speaking.

About 1850 a colony of Benedictine Fathers from the famous monastery of Our Lady of the Hermits, Einsiedeln, Switzerland, founded the monastery of St. Meinrad's in Indiana, which has furnished excellent priests to that State, and subsequently the Abbot Martin Marty undertook Indian missions in Dakota Territory among the Sioux. His attempt met with great success, and, resigning his abbey, he devoted himself entirely to his new work, having been made Vicar Apostolic of that Territory. This Order has also given to the American Episcopate the Right Rev. Louis M. Fink, Vicar Apostolic of Kansas, and subsequently Bishop of Leavenworth, and Right Rev. Rupert Seidenbush, Vicar Apostolic of Northern Minnesota.

Another accession to the clergy was a colony of Passionists, an Order of most austere missionary priests founded in the last century by Saint Paul of the Cross. These religious, who opened a Retreat at Pittsburgh in 1852, have since established houses at Dunkirk, N. Y., and Hoboken, N. J. Their zeal and eloquence in missions in all parts of the country have converted many, and revived piety and devotion far and near.

In Ohio the self-denying and devoted priest, Rev. Francis de Sales Brunner, introduced the priests of the Most Precious Blood, a congregation founded by the Venerable Caspar di Bufalo. The community has grown, and has for years rendered efficient service in the West, and Sisters of the same rule are engaged in teaching. This body of regulars has given to the hierarchy Bishop Dwenger, of Fort Wayne.

The teaching Orders developed greatly. In 1848 some Brothers of the Christian Schools, a community founded in France in the seventeenth century by the Venerable John Baptist de la Salle, were invited to New York by the Rev. Annet Lafont, pastor of the French Church, who confided his schools to their care. They produced so favorable an impression as teachers that they soon opened an academy, which is now Manhattan College, with dependent institutions, and their services are sought in many dioceses, to direct the parochial schools for boys.

The Brothers of Mary about the same time began in the Diocese of Cincinnati, and have now many schools under their care. The Brothers of the Third Order of St. Francis, introduced at Pittsburgh in 1847, have also extended to other dioceses.

The School Sisters of Notre Dame, founded by the Blessed Peter Fourrier, and revived in Germany, were introduced to direct the parochial schools for girls in the German churches of Wisconsin; but the care taken to train the Sisters as teachers gave them a reputation far and wide, and they have spread over many dioceses to the Atlantic coast.

The higher education of girls led to new foundations in various cities of Ladies of the Sacred Heart. Visitation Nuns, Sisters of St. Joseph, and the Benedictine Nuns, founded in the Diocese of Erie, have academies and free schools in various parts of the country.

In the works of mercy, the Sisters of the Good Shepherd multiplied their houses; and the Sisters of Mercy, faithful to their work by visits to the sick and poor, to the erring and the prisoner, relieve human suffering and revive faith, too often obscured by ignorance and passion.

The country was now divided into several ecclesiastical provinces, and separate provincial Councils had been held.

It was deemed, however, important, in order to secure unity of discipline as much as possible, to hold a Council for the whole country. This was proposed to Pope Pius IX., who, on the 19th of August, 1851, authorized the Most Rev. Francis P. Kenrick, Archbishop of Baltimore, to convene it, appointing him Delegate Apostolic for that purpose.

This imposing assembly met on the 8th of May, 1852, in the Cathedral of Baltimore, and was attended by the six Archbishops of Baltimore, Oregon, St. Louis, New Orleans, New York, and Cincinnati, and the twenty-three Bishops of Mobile, Dubuque, Nashville, Natchez, Wheeling, Galveston, Pittsburgh, Little Rock, Albany, Charleston, Boston, Cleveland, Buffalo, Louisville, Chicago, Nesqually, Hartford, Savannah, Richmond, and St. Paul; the Bishop Administrator of Detroit, and the Vicars Apostolic of New Mexico and Indian Territory, as well as by the Bishop of Monterey, who was subject directly to the Holy See. Among these were the great theologian Archbishop Kenrick, Archbishop Hughes, Bishop Spalding, of Louisville, Bishop O'Connor, and the future Cardinal, then Bishop McCloskey. There were also present the Abbot of St. Mary of La Trappe, the Commissary General of the Augustinians, the Visitor General of the Dominicans, the Superior of the Benedictines, the Superior of the Franciscans, and, representing the four divisions of the Society of Jesus laboring in the country, the Provincial of Maryland, the Vice Provincial of Missouri, and the Superiors of New York and New Orleans; the Provincial of the Redemptorists, the Rector of the Sulpitian seminary, and a Superior of the Priests of the Mission.

In their decrees, the Fathers of the Council recognized the Sovereign Pontiff as the head of the Church, the successor of St. Peter, and the father and doctor of all Christians, with full power from Christ to feed, rule, and govern the whole Church.

Among the important steps advised were the establish-

ment of a Chancery in each diocese, for the more orderly
transaction of ecclesiastical business, and the preservation
of archives; the appointment of a Council in each diocese, to aid the Bishop; a strict revision of prayer-books;
the laying off of parochial districts, the publication of banns,
the establishment of schools, and of a seminary at least for
each province, and the extension of the Association for the
Propagation of the Faith.

The Holy See approved the decrees of the Council, and,
at its request, erected new sees at Portland—Maine and
New Hampshire forming the diocese; at Burlington for
Vermont; at Brooklyn for
Long Island; at Newark for
New Jersey; at Covington
in Kentucky; at Quincy in
Illinois; at Natchitoches in
Louisiana; at Santa Fé in
New Mexico; and at San
Francisco in California, of
which Dr. Alemany, of Mon-
terey, became Archbishop.
Upper Michigan became a
Vicariate Apostolic, under
the zealous and devoted
Indian missionary, Right
Rev. Frederic Baraga.

Right Rev. Frederic Baraga.

The Bishop of Burlington, Right Rev. Louis Count de
Goesbriand; the Bishop of Newark, Right Rev. James
Roosevelt Bayley, a nephew of Mother Seton, foundress
of the Sisters of Charity; and the Right Rev. John Lough-
lin, Bishop of Brooklyn—were consecrated in the Ca-
thedral at New York on the 30th October, 1853, by the
Most Rev. Cajetan Bedini, Archbishop of Thebes and
Nuncio of Pope Pius IX.

The Apostolic Baraga was subsequently made Bishop
of Sault Ste. Marie and Marquette, and devoted his whole life

BISHOP BARAGA VISITING AN INDIAN STATION.

to his flock, visiting assiduously the scattered Indian stations, laboring by word and pen to instruct his flock.

Pope Pius IX. had taken a deep interest in the growth of the Church in the United States, and, to secure it a supply of thoroughly trained priests, proposed the establishment of an American College at Rome, where clergymen could reside and attend the courses in the great theological schools there, and become familiar with the management of ecclesiastical affairs and the solemn rites of the Church, as used in the capital of Christendom. He gave a house for the purpose, and the hierarchy of the United States co-operated in founding the college. It has rendered great service to the Church, but unfortunately has not attracted the attention of wealthy American Catholics, whose donations and legacies long ere this should have endowed it with means to enable it to increase its usefulness to meet the wants of the country.

The illustrious Pope showed his interest in America also by sending a Nuncio to the United States. Our government some years previously had sent an Ambassador to Rome, apparently without any knowledge of the long established system of diplomatic intercourse between the Popes and foreign powers. No intimation was given to the Holy See of any wish on the part of the American government to derogate from the custom of centuries. The Sovereign Pontiff did not at once send a Nuncio to this country, but in 1852 he despatched Mgr. Cajetan Bedini, Archbishop of Thebes, a prelate of great ability, learning, and mildness, as Nuncio to Brazil, and intrusted him with a letter to the President of the United States, so as gradually to open official intercourse.

At this moment an anti-Catholic excitement had again arisen in the United States. An organization known as the Order of United Americans had spread over the country, the object of which was to exclude Catholics from office, business, and as far as possible from all civil rights.

The party of which this society was the nucleus was popularly called the Know-Nothings. Gavazzi, an apostate priest from Italy, gathered crowds to hear his denunciations of the Church. A fanatic named Orr, who called himself the Angel Gabriel, went from place to place exciting the mob to violence by incendiary appeals. The arrival of Mgr. Bedini gave fresh impulse to the intolerant spirit, and the great German infidel element in the country, with similar refugees from other parts of Europe, whose great object was the overthrow of the Papal power in Rome, gave all their aid. Mgr. Bedini had been Governor of Bologna when that city was occupied by the Austrians, who arrested and shot several revolutionists, including a priest named Bassi. All these executions were now ascribed to Mgr. Bedini as his work, although he was utterly powerless and had taken no part in the affair. A plot was formed to assassinate the Nuncio, and though he escaped by a timely warning, his informant was poniarded in the streets of New York, and the authorities dared not investigate the affair. As the Nuncio visited other cities he was mobbed, especially at Pittsburgh and Cincinnati. At Washington the question of his reception led to most pitiable equivocation, and they finally took the ground that under our Constitution a Nuncio could not be received, but that a simple Ambassador would be, although from the outset they knew that the Popes never sent any.

All this fed the anti-Catholic excitement, which soon culminated in acts of violence. As usual the cry was raised that Catholics wish to drive the Bible out of the common schools, and meanwhile they forced Catholic pupils in the schools to take part in the reading of the Protestant Bible and the offering of Protestant prayers. In their blindness they accused of intolerance those who merely protested against their intolerance. In the spring of 1854 the Catholics at Ellsworth, Maine, finding the position intolerable, by the advice of their pastor, Rev. John Bapst, S. J., petitioned that their children should be exempted from attendance at this part of the school exercises, and, when it was refused, applied to the courts for redress. On this, a town-meeting was held and a resolution passed by that body to tar and feather Father Bapst on his next visit to the town. In pursuance of this, when the Catholic priest arrived on the 14th of October to celebrate Mass, the next day he was seized, stripped naked, vilely abused, ridden on a rail, and covered with tar and feathers, amid the most blasphemous imprecations. When the town authorities had wreaked their vengeance on him for two hours, these officials left him after midnight in the muddy road, to drag himself as best he might to the house where he usually stayed. The heroic priest reached it at last, in most intense suffering, and removed the evidences of the outrage as far as he could; then, without the slightest refreshment, went up to the altar, with his bruised and lacerated body, to offer the Holy Sacrifice for his little flock.

A grand jury met, took the oath to present all offenders, but could find no evidence of any injury to Rev. Mr. Bapst. No one was indicted for the outrage, or for the theft of his watch and purse.

Indignant protests came from many Protestants at this fearful act, but the "Native American" party gained adherents and carried elections in many States, especially in New Hampshire, a State where even now Catholics are excluded from office.

Other cases of violence had occurred in that State. In July a mob held possession of Manchester for two days, wrecked the houses of many Catholics, and actually tore the church to pieces, destroying it from top to bottom. At Dorchester in the same State the Catholic church was undermined and blown up with gunpowder. At Bath in Maine a mob, led by Orr, burst in the church doors, tore down the altar and pulpit, and placing on the pile the cross from the steeple, set it afire, and reduced the edifice to ashes.

The fierce hatred had not died out a year later, for when Bishop Bacon attempted to lay the corner-stone of a new church, a mob took possession and prevented the ceremony.

In September an armed procession paraded the streets of Newark, New Jersey, and demolished a German Catholic church. Two months later a mob attacked a church in Williamsburg, N. Y., and, after wrecking it completely, set it afire, but the military arrived in time to save it. Even as far South as Mobile the spirit spread; a priest was beaten, and threatened with further violence, if he did not stop visiting a neighboring village to say Mass.

Even legislative bodies felt the influence. New York passed laws to prevent bequests to Catholic institutions, and to vest in trustees elected by the congregations, all property held by the bishops, even where they had bought it as individuals at public sale, ordered by the court on the bankruptcy of the trustees.

The Legislature of Massachusetts, which numbered several ministers, appointed a committee to investigate the condition of the Catholic convents; and in that of Notre Dame, Roxbury, these legislators of the proudest State in the Union acted as the lowest and most degraded ruffians. In fact, the conduct of one member in his travels was in such defiance of all decency that the Legislature expelled him.

The most fearful scenes of bloodshed were enacted in Louisville in August, 1855, when an attempt was made to burn the Cathedral, and numbers of houses of Catholics were fired and destroyed, and more than twenty of the inmates were burned alive or shot down by the mob.

All this violence was of no avail. Catholicity grew in spite of all such outrages and injustice, whether from the government or the mob.

The Catholics in the United States at this time numbered at least two millions and a half, but were almost entirely unrepresented in the Legislatures of the States and in Congress. It was almost impossible for a Catholic to be elected to any position of influence. Neither of the political parties would nominate a Catholic, the bigoted opposition being such that thousands would vote against their own party rather than give a vote to a Catholic; and this feeling prevails to no slight extent even to this day.

In all this storm against the Church, the press, too, sided generally against it, pandering to the bigotry of the masses, and reluctantly giving place to any defence of Catholics.

Most Rev. John Hughes, D.D.

The advocacy of their cause in a way to reach the better class of minds in the country, devolved on a few, whose recognized ability, intellect, and eloquence commanded a hearing. Among these prominently stood the great Archbishop of New York, the Most Rev. John Hughes, whose courageous words, full of manliness, vigor, and truth, came with crushing power on the insincere who perverted truth and reason to assail us. No Catholic writer in the country was ever so widely read; and, as his merciless logic left little chance for even such a plausible answer as would satisfy people of average education, his influence was most beneficial. During both anti-Catholic movements his writings had been timely and effective. His letter to James Harper, the Native American Mayor of New York, on the evil spirit of the times; his crushing of Stone, Bennett, Hale, and other assailants of the Church; his letter to Hon. Lewis Cass on the affair of the Madiai; his controversy with Senator Brookes on the Church Property bill—all tended to give the public mind a fair view of the position held by those whom he represented. The Protestant public looked to Bishop Hughes as the great exponent of Catholic thought, impressed by his honesty, uprightness, and disinterestedness; for he never sought the great influence he acquired, and never employed it for any ends but those of truth and justice. In his own diocese his views were grand, looking to the future with sanguine hope. He wished to endow it with all necessary institutions of learning, secular and theological; with every institution for the exercise of the works of mercy: he wished to give dignity to the divine worship and all the services of the Church, that every Catholic might feel a pride in being a child of such a mother. In this view he laid, in 1858, the corner-stone of a new Cathedral in New York on the site of the college occupied by the Jesuits nearly half a century before, but which the growing city had encircled. This edifice, the noblest in its design and proportions yet seen on the Continent, was completed by his successor, Cardinal McCloskey, and dedicated, with a pomp never before witnessed in the United States, on the 25th of May, 1879.

In the West, Bishop Spalding, of Louisville, who had impressed Rome with the depth and soundness of his theological learning, showed also the ability to reach the popular mind in America on Catholic questions. Typically American in thought and manner, his sincere manliness, mental vigor, and honesty told irresistibly, and prepared all for the influence which he exerted in America, and which he displayed in the Vatican Council after his elevation to the Archiepiscopal See of Baltimore.

CHAPTER XI.

Services of the Clergy and Orders in Yellow-Fever Times—The Franciscans in the United States—Position of the Church in 1861—The Civil War—Priests and Sisters on the Battle-field and in Hospitals—A Benedictine killed in his Good Work—The Church's Losses—Treatment of Bishop Elder—The Second Plenary Council—Work among the Negroes—Great Progress in North Carolina—Georgia—New Dioceses in Texas—Indian Territory a Prefecture—Revival of Anti-Catholic Feeling—Bigotry on the Bench—Catholic School Books—Missions by the Redemptorists and Others—Diffusion of Catholic Books and Periodicals—Theological Seminary—The Yellow Fever in 1878—The Indian Missions—An American Cardinal—His Eminence John, Cardinal McCloskey, Archbishop of New York.

IN the lull that followed the Know-Nothing madness, the Church kept on its course, and, even amid that excitement, she gave a lesson more potent than words. While fanatics were destroying Catholic churches in the North, the people saw with admiration the zeal of the clergy and religious at Savannah, then ravaged by yellow-fever. They cheerfully attended the sick to the last, the Bishop, Right Rev. F. X. Gartland, with another prelate, Bishop Barron, and two Sisters of Mercy dying of the pestilence.

Undeterred by the hostility they might encounter, a colony of Reformed Franciscans, under the Very Rev. Pamphilo da Magliano, came from Italy in 1855 to found a house of their order at Ellicottsville, N. Y., and, entering fervently into the mission work, soon established a college and seminary, and directed churches in various parts of New York and Connecticut. Other communities of the same Order from Germany founded flourishing convents in Ohio and Indiana; the oldest, however, being those in California, which date back to the settlement of that colony.

When the Civil War broke out in the United States in 1861, the Church, which in 1808 had in that territory two dioceses, two bishops, and less than a hundred churches and priests, had increased so as to form seven ecclesiastical provinces, forty-three dioceses, three vicariates apostolic, with two thousand two hundred and thirty-five priests, who attended nearly twenty-four hundred churches and twelve hundred stations and chapels. The number of the faithful was more than three millions, and their spiritual wants were much better supplied. There were eighty-nine colleges and male academies, and two hundred and two institutions for the higher education of girls. The parish schools were rapidly advancing in numbers and proficiency, and numbered nearly five hundred, with a hundred thousand pupils. More than a hundred orphan asylums were dotted over the country; there were twenty-five Catholic hospitals, five Magdalen asylums, many widows' homes, industrial schools, and other institutions of a charitable character.

The great mass of the population lay in the Northern and Western States, those south of Maryland on the east and of the Ohio river on the west containing only four hundred and sixty-three out of the two thousand two hundred and thirty-five priests.

A terrible civil war broke out at this time. A fanatical spirit at the North, which from time to time excited hostility to the Church on other occasions, sought the abolition, or at least the restriction, of slavery in the South. Numbers of Protestant clergymen took an active part in stirring up a bitter sectional feeling; and when troubles began in regard to the extension of slavery in Kansas, the Protestant pulpits of the East rang with appeals to their flocks. In this matter the Catholics stood aloof. When the war came no one could accuse them of having done aught to precipitate it. Yet, as we have seen, they were chiefly in the Northern States which invited immigration,

THE CHURCH IN AMERICA. 403

while the South discouraged it, and ignorant prejudice against the Church prevailed as much at the South as at the North.

The South acted with energy, not only in the field, but

Consoling the Dying.

by securing sympathy from the governments of Europe. To counteract this the Government sought the aid of a Catholic prelate. At the request of the President, Archbishop Hughes visited Europe, and labored there to secure the great object—the restoration of peace and union in the country. When the war went on and large armies were called into the field, there were thousands of Catholics in the ranks, and Catholic chaplains and Sisters did their duty nobly on the battle-field and in the hospitals, where so many lay in suffering and pain. One Benedictine Father, Dom Emeran Blümel, lost his life on the battle-field of Jonesborough while attending the dying; and many priests and religious brought back the seeds of death from the scene of their labors. These sacrifices were not in vain. Men from parts of the country where the Church was known only by vague rumors as of some monstrous thing, looked with wonder at the devoted priest or sister; and when warned to prepare for death asked the aid of those who came nearest to their highest ideal of the Christian ministry, and died with the prayer of Catholic faith on their lips.

The war was disastrous to the South. Nearly all the battles were fought in the Southern States; and, as the Northern armies advanced, the officers frequently could not repress, or encouraged, the destruction of Catholic Church property. St. Finbar's Cathedral, with the bishop's house, in Charleston, and its valuable library, perished in the bombardment. Sherman's destruction of Columbia swept away St. Mary's College, the convent of the Sisters of Mercy, and that of the Ursulines. In Georgia, St. Mary's, in Camden County, and the church at Dalton perished; in Florida, Jacksonville and Pensacola saw the Catholic churches destroyed, and that at Warrington perished during the bombardment. In various places churches were taken as hospitals or for other military purposes, and left utterly unfit for use.

Besides this many communities abandoned their institutions, unable to struggle against adversity. Schools were broken up and works of mercy forgotten.

In the progress of the war the fanatical anti-Catholic spirit began to manifest itself in various ways. Oaths were imposed which Catholic clergymen could not in conscience take, and those who refused were subjected to various annoyances and petty persecutions. This was especially the case in Kentucky. The grossest violation of law, no less than of the whole spirit of American institutions, was displayed in Mississippi, where Colonel Farrar, post commandant, issued an order requiring all clergymen in their public worship to offer a prayer for the President of the United States. Against this Bishop Elder, of Natchez, remonstrated, taking the broad ground that as Congress could make no law establishing or regulating religion, no official could do what Congress could not do, and that no official could require the Catholic Church to alter her liturgy and introduce or omit prayers to suit his fancy.

Bishop Elder had been unremitting in his attention to the sick and wounded on the battlefield and in the hospital, and one of his scanty band of priests had died in his zealous mission. In spite of this, the Bishop was arrested and carried to Vidalia, in the State of Louisiana. He was there detained till General Brayman, to whom the case was carried, revoked the illegal order, but in terms insulting to the Bishop.

Soon after the close of the Civil War steps were taken for convening another Plenary Council at Baltimore. It met on the 7th of October, 1866. Besides Archbishop Spalding, who presided as Apostolic Delegate, there were present the six Archbishops of Oregon, St. Louis, Cincinnati, San Francisco, New Orleans, and New York, and thirty-seven Bishops, besides three Mitred Abbots, the local Superiors of thirteen religious Orders, and one hundred and twenty Theologians. In this Council it was resolved to treat the whole subject of doctrine and discipline, so as to make the decrees a manual on all important questions. Each topic was long and carefully studied before the Council met. The decrees were approved at Rome, and, couched in pure, clear Latin, excited general admiration. Cardinal Cullen, primate of Ireland, declared them a mine of every sort of knowledge necessary for an ecclesiastic; and at the Council of the Vatican, where the bishops of the whole world assembled, these decrees were in the hands of many of the Fathers.

In the Southern States the emancipation of the negroes opened that race as a field for Catholic zeal; not only did the priests at various points labor to explain to them the pure truths of the Gospel, but a number of clergymen came from England to devote themselves especially to this neglected race. They belonged to St. Joseph's Society for Foreign Missions.

Most Rev. James Gibbons, D.D.

The war left Catholic affairs in the Southern States in a most desolate condition, and the succeeding years of misrule prevented any immediate improvement. Emigrants shunned States where nothing was safe, and the general inflation, with the financial distress that followed, increased their difficulties. This appealed to Catholic charity everywhere, and Archbishop Spalding of Baltimore exerted himself earnestly to relieve them amid their trials.

Yet Catholicity began to look hopefully forward in a quarter that seemed to promise least. On the appointment of the Right Rev. James Gibbons as Vicar Apostolic of North Carolina, attention was drawn to the claims of the Church. The Bishop, devoting himself entirely to extending Catholicity in the State, presented its doctrines and practices in so clear a light that numbers, aided by God's grace, opened their hearts to the faith, and congregations of converts were formed in several places in that State, which seemed impenetrable to the truth

In Georgia, under Bishops Verot, Persico, and Gross, the Church began to recover, and a body of French Benedictines began a mission in the Isle of Hope, laboring especially among the colored people. The superior, Dom Gabriel Bergier, and some of his associates died of yellow-fever in 1875, amid their labors, but the good work was not abandoned. The Abbot of St. Vincent's, in Pennsylvania, resolved to carry on the good work, and Father Oswald Moosmüller, a man of learning and research, renounced his studies to devote himself to the service of this benighted people.

Texas recovered more rapidly from the prostration caused by the war, and received a steadily increasing immigration, chiefly German and Polish. The Mexican population also grew. On the 3d of September, 1874, Pope Pius IX. divided the Diocese of Galveston, which now had a Catholic population of nearly a quarter of a million, with two hundred and fifty churches and chapels scattered over the vast territory. A new see was erected at San Antonio, and the zealous Bishop Pellicer was soon giving a new impulse to the faith and laboring to supply the spiritual wants of his flock. On his death, in 1880, his diocese had gained greatly in numbers and Catholic spirit.

The district along the Rio Grande, with a large Mexican population in scattered ranches, among whom it was necessary to revive the faith and especially the practice of Christian duties, became the Vicariate Apostolic of Brownsville, where Bishop Manucy, struggling with peculiar difficulties, labored for years with consoling results.

The Indian Territory west of the State of Arkansas also invited the zeal of the Fathers of St. Benedict, and Dom Isidore Robot began a mission there. Catholic Indians had been transported to that territory by Government, and were destitute of clergymen; there were scattered Catholics in several tribes; and a band of Spanish Catholic Indians from Florida were to be recalled to long-forgotten duties. Ere long, in 1876, Dom Robot was made Prefect

Apostolic of Indian Territory, and his monastery became the Abbey of the Sacred Heart. The Diocese of Little Rock, on which the Territory had depended, began to increase at last by immigration.

Throughout the Northern States there had been general progress, but the close of the war was a signal for the revival of old bitterness against the Church. An attempt was made to make the school question not a State but a national matter. General Grant, elected President in 1869, showed a disposition to unite with the old Know-Nothing party, and on several occasions alluded to the school question, taking ground, however, in favor of absolutely godless schools. The question of the right of bigoted Protestants to force their erroneous and mutilated translation into schools as being *the* Bible, came before the courts in Ohio; but the judiciary there, as in Massachusetts, New York, and Pennsylvania, listened to prejudice, and, when Catholic cases came up, sought to warp the law so as to annoy the Church. Thus, in Massachusetts, a priest was cast in heavy damages for cautioning his flock against those who favored assailants of Catholicity while pretending to be Catholics; in Pennsylvania, a judge declared that a priest who refused to give to his bishop any account of his administration of the affairs of his church, could not be removed, but had a legal right to the possession of the church and the receipt of the pew-rents; in New York, a judge decided that a Protestant and Freemason had a right to be interred in a lot he had bought for his Catholic wife and children. Higher courts set aside such law, but the spirit of hostility was made painfully apparent.

These signs induced new and greater exertion to expand our system of parochial schools, so as to avoid any necessity for Catholics to send their children to the public schools, which it was evident must soon be either absolutely Protestant or utterly infidel. New schools were established in many parts, notably in New England, where the parochial system had made little progress. The teaching Orders already in the country spread, and were aided by others from abroad, like the Presentation Nuns, the Sisters of the Holy Child Jesus, the Sisters of Christian Charity. The preparation of suitable school-books received greater care, and not only Readers, but series of Geographies and School Histories were prepared equal to any published for use in the public schools. Some of these were mere modifications of Protestant works, but others were intrinsically Catholic.

Among the means of elevating the tone of Catholic religious feeling, and increasing the general frequentation of the sacraments, was the system of missions. One of the great propagators of this was the Count de Forbin Janson, who spent some years in Canada and the United States. In this country the good work was taken up seriously by the Redemptorists, first among the German population, and in time among those speaking English; the Jesuit Fathers, as well as the Passionists, Paulists, and Dominicans, Oblates and Priests of the Holy Cross and of the Precious Blood, all joining in the good work. There are now few parishes in the country where a mission is not given once in five years, and at such times not many are deaf to the call of religion. Hundreds return to the practices of religion; domestic piety revives; good books are read; the children instructed; Protestants whose doubts have been excited come to listen and be convinced.

The permanent good is shown by the great diffusion of works of piety, books of meditation, the spiritual works of Father Faber, translations of the best ascetical works in French, German, Italian, and other languages, and in the existence of periodicals like the *Ave Maria* and the *Messenger of the Sacred Heart*. America has, too, produced the remarkable "Imitation of the Sacred Heart," by the Jesuit Father Arnoudt; and the "Sacrifice of the Mass,"

"The Holy Eucharist," and other works of a similar character, by Father Müller of the Congregation of the Most Holy Redeemer.

In the higher and more careful training of the clergy great progress has been made. Besides the American College at Rome, a Missionary College was founded at Louvain, chiefly through the exertions of Bishop Lefevre of Detroit and Bishop Spalding of Louisville, to draw recruits for the American Mission from Catholic Belgium, the land of Nerinckx and De Smet. In the United States, the Seminary of St. Mary's, Baltimore, with its preparatory college, and Mount St. Mary's developed; the Seminary of St. Charles Borromeo, near Philadelphia, became an institution of great merit; a provincial Theological Seminary for New England, New York, and New Jersey was established at Troy, and has students enough to occupy a faculty of great learning and ability. The Seminary of Mount St. Mary's, Cincinnati, was long a thriving institution, and the Lazarists not only continued their good work in Missouri, but established a successful seminary at Niagara.

Besides these, the Society of Jesus, founded at Woodstock, Maryland, a college for the thorough ecclesiastical training of all its scholastics in the United States; and the fame of its professors is recognized everywhere. The Redemptorists have a similar house of studies at Ilchester; the Franciscans at Alleghany, N. Y., and the Benedictines at St. Vincent's, Pennsylvania, have theological schools for members of their Orders as well as for candidates for the ranks of the secular clergy.

Catholic devotedness was shown in a remarkable degree during the yellow-fever which ravaged the Mississippi Valley in 1878. Several priests and sisters of various Orders died nobly at New Orleans; Vicksburg, which became a perfect plague-stricken city, saw the bishop of the diocese facing every danger, three of his priests and a number of his religious dying while attending the sick. At Memphis, another stricken city, priest after priest died, volunteers constantly arriving to take their place or aid those who sank under their labors. Zealous priests formed, outside the city limits, Camp Father Matthew as a refuge for those who could remove from the city, and before the pestilence ended nine priests and thirteen sisters died.

The Indian missions had been the care of the Church from the period of the discovery. Spanish missions extended from the Chesapeake to the Rio Grande, and from its shores to the Pacific; Maryland had its Catholic converts before the Protestants in the colony had a minister; the missionaries of France had converts from the mouths of the St. Lawrence, Mississippi, and Columbia, throughout the valleys of those great rivers. When our republic was established it contained Catholic Indians; and the acquisitions from France and Spain added a large body of Indians who professed our faith. The second Council of Baltimore assigned this field especially to the Jesuits, and they labored in it with zeal and success among the Pottawatamies, Kansas, Osages, Blackfeet, Flatheads, Nez Perces, Ponds d'Oreilles. The Canadian missionaries and Oblates in Oregon won the Yakamas and other tribes. Lakes Superior and Michigan were dotted all around with Catholic Missions. Many of the early treaties with Indian tribes recognized Catholicity as established among them. These missions were injured by the frequent removal of the Indians to points west of the Mississippi, and finally by the establishment of reservations with a monstrous agency system, under which the most arbitrary powers are conferred on a class of men notoriously unworthy, by whom they are most tyrannically exercised.

This was a great obstacle to the progress of the missions; yet after the civil war one-sixth of all the missionaries employed among the Indian tribes were Catholics, although the Protestant establishments were aided by large missionary societies, which spent money freely. They took alarm, and General Grant established a policy by which the various agencies were divided among religious denominations. In this division no regard was had to what the religious body was doing in the field, or the religion of the Indians. Out of all only two or three agencies were allotted to the Catholics; and nearly every tribe with Catholic Indians was assigned to some Protestant body, who appointed the agent, and made their form of faith the established religion of the agency. Catholic missionaries were driven out and beaten for attempting to visit their flocks; churches seized by military force; and the Indians prevented from enjoying the consolations of their faith on the reservation, and forbidden to leave the reservation to reach a Catholic chapel or priest. One man claimed that, as agent, he had an exclusive right to baptize the Indians, and made a formal complaint to Washington against the Catholic priest for telling his flock that they must bring their children to him.

His Eminence John, Cardinal McCloskey.

As the Catholics had no missionary society in the country, Government ignored the Catholic bishops and priests, and their remonstrances were unheeded. This led to the formation of an Indian Missionary Association, due to the zeal of the Very Rev. Mr. Brouillet, and to the appointment of a Catholic Commissioner at Washington, to represent to Government the claims of the oppressed and enslaved Catholic Indians. Little, however, has been effected. The Catholic Indians of New Mexico, California, Oregon, and elsewhere are still almost entirely under the control of Protestant agents, who employ teachers and call in missionaries whose sole object is to tamper with their faith.

The development and increase of Catholicity in America are seen in the presence of so many of the Archbishops and Bishops at the Vatican Council; in the elevation of the Most Rev. John McCloskey, Archbishop of New York, to the rank of Cardinal; and in the numerous band of pilgrims, including bishops, priests, and lay persons of both sexes, who a few years ago joined in a pilgrimage to Rome and the great shrines in Europe.

CHAPTER XII.

The Saints in America—St. Turibius, Archbishop of Lima—St. Francis Solano—St. Louis Bertrand—Blessed Peter Claver—Blessed Ignatius Azevedo—St. Philip of Jesus—Blessed Sebastian of the Apparition—Blessed John Masias—Blessed Martin Porras—St. Rose of Lima—Blessed Mariana of Quito—Venerable Antonio Margil—Venerable Mary of the Incarnation—Venerable Margaret Bourgeoys—Venerable Francis de Laval, Bishop of Quebec—"The Good Catharine," the Holy Indian Girl.

THE sanctity of the Church has been shown by the holy lives of many, whose virtues have been attested by their canonization or proceedings for it. Among these stands foremost St. Turibius Mogrobejo, Archbishop of Lima. His early life was marked by tender piety, and as he grew up he led a life of austerity and fervor. When he was judge at Granada he was appointed Archbishop of Lima; he sought to escape the dignity, but, yielding to an express order, he was ordained and consecrated. On arriving in his diocese he began a visitation which occupied several years, for he visited every hamlet as an apostle instructing the ignorant, introducing devotion, correcting abuses, and exciting all to a holy life. When pestilence came, his zeal was unremitting. He held several synods of his clergy, and convened Provincial Councils, the decrees of which were adopted throughout Spanish America. His life was one of prayer, mortification, and labor, till he died at Santa in 1606 during one of his missionary visitations. Miracles had attested his sanctity, and he was canonized in 1726.

St. Francis Solano, after a holy youth in Spain, entered the Franciscan Order, and in his zeal asked to be sent to America. He was regarded as a saint wherever he had preached and labored. He entered on the mission in America with

THE CHURCH IN AMERICA. 415

all his zeal, and his preaching was rewarded by wonderful conversions throughout the country from the river La

St. Francis Solano.

Plata to Lima. In that city, where vice was prevalent, he announced the judgments of God with such force that thousands returned to the practice of virtue. He died there in 1610, and was canonized in 1726. St. Francis Solano was renowned for most extraordinary miracles, and is invoked with fervor for protection against earthquakes.

St. Louis Bertrand, one of the ornaments of the Dominican Order, labored for several years on the coast of South America, from Panama to Venezuela, converting many Indians to the faith and reforming many lives of the Spaniards. His denunciation of vice led to attempts on his life, from which he escaped miraculously. He was canonized in 1671.

Blessed Peter Claver, of the Society of Jesus, labored in the same district, but devoted his whole life to the comfort, instruction, and salvation of negro slaves, whose condition on the ships that brought them from Africa, and in America, was most wretched. The holy Jesuit, who had learned the science of the saints from the Blessed Alphonsus Rodriguez, not only endured with cheerfulness the trials he encountered amid these degraded people, but added other austerities, which should fill with confusion those who seek only their own ease and comfort. Even during his last sickness, which kept him in his bed for four years, he continued to hear the confessions of his negroes and instruct them. He died September 8, 1654, and was beatified in 1852.

The Blessed Ignatius Azevedo and his thirty-nine companions, beatified in 1854, were holy Jesuit missionaries on their way to Brazil to labor in converting the Indians to the faith. They were captured by a Calvinist pirate, who threw them all into the sea.

St. Philip of Jesus, a native of Mexico, of which he is the patron, as well as several others who have been canonized or beatified as martyrs in Japan, were born in America, or labored with zeal here in the missions.

The Blessed Sebastian of the Apparition, the patron of

the city of Puebla, in Mexico, was in the world a model of piety, although engaged in distracting occupations, having established conveyances for goods and passengers from Vera Cruz to Mexico. He entered the Franciscan Order, and was illustrious for his spirit of prayer, his love of the poor, and his patience under all trials. His purity was so angelic that animals obeyed him as they did Adam in Paradise.

The cloister produced other saints among the humble lay brothers. Blessed Brother John Masias and Brother Martin Porras, at Lima, led such holy lives that they have been beatified and presented to our imitation by the Church.

But America has produced saints not only among her bishops, priests, and religious men, but feeble women have taken heaven by violence, and, while avoiding the applause of men in life, have won a fame above that of mighty conquerors.

St. Rose of Lima from her childhood sought to copy the virtues of St. Catharine of Siena, and gave her time wholly to prayer, work, and pious reading. She shunned every occasion of sin, and, when praised for the beauty of her hands, thrust them into lime to disfigure them so that they should be a snare to no one. When her family was reduced to poverty she accepted the cross joyfully and became an humble seamstress. As her family importuned her to marry, she entered the Third Order of St. Dominic, and, making a little cell for herself in a garden, subjected herself to the greatest mortification. She was raised to a sublime degree of prayer, and her example as an offering to avert God's anger from the people moved many to penance. She was honored as a saint in life and at her death, in 1617. Such miracles attested her favor with God that she was canonized in 1671.

Blessed Mariana Paredes, born at Quito in 1618, was an imitator of St. Rose; she was zealous in instructing children in their religion, and in the practice of devotion.

Her own example of piety and mortification was the best of lessons. Nothing could exceed her desire of consecrating her life to God in the religious state, but, whenever she attempted to enter a convent, obstacles arose. She therefore made a cloister in her own home, and labored for her own sanctification and that of her neighbors, converting many, and miraculously curing many afflicted with disease. She is recorded even to have raised a dead woman

Venerable Margaret Bourgeoys.

to life. During a season of pestilence and earthquake she offered her life to God for her countrymen, and, as her sickness increased, the scourges were arrested. She died in 1645, and was beatified by Pope Pius IX. in 1853.

Several of the archbishops of Mexico led such holy lives that the process of their canonization was introduced, as was that of the holy founder of the Texas missions, the Venerable Antonio Margil, who, after a life of apostolic labors, prayer, and mortification, died at Mexico in 1726.

In the northern part of the continent, Canada was a holy land. Among the saintly personages who have been declared Venerable, and whose canonization some may live to witness, are the Venerable Mother Mary of the Incarnation, foundress of the Ursuline Convent at Quebec, who for forty years adorned the colony by her zeal and virtues. She was especially devout to the Sacred Heart of Jesus, and introduced the devotion into America. For her sublime gift of contemplation and the depth of her spiritual writings, she has been called the St. Teresa of the New World.

The Venerable Margaret Bourgeoys, foundress of the Sisters of the Congregation at Montreal, whose schools cover Canada, is another servant of God, the proofs of whose heroic virtues and miracles are undergoing examination.

The same is true, also, of the Venerable Francis de Laval, first bishop of Quebec; and a holy Indian girl, honored to this day as "The Good Catharine," was famous for the miracles wrought at her tomb.

The history of the Church in America thus presents a strange contrast, for the consideration of all who pause to reflect. In one part, Catholicity, fostered by the piety of Spanish, French, and Portuguese monarchs, throve and prospered, the faithful receiving the fullest instruction in the pure word of God, and the ablest guidance, edified by the lives of persons in all ranks who rose to the highest degrees of sanctity: and then in a great portion of that very field a fearful falling away—governments given up to infidelity, swayed by secret societies warring on the Church and in every way crippling its power for good, and the people losing almost all semblance of Catholicity.

On the other hand, settlements formed under Protestant governments or conquered by them, where at the outset the faith encountered every opposition from the aborigines and from settlers, seventy-eight missionaries dying by the hands of Indians in the limits of the United States alone, and every colony almost putting Catholics under a ban; and then, just as the part that was once the pride of the Church began to fall away, a new Catholicity arising in the United States, animated by that of Canada which never wavered, and exhibiting in our time a wonderful vigor, energy, and devotedness, that covers our vast territory with Catholic churches, convent schools, and institutions inspired by faith and consecrated to every work of mercy that human ills can call upon religion to solace with her angelic charity.

CONTENTS.

	PAGE
PREFACE	5

CHAPTER I.—THE CHURCH AND HER HISTORY.

1. What the Church is 11
2. Why the Church is the Pillar and Ground of Truth.... 16
3. What is Church History ?............ 21
4. Whence are derived the Truthful and Genuine Recitals of Church History ?............ 23
5. False Church History............ 25

CHAPTER II.—HISTORY OF THE CHRISTIAN MISSIONS.

6. The First Congregation at Jerusalem............ 27
7. The Life and Mission of St. Peter............ 29
8. The Conversion of St. Paul............ 32
9. The Missionary Labors of St. Paul............ 34
10. Imprisonment and Execution of St. Paul............ 38
11. The Missionary Labors of the Other Apostles......... 41
12. The Growth of the Church in Europe............ 45
13. The History of the Church in Asia............ 55
14. The History of the Church in Africa............ 60
15. What America owes to the Catholic Church......... 62
16. The Church planted in America—Its Growth......... 67
17. The History of the Church in Australia............ 73
18. The Catholic World............ 74

CHAPTER III.—THE HISTORY OF CATHOLIC WORSHIP.

19. What is Catholic Worship ?............ 78
20. Places of Worship............ 79
21. The Holy Sacrifice of the Mass............ 83
22. The History of Baptism............ 87
23. The History of Confirmation............ 89

		PAGE
24.	The History of the Holy Eucharist	90
25.	The History of the Sacrament of Penance	92
26.	The History of Extreme Unction	94
27.	The History of Matrimony	95
28.	The History of Holy Orders	98
29.	The History of Sunday	99
30.	The History of the Festivals of Our Lord	101
31.	The Festivals of the Blessed Virgin	106
32.	The Festivals of the Saints	109

CHAPTER IV.—THE HISTORY OF THE TEACHING-OFFICE IN THE CHURCH.

33.	The Church Fathers	114
34.	The Four Great Fathers of the Western Church	119
35.	The Four Great Fathers of the Eastern Church	121
36.	The History of the Church Councils	123
37.	History of the Twenty General Councils	125
38.	The Infallibility of the Pope	128

CHAPTER V.—THE HISTORY OF THE HIERARCHY, OF CHURCH RIGHTS, AND OF CHURCH PENALTIES.

39.	The Kingly Office in the Church	132
40.	The Hierarchy	133
41.	The History of Church Rights	137
42.	Selection and Appointment of the Clergy—Their Maintenance	142
43.	The History of Church Temporalities	145
44.	The Temporal Power of the Popes	147

CHAPTER VI.—THE HISTORY OF RELIGIOUS ORDERS.

45.	Holiness in the Catholic Church	154
46.	History of Monastic Life in General	156
47.	History of the Benedictines	160
48.	History of the Crusades	162
49.	History of the Franciscans	168
50.	History of the Dominicans	171
51.	The Jesuits	172
52.	The Redemptorists	175

53. History of the Religious Bodies dedicated to Schools, or to the Care of the Sick and Destitute............... 176
54. Concluding Remarks on the History of Monastic Life.. 184

CHAPTER VII.—THE HISTORY OF THE SAINTS.
55. The Martyr Saints................................. 187
56. History of the Bishops............................ 191
57. History of the Priesthood......................... 194
58. The Saintly Hermits............................... 195
59. The Royal Saints.................................. 198
60. The Saintly Workmen............................... 202
61. The Saintly Farmers and Shepherds................. 204
62. The Saintly Matrons............................... 207
63. The Virgin Saints................................. 210

CHAPTER VIII.—THE HISTORY OF HERESY AND ITS AGGRESSIONS.
64. Nature and Origin of Heresy....................... 214
65. Heresies concerning Creation...................... 216
66. Heresies against the Blessed Trinity.............. 218
67. Heresies against the Divine Person of Jesus Christ. ... 220
68. Heresies concerning Grace......................... 221
69. Iconoclasm.. 222
70. The Greek Schism.................................. 223
71. The Albigenses and Catherers...................... 224
72. The Hussites...................................... 226
73. The So-called Reformation......................... 228
74. Catholic and Protestant Teachings................. 231
75. Martin Luther..................................... 234
76. Ulrich Zwingli.................................... 236
77. John Calvin....................................... 237
78. The Effects of the Reformation.................... 238
79. The False Liberalism of our Day................... 241

CHAPTER IX.—THE HISTORY OF THE PERSECUTIONS.
80. Persecutions from the Jews........................ 245
81. The Ten Roman Persecutions........................ 249
82. Persecutions by the Emperors of the East.......... 251
83. Persecutions in the Middle Ages................... 252
84. Modern Persecutions 255
85. The Church and the Governments in Modern Times . 257

CHAPTER X.—THE TRIUMPH AND GLORY OF THE CATHOLIC CHURCH.

                                                                                         PAGE

86. The Triumphant Existence of nearly Nineteen Hundred Years... 262
87. The Triumph of the Church in her Martyrs........... 265
88. The Triumph of the Church over Heathen Powers..... 267
89. Triumph of the Church over the Barbarians in the Days of the Northern Invasions........................ 270
90. Triumph of the Church in the Persons of her great Pontiffs.. 271
91. Triumphs of the Church over the Heresies........... 274
92. Triumph of the Church in her Conversions—The Converts... 276
93. Triumph of the Church in the Arts and Sciences..... 278
Conclusion... 281
94. Retrospect of Church History, according to Ages and Centuries.. 285

THE CHURCH IN AMERICA.

CHAPTER I.—Spanish America—Iceland and Greenland—The Voyage of Columbus—Missions—A See at St. Domingo—The Church in Mexico, Central and South America—A Bishop Martyr—The Dominicans oppose Indian Slavery—Indian Missions—Saints in the Episcopate and in the Clergy and Regulars—Negro Slavery and Blessed Peter Claver—Brazil—Martyrs on the Sea—The Suppression of the Jesuits—The French Revolution—Decline of Religion—Efforts of the Holy See—Pius IX. in America—Famous Shrines.. 315

CHAPTER II.—The Church in the United States—Catholic Explorers—Spanish Attempts at Settlement—Lord Baltimore—Progress—Oppression of the Catholics—The Church in Pennsylvania—The Acadian Confessors—The Revolution—Services of Catholics—Influence of the Alliance with France.. 321

CHAPTER III.—American Catholics ask a Prefect—Very Rev. John Carroll appointed—His Visitation—The See of Baltimore established—Extent of Bishop Carroll's Diocese—Religion in Canada—Its missions and Martyrs—English Conquest—Present State...................................... 327

CHAPTER IV.—French congregations in the West—Bishop Carroll is consecrated—Sulpitians—Georgetown College—Carmelite Nuns—First Synod of Baltimore—Controversies—Spread of the Church—Baltimore an Archbishopric—Sees at Boston, New York, Philadelphia, and Bardstown—Religious Orders—Diocese of Louisiana confided to Archbishop Carroll—Bishop Dubourg appointed...................... 336

CHAPTER V.—The Church in New England—Trial of Rev. Mr. Cheverus—Rev. John Thayer—New York—Bishop Connolly—Mrs. Seton and the Sisters of Charity—Bishop Egan of Philadelphia—The Hogan schism—Western Pennsylvania—New Jersey—Bishop Flaget and the Church in Kentucky—Dominicans in Ohio—Devotion of Priests and Sisters during the Cholera... 343

CHAPTER VI.—Sees of Charleston and Richmond—Religion in Virginia—North Carolina—Bishop England and the Carolinas—Religion in Florida, Louisiana, and Missouri—Miraculous cure of Mrs. Mattingly—First Provincial Council. 353

CHAPTER VII.—Religion in Michigan—The See of Detroit—Bishop Rézé—Bishops at Vincennes and Dubuque—Early history of Natchez—Religion in Tennessee—Anti-Catholic movements—Vile fictions and libels—the Ursuline Convent destroyed—Increase of German Catholics—The Redemptorists—Councils at Baltimore—Missions to Oregon—Church in Minnesota—Rate of Progress....................... 359

CHAPTER VIII.—Catholic Schools—State Schools hostile to the Faith—The Fourth Council of Baltimore—The School Question in New York—Spread of Catholic Educational Institutions—Death of Bishop England—New Dioceses and Orders—Texas annexed—Bishop Odin—The Native American Party—Philadelphia Riots and Destruction of Catholic Churches—A Priest in Indiana Unjustly sent to Prison—Conversions—Madame Gallitzin—Catholic Literature—Dr. O. A. Brownson...................................... 368

CHAPTER IX.—The Mexican War—Military Chaplains—Catholic Territory Annexed—Religion in New Mexico—Bishop Lamy, Vicar Apostolic—California and Father Juniper Serra—The Bishop of both Californias—See of Monterey—Right Rev. Joseph S. Alemany—Emigration—Archbishopric of Oregon and Diocese of Nesqually—Sees at Albany, Buffalo, Cleveland—Bishop Creton....... 382

CHAPTER X.—The Blessed Virgin chosen Patroness of the

Church in the United States—Benedictines in the United States—Passionists—Brothers of the Christian Schools—Brothers of Mary—Sisters of the Good Shepherd—First Plenary Council of Baltimore—New Sees—American College at Rome—Archbishop Bedini Nuncio to the United States—The Know-Nothings—Violence—Father Bapst—Churches destroyed in New Hampshire and Maine—At Williamsburg and Newark—Anti-Catholic Laws—The Louisville Riots—Archbishop Hughes—Bishop Spalding........ 389

CHAPTER XI.—The Clergy and Orders in Yellow Fever Times—Franciscans in the United States—Position of the Church in 1861—The Civil War—Priests and Sisters on the Battlefield and in Hospitals—A Benedictine Monk killed—The Church's losses—Treatment of Bishop Elder—The Second Plenary Council—Work among the Negroes—Great Progress in North Carolina—Georgia—Texas—Indian Territory a Prefecture—Revival of Anti-Catholic Feeling—Bigotry on the Bench—Catholic School Books—Missions by the Redemptorists and Others—Diffusion of Catholic Books and Periodicals—Theological Seminary—Yellow Fever in 1878—The Indian Missions—His Eminence John Cardinal McCloskey, Archbishop of New York..................... 401

CHAPTER XII.—The Saints in America—St. Turribius, Archbishop of Lima—St. Francis Solano—St. Louis Bertrand—Blessed Peter Claver—Blessed Ignatius Azevedo—St. Philip of Jesus—Blessed Sebastian of the Apparition—Blessed John Masias—Blessed Martin Porras—St. Rose of Lima—Blessed Mariana of Quito—Venerable Antonio Margil—Venerable Mary of the Incarnation—Venerable Margaret Bourgeoys—Venerable Francis de Laval, Bishop of Quebec—"The Good Catharine," the holy Indian girl............ 414

www.ingramcontent.com/pod-product-compliance
Lightning Source LLC
Chambersburg PA
CBHW032141010526
44111CB00035B/849